Library of Southern Civilization
Lewis P. Simpson, Editor

THE CAUSE OF THE SOUTH

THE
CAUSE OF
THE SOUTH

SELECTIONS FROM *DE BOW'S REVIEW*
1846–1867

Edited, with an Introduction, by
Paul F. Paskoff and Daniel J. Wilson

Louisiana State University Press
Baton Rouge and London

Library of Congress Cataloging in Publication Data

The Cause of the South.

(Library of Southern civilization)
Bibliography: p.
1. Southern States—Economic conditions—Ad-
dresses, essays, lectures.   2. Southern States—
History—Civil War, 1861–1865—Addresses, essays,
lectures.   3. Slavery—Southern States—History—
Addresses, essays, lectures.   4. Southern States—
Social life and customs—Addresses, essays, lec-
tures.   5. De Bow's review.   I. Paskoff, Paul F.
II. Wilson, Daniel J., 1949–   .   III. De Bow's
review.   IV. Series.
HC107.A13C34 1982   975'.03   81-23680
ISBN 0-8071-1009-4   AACR2
ISBN 0-8071-1039-6 (pbk.)

Published with the assistance of a grant
from the National Endowment for the Humanities.

For
Marjorie and Stewart Wilson
and for
Ann, Benji, and Alberto Villeñ

CONTENTS

PREFACE

De Bow's Review, though often cited in works on southern history, has long been inaccessible to the nonspecialist and student. Widely known for his views on slavery and secession, J. D. B. De Bow was much more than a polemicist for southern institutions and rights. His commitment to southern economic development and southern culture makes his journal a mirror of the concerns of southern society and an invaluable source for the study of antebellum America. This volume of selections from *De Bow's Review* presents the reader with a comprehensive and representative cross section of the magazine's contents from its inception in 1846 until the end of De Bow's editorship in 1867.

For the most part, the selections are printed in full. Where we have deleted portions of an essay because of length or the presence of extraneous matter, we have taken care to preserve the integrity of the argument and have indicated our deletions by ellipses. Except in cases of obvious typographical errors, which have been silently corrected, original usage has been maintained (*e.g.*, negro).

We have organized the selections according to their dominant themes as reflected in the chapter headings. Within each chapter, the articles are arranged in the chronological order in which they appeared in the journal. In our annotations, we have attempted to provide such biographical and contextual material as would enhance the reader's understanding.

This has been a joint venture from the beginning, and we have benefited from the assistance and encouragement we received. We are grateful for the financial assistance provided by a Muhlenberg College Pre-Publication Grant and a Louisiana State University Graduate Council-on-Research Summer Grant. Through their support, John Loos, chairman of the Department of History at L.S.U., and Katherine S. Van Eerde, chairman of the Department of History at Muhlenberg, facilitated the completion of the manuscript. Ernestine Trahan removed obstacles at every turn, and Christine Angelloz typed the manuscript superbly. The cooperation of Evangeline Lynch, curator of the Louisiana Room of L.S.U.'s Middleton Library, and of the staff of the L.S.U. Archives was invaluable. William J. Cooper, Jr., Lewis Simpson, and Gary Crump offered helpful advice. Beverly Jarrett, Martha Hall, and Margaret Fisher Dalrymple, our editors at Louisiana State University Press, eased our task. Ann Wonsiewicz-Schlecht, Ludwig Schlecht, Joanne Mortimer, Robert Becker, and Burl Noggle kept morale high. Finally, we wish to thank Beth for making it possible and Catherine and Martha for making it interesting.

I

J. D. B. DE BOW AND THE
COMMERCIAL REVIEW

Among the impressive array of nationally prominent men produced by southern antebellum society, James Dunwoody Brownson De Bow was an oddity. Neither politician nor military leader, he nonetheless exerted considerable influence in shaping articulate southern opinion, particularly with respect to the South's increasingly acrimonious debate with the North over the issues of slavery and the territories. De Bow's adult life was bound up—at first peripherally, but later more intimately—with the substance of this debate. His New Orleans-based magazine, variously titled over its lifespan but always familiarly known as the *Commercial Review* or simply *De Bow's Review*, became an articulate champion of southern interests and positions, thereby propelling its editor into the not-entirely-unsought position of southern advocate and spokesman—a position which, by virtue of his convictions, education, and experience, De Bow felt eminently qualified to assume.

Born in Charleston, South Carolina, on July 10, 1820, to transplanted northerners, De Bow spent his early childhood in the comfortable home provided by his father's success in business. The collapse of this business shortly before his father's early death when De Bow was six left the family of four children and their mother in difficult straits. Fortunately, the elder De Bow's land investments and the business acumen of his older son and his widow enabled the family to weather the economic difficulties and even to recoup, in part, their former position. In his teens, De Bow received firsthand experience in commerce working as a clerk for a wholesale grocer while at the same time pursuing his own course of study in Charleston.

De Bow's early education proceeded unevenly and very much reflected his own interests, his circumstances, and the nature and quality of the available schools. Having read widely in history and moral philosophy, he embarked in 1836 on a short-lived career as an unenthusiastic "country pedagogue" in a log cabin schoolhouse outside Charleston. De Bow soon had his fill of his unruly charges, and, after challenging the father of one of his students to a duel, he decided to change careers in 1838. The following year he entered the Cokesbury Institute, a Methodist vocational institution in Abbeville, South Carolina, and pursued a course of study in agriculture. Husbandry proved uncongenial, and De Bow quickly turned his attention to scholarship and writing. In the winter of 1840, he entered the College of Charleston, where he took up studies in natural science, law, and economics. Until his senior year, when he inherited $800 from his father's estate, he led a penurious existence. While at the college, De Bow seems to have nourished his taste for classical history and literature, which he would later parade in his many articles for the *Review*.

Graduating first in his class in 1843, De Bow read law for a year in Charleston, was admitted to the bar, and quickly realized that he was not cut out to be a lawyer. With his interest in law waning, he returned to his intellectual pursuits and resolved to become a writer. He began to contribute philosophical and political essays to the *Southern Quarterly Review*. After a dispute with the editor over his role on the journal, De Bow left the *Quarterly* and soon found himself, in October, 1845, a delegate to the Southern Commercial Convention in Memphis, Tennessee. As a result of his experiences at the Commercial Convention, De Bow became convinced that the South and the Mississippi Valley could benefit from a journal devoted to their unique agricultural and economic interests. This conviction led De Bow to establish *The Commercial Review of the South and West* in New Orleans. The first issue appeared in January, 1846.

De Bow consciously modeled his new journal on *Hunt's Merchants' Magazine*, a journal of commerce and finance edited and published in New York. In the lead article of the first issue (reprinted below), De Bow set forth the *raison d'être* of the *Review* and expressed his hope that it would contribute to the economic improvement of the South, the West, and the Southwest. He envisioned a journal that covered the trade, commerce, agriculture, manufacturing, and internal improvements of the region and promised a magazine of "active *neutrality*," open to all viewpoints and committed to "fair, honest, and calm discussions" in the pursuit of truth.

Though nothing like it existed for the region, De Bow was hard pressed to sustain his *Review*. Problems of circulation, budgets, printing, and soliciting contributors, common to all antebellum southern journals, taxed the editor's patience and resources. In these early years, the *Review* survived only because of a subvention from Maunsel White, a wealthy New Orleans merchant and sugar planter. While working to keep his struggling *Review* alive, writing nearly the entire contents of several early issues, De Bow became deeply involved in the cultural and commercial life of his newly adopted city of New Orleans. An advocate of the "moral advance" of New Orleans, De Bow pushed for the establishment of such cultural institutions as the Louisiana Historical Society and the University of Louisiana. He could not, however, ignore the continuing financial difficulties of the *Review*, which caused him to suspend publication for six months in 1847 and again in 1849. Some of the problems of the *Review* in this period may have stemmed from the editor's other commitments, notably his acceptance of the Chair of Commerce, Public Economy, and Statistics at the newly founded University of Louisiana in 1848 and his appointment as director of the state Bureau of Statistics in the same year. Both positions permitted De Bow to pursue his interest in compiling statistical data on southern economic and social conditions. The initial results of these efforts were published first in installments in his *Review* and, later, in 1852 and 1853, in his three-volume study, *The Industrial Resources, etc., of the Southern and Western States*. These publications soon served their author in a way that he had not anticipated, one which had its roots in presidential politics.

The election of Franklin Pierce in 1852 was followed by the usual squabbles over patronage and influence that had long accompanied the advent of new presidents. One of the more capable but vulnerable targets of the new Democratic administration's head-hunters was Joseph C. G. Kennedy, the Whig superintendent of the Seventh Census of the United States. Kennedy had incurred the animosity of a numerous and powerful body of Democrats and Whigs even before the 1852 election. His doom was sealed—despite his conscientious discharge of his duties, including the publication of preliminary reports on the census—when Pierce intimated before his inauguration that Kennedy and others "known to be under the influence of political hostility and partisan prejudice" were expendable.

Despite his Democratic ties, De Bow had praised Kennedy and his work in the *Review* and had eagerly published his reports. After Kennedy's dismissal, Pierce's inclination to replace him with a well-connected Democrat and the sponsorship of the powerful Louisiana Democratic organization assured De Bow's appointment as superintendent of the census in early 1853. Fortunately, in this instance the spoils system coincided neatly with competence.

De Bow eagerly assumed his new post and immediately imposed a new regimen on the census office staff with the aim of increasing its efficiency. He scrutinized and, where possible, substantially revised the procedures for tabulating the schedules of population, agriculture, and manufactures. When the *Compendium of the Seventh Census* appeared in 1854, it met with a generally favorable reception, the consensus being that it represented a significant improvement over earlier censuses, and De Bow properly received the largest share of the credit.

Not everyone, however, was pleased, and more than one critic assailed De Bow for what appeared to be his pro-South bias in the tabulation and reporting of data on pauperism in various states. De Bow, of course, denied any bias, perhaps believing that, with his denial, the issue had been laid to rest. The controversy over the relative degree of pauperism in free states and slave states was, however, by no means dead. Ironically, De Bow was the one who revived it in his magazine in an effort to demonstrate that the slave-based economy worked fewer hardships on whites than did the free labor system of the North.

De Bow's experiences as superintendent of the census and particularly his work comparing the demographic and economic statistics of the states seem to have reinforced his growing conviction that the longstanding inferiority of the South relative to the North in terms of population and economic power was increasing. From the inception of the *Review*, he warned southerners that continued inferiority was dangerous to southern institutions, especially slavery, and repeatedly urged contributors to address the problem and to suggest remedies. William Gregg's essays on manufacturing in 1850 and 1860 (reprinted here) reveal the growing perception of the severity of the problem by informed southerners; the 1850 essay is a reasoned argument for southern manufacturing, whereas the 1860 article is the jeremiad of a frustrated and desperate advocate of the southern cause. As the decade of the 1850s progressed, numerous other writers echoed Gregg's alarm in the pages of the *Review*.

In the 1850s, southern nationalism and the defense of slavery drove all other considerations from the marketplace of southern ideas. The "active *neutrality*" open to all views that De Bow had promised in 1846 soon gave way to open partisanship for the cause of the South. The first volume of the *Review* saw articles on education and medical frauds that were as applicable to the North as to the South. By the end of the decade of compromise and controversy over slavery and its expansion, even essays on such subjects as the character of school books and the place of southern womanhood had become vehicles for the expression of southern nationalism and the superiority of southern institutions.

De Bow and many of his contributors did not flinch from confronting even more directly the key issues dividing North and South. The political disputes of the decade centered on the question of expanding slavery into the new territories, and as early as 1850 De Bow warned his fellow southerners against the "reckless fanaticism or ignorant zeal of the 'cordon of free States' surrounding us on every hand." The pages of the *Review* saw both reasoned arguments grounded in the Constitution supporting the right of southerners to take their slaves with them into the territories and, after 1854, shrill propaganda against the free-soil advocates in Kansas.

Although by no means a peripheral concern of the South, the territorial question was bound up with more fundamental issues of the morality and constitutionality of slavery and the growing antagonism between two divergent cultures. To the disgust of many northerners, men like Samuel A. Cartwright and Josiah C. Nott repeatedly advanced moral, biblical, biological, and historical arguments in defense of the peculiar institution. Edmund Ruffin, meanwhile, warned of the growing northern abolitionist sentiment and of its potentially decisive political consequences for the South.

As secessionist sentiment mounted in the South at the end of the decade, *De Bow's Review* became the major platform for the more extreme advocates of southern rights and interests. By 1860, the intelligent reader of De Bow's magazine could not avoid the conclusion that insofar as the *Review* reflected articulate southern opinion, the question before the South was not whether it should secede, but when. With De Bow's encouragement, men like Edmund Ruffin, George Fitzhugh, and Joseph A. Turner used the pages of the *Review* to press their view that the South could protect its institutions and culture only by dissolving the Union.

De Bow's advocacy of secession in 1860 was a logical culmination of his fourteen years of effort on behalf of southern institutions. In his *Review* he had long argued the necessity of southern economic independence—the improvement and diversification of southern agriculture, the creation of a southern industrial base, and the development of an adequate transportation network. The events of the 1850s convinced him that these goals and the protection of slavery could only be achieved through political independence. De Bow's own odyssey toward secession thus, in large part, mirrored that of his region.

Like many southern nationalists, De Bow cheered the formation of the Confederacy and its early successes in the war against the Union, but by mid-1862 the fortunes of the Confederacy had dimmed and, with them, De Bow's own and those of the *Review*. He was forced to suspend publication in April, 1862, due to financial difficulties and scarcities of paper and printing supplies. The deteriorating military situation of the Confederacy, such as the fall of New Orleans in April, 1862, contributed to De Bow's difficulties and, combined with the other problems, led to a two-year suspension of the *Review* from August, 1862, until August, 1864. De Bow published only the August, 1864, issue and then was forced to suspend publication again until January, 1866.

The publication problems of the *Review* notwithstanding, De Bow placed his talents at the service of the Confederacy. In August, 1861, C. G. Memminger, Confederate Secretary of the Treasury, appointed De Bow to the Produce Loan Bureau, where he attempted to secure revenue from the sale of commodities loaned to the Confederacy by planters. Though De Bow's relationship with Memminger was frequently marred by misunderstanding and friction, he served in this and similar capacities throughout the war. The source of much of that friction was De Bow's feeling that his abilities could have been put to better use. Charges of malfeasance against his subordinates led to charges against De Bow himself, though no evidence was produced to suggest that his own conduct was anything but exemplary. In spite of these difficulties, De Bow managed early in the war to accumulate a considerable fortune as a result of well-timed investments in gold, cotton, land, bonds, and railroads. Though De Bow suffered some financial reverses during the war, including the loss of plantation land in Mississippi, he was, nevertheless, better off at the end of the war than he had been at its beginning.

More than any other southerner, De Bow should have been cognizant of the weaknesses in the Confederacy's capacity to wage war. Faith more than logic must have induced him to count on European intervention, southern morality, and southern manhood to achieve independence. During the two years of the war in which the journal appeared, De Bow's contributors moved from optimism, even cockiness, to a more realistic and sober appreciation of the odds facing the Confederacy. With the failure of King Cotton to swing the balance in favor of the South through European intervention against the North, essayists such as J. H. Thornwell appealed to southern pride and manhood to "redeem a land from bondage, and a continent from ruin." Thornwell's brave words and the brave men inspired by them could not stem the growing tide of Union victories that would, in 1865, destroy the hopes of southern nationalists. *De Bow's Review*, which had chronicled the rise of southern nationalism, was not there to record its fall.

The end of the war found the South devastated and in a state of chaos. By August, 1865, De Bow had begun efforts to revive his journal, and by December of that year he had succeeded in surmounting such familiar problems as financing, securing subscribers and contributors, and procuring adequate printing supplies. The new title he chose—*De Bow's Review, Devoted to the Restoration of the Southern States, and the Development of the Wealth and Resources of the Country*—reflected his recognition of the changed circumstances of the South. Though some familiar contributors, such as George Fitzhugh and Josiah Nott, returned, the postwar *Review* never achieved the popularity or influence enjoyed by the journal in the antebellum South. The cause of the South was now the Lost Cause, and the reappearance of the *Review* reminded many southerners of that fact. Moreover, many northerners persisted in viewing the *Review* as the voice of treason and secession. Nevertheless, although diminished in influence, the revived *Review* reflected the efforts of articulate southerners to come to terms with defeat, reunion, and reconstruction.

For the most part unrepentant, De Bow and his contributors asserted the nobility of a lost cause, pleaded a case for leniency based on common northern and southern interests, and argued for the continued subordination of black to white. De Bow, for example, in one of the last articles he wrote for the *Review*, attempted to convince the Radicals in Congress of the virtues of magnanimity and of permitting the South to solve the race question in its own fashion. Southerners like De Bow and Fitzhugh, who welcomed the lenient policies of Andrew Johnson, were appalled by the harsher measures introduced under Congressional reconstruction beginning in March, 1867. However, by the end of that year even an unreconstructed southerner like George Fitzhugh could find cause for optimism and would hail the return of good feeling between the North and South. Though premature, Fitzhugh's conviction that the North had begun to acquiesce in the southern view of race relations would be borne out over the next decade.

Much as it had in the antebellum years, the revived *Review* addressed the problems of southern economic development and linked that problem with the question of labor, particularly black labor. Before the war, southerners assumed that blacks were particularly suited to agriculture and could be compelled to work only as slaves. In the aftermath of the war, the South found itself confronting a scarcity of labor and an abundance of free Negro laborers. There were two questions: would free blacks work at all, and could white labor be induced to migrate to the South? Men like Fitzhugh and Edwin Q. Bell could only ask the questions; in the short time left to the *Review*, there was little opportunity to provide answers.

The *Review*, which had been unable to regain its prewar eminence, suffered a fatal blow with De Bow's death on February 27, 1867. De Bow's widow and two business and editorial associates, R. G. Barnwell and Edwin Q. Bell, attempted to carry on with only indifferent success. The *Review* was sold in March, 1868, but the new owners were unable to resolve the difficulties that had plagued even De Bow after the war, and they were forced to suspend publication in July, 1870. An effort to revive the journal in October, 1879, failed after four issues had been published. Ironically, the once powerful and militant voice of southern nationalism ended its existence as the property of the *Agricultural Review*, a financially troubled journal published in New York. Because the *Review* was so closely identified with its founder, it is not surprising that the quality of the journal declined dramatically after his death and that his successors were unable to sustain an enterprise that had, even in its best years, led a precarious existence.

Despite De Bow's frequent difficulties and a circulation that never exceeded 5,000 paid subscriptions, the *Review* was undoubtedly one of the most important southern publications, with an influence extending north of the Mason-Dixon line. The journal's influence stemmed from the force of the editor's personality and commitment, a solid statistical basis and economic emphasis unique among southern journals, and, in the late 1850s, its militant defense of slavery and southern nationalism. Though often taken as representative of southern opinion as a whole, *De Bow's Review* spoke most directly to the interests of commercial planters, merchants, bankers, and manufacturers—in short, to those elements within southern society furthest removed from the southern agrarian and cavalier ideal. De Bow's vision of southern society was thus a commercial and industrial, indeed a bourgeois, conception somewhat at odds with the dominant southern culture of mid-century. It did, however, reflect in part the dynamism and self-confidence of the cotton South and particularly the booming economy of New Orleans and the Southwest. Although preoccupied with the creation of a commercial and industrial economy and the defense of southern institutions, De Bow recognized that "something higher must be aimed at than mere trade and commerce," and to that end he attempted to "encourage a taste among our citizens for those things that are high and ennobling in themselves": art, literature, history, and public decorum. He began and ended his *Review* by attempting to improve the South's position within the Union. For much of its existence, however, *De Bow's Review*, like the South itself, felt compelled to champion uniquely southern interests, even to the point of secession and war. In this, *De Bow's Review* was at its best and made the cause of the South its own.

J. D. B. De Bow

THE *COMMERCIAL REVIEW*
Its Position in Relation to Southern and Western Periodical Literature, and Southern and Western Interests

The design and object of an enterprise, new in its character, which is to be dependent upon public sympathy for support, ought to be distinctly stated in the outset, and clearly understood.

If purposes of an elevated nature are to be achieved—the occupation of ground rich in resources and hitherto untilled—the diffusion of instruction and light upon interests most practical and important—the advocacy of widest sections, and everything that contributes to their moral and physical advance—if the aims be high as these, and guarantees be furnished for their attainment, then we conceive, beyond all question, the enterprise places itself at once upon a basis of enduring strength, and commands the approval and support of every citizen wishing well to his country.

But if, on the other hand, the scale be reversed, and that which is proposed be in reality valueless, even when accomplished—if the field to be occupied is already ably and adequately commanded, or the would-be occupiers are meagre in resources, of inefficient action and circumscribed views—in such a case, we imagine, no prophetic vision can be required to pierce into destiny, and determine that declension and decay which are following inevitably on—rapid—certain—unlamented. There is no power long to deceive mankind in matters of this nature. A keen sensitiveness happily prevails in the world, whose benign influence it is to rescue society and literature from the excrescences which would otherwise grow up upon them—a sensitiveness which chastises pretension with neglect.

The Journal which is now ushered upon the world, and subjected to the ordeal delineated, will, of course, stand or fall as it approximates to the one extreme or the other of the contrast which has been drawn. That the Editor will have a powerful incentive, demanding his whole resources and energy to reach the happier and better fortune involved, will be conceded without argument; and, indeed, if a long and careful

Vol. I (January, 1846), pp. 2–6.

study of the history, the wants and resources of the Southern and Western States—if a practical as well as theoretical acquaintance with Commercial movements, internal and foreign—if an acquaintance with the principles of international and local law, acquired in the studies and duties of a profession, and an editorial experience in the conduction of one of the first literary works in the Union, superadded to that which is equal to all the rest, and, perhaps, above them all, industry, application, and devotion to the interests of the sections advocated, can be of any avail and at all an earnest of the future, that happier and better fortune will be won.

To those who have any experience in the conduction of Southern or Western periodical literature, the difficulties and embarrassments under which it has always been doomed to struggle are matters of familiar knowledge. In the higher departments little has yet been accomplished among us. Able monthlies and quarterlies, devoted *exclusively* to literature, in its lighter walks of fancy, or its statelier tread of philosophy, have run their brief career, and expired almost in the very throes which gave them birth. We have seen some of them live on, however, live in spite of the strewn wrecks around, but it has been a galvanized life—action without the heart-work and the blood—without the power from within of supplying the elements of its continuance. There is not one of these, and we speak it with knowledge—not one remunerating its proprietors now in any degree proportionate with their labors. The remuneration, if it come at all, must come in the doubtful future, or it must come, as the starved devotee to literature and science too frequently greets it, in the simple consciousness of extending the influence and the empire of letters.

We shall not pause here to inquire into the causes of what is so lamentable in itself. We have seen speculations to this effect, and heard various explications attempted. To us, at present, the simple fact is sufficient, and the corollary which is deducible from it. Disguise the painful truth as we may, it is still stubbornly there, that the South and West have not yet, whatever the reasons, attained to that happy preeminence when a reading population, heartily appreciating literature and sympathizing with it for itself, and for itself alone, can be afforded, large enough to give character and permanency to literary movements in their midst. The confession is wrung from us with regret. If we take the South, from the Old Dominion as it stretches itself to the gulf, there is a population scattered and difficult to be reached by the influences of letters. If we take the West, sweeping away through the valley of the Mississippi, there are States forming and developing, there are men struggling with the wilderness, subduing soil into cultivation, opening trade and creating for it avenues. The first efforts of these men have their aim and end in physical good. The physical want precedes, in the order of time, the intellectual. Ploughshares come before philosophy. The *utile* and then the *dulce*, the body first and the intellect which is beyond it. No demonstrations of Malthus are needed here.

With convictions of this kind, there would be, in our case, something of the nature of fatuity were we to enter the literary field with a new enterprise, to be sustained amid all its hazards, and to rest *solely* for its success upon the votaries which literature may chance to have. We should rather marvel at such temerity in another than be inclined to imitate it ourself. Our individual resources, though they might be sustained by ever so large an amount of public spirit, would unquestionably be exhausted in the large outlays and the meagre revenues which our literary friends now and then dolefully count up. We should yield ourself in the struggle, to place others on their feet, and prejudice a good cause by a premature advocacy, and a forced abandonment of it.

What, then, can be done, and why are we moving at all? By what process have we been lulled into the pleasing assurance that our present connection with the publishing world will be a successful, an enduring, and an influential one? We answer, in brief, that we address ourselves to the times as they are, and to the circumstances as they exist. The class of wants which comes within our cognizance, and which we volunteer to supply, is the class which our region of country is now feeling, must feel, and continue to feel, before any other class can be thought of, or even exist. They are the practical wants of every-day life, developed in the first movements of private or public enterprise, in the business relations of man with his fellowman. Falling in with the spirit of the age and the country, without dropping behind on the one hand, or outstripping it on the other, we seize upon the practical field of labor. We hold up the "map of busy life," with its broad, deep lines of struggles, and toils, and hazards, in conquering wildernesses into fields, in rearing up States out of adventurous woodsmen, in advancing individual fortune, in connecting section with section, and region with region, by ties of reciprocal interest and fraternal affection, and in marching on with the whole to those high destinies which, as a people, it seems to be the will of God we are to reach.

We entitle our work the COMMERCIAL REVIEW, not that the appellation entirely satisfies us, or that it comes up to an adequate expression of its nature and objects; but that, in the defects of our language, we could not, without a circumlocution, find another phrase which would answer as well. Had we said Practical Review, there would have been, to say the least of it, some inelegance, and no little ambiguity. We establish, to be sure, a Commercial work, as much so as Hunt's is one, with its remarkable merits, its high and well-earned influence; but it is Commercial only, in the widest and most liberal construction of the term. There is no end to the diversities and ramifications of commercial action. You cannot touch a practical interest, in fact, whatever its nature, which does not, to a greater or a less extent, trench upon commerce, affiliate itself with, and affect it. Touch agriculture, touch the arts, the professions, fortifications, defenses, transportations, legislation of a country, and the chances are a thousand to one you touch commerce somewhere. With this understanding, our Review is not inappropriately named; but, in the ordinary sense of the term, we are more than commercial. Not to dwell, however, too long upon mere technicalities, we shall hastily reconnoitre the field of action before us, and furnish what may be considered a fair index of our future labors.

And first, our position is one which has not yet been taken by a single periodical in the Southern or Western States, and by but one in the whole country. It is evident that a nation vast as ours, and of such resources, cannot be adequately represented by a solitary work upon this principle. A wide sphere of action may yet be discovered, and the co-labors, and not otherwise than generous rivalries, which will hereafter be called into action between two works, the one established at the heart of the commerce of the North and the East—New York, and the other at the great emporium of the South and West—New Orleans, will exert an influence in the highest degree favorable to the interests of the whole country. The exalted position of our contemporary has been long understood, and our aspirations are not lower than his, whether or not we ever reach them. We differ somewhat, however, in the departments undertaken. For us it shall be to adhere to the West, the South, and the South-west; to take the highest views on their great, ever-arising, ever-augmenting interests, to advocate their true and best policy, to defend their rights and develop their resources, to collect, combine, and digest in a permanent form for reference, their important statistics. These shall be the characteristics of our enterprise.

As a *Journal of Trade*, each and all of the commodities it embraces will come under repeated examination. The history of these commodities, their production, consumption, valuation, transportation, and the principles which govern their interchange and distribution.

As a *Journal of Commerce*—Commerce in its various and multiform relations will be analyzed; commerce in its origin; in its history and statistics; commerce in its exchange of the products of distant climes and nations, and its civilizing, enlightening and peace-perpetuating influences upon the world.

As a *Journal of Commercial Polity*—the field is wide and in the highest degree important. The regulations of trade, inter-state and inter-national; treaties, foreign and domestic; tariffs, excises and posts; maritime regulations; mercantile systems, codes, laws, and decisions, ancient and modern; banking, insurance, exchange, partnership, factorage, guarantee, brokerage, bankruptcy, wreck, salvage, freights, privateering, marque and reprisal, piracy, quarantine and custom-house regulations, etc.

As a *Journal of Agriculture*—the soil and its capacities for improved growth and cultivation, the variety and tests of soils, their relative value and productiveness, their yield in the most and least favorable circumstances, their best sites and locations.

As a *Journal of Manufactures*—the gradual advancement of this branch of industry among us shall be noted; the capacities of the south and west for their larger introduction and extension, and such general information in relation to their establishment as may be embraced within the limits of the work.

As a *Journal of Internal Improvement*—Canals, turnpikes, and railroads, steamboats, and river navigation, new and projected routes and enterprises, with their respective advantages, facilities, economy, productiveness, mail conveyances, etc., will be embraced.

As a *Literary Work*—the least pretending, but not unimportant department. Literature cannot be entirely neglected even in the workshop or in the press of stirring enterprise. The biographical sketches of distinguished, practical, and business men, of public benefactors, and high-reaching directors and controllers of a struggling age, will stimulate similar efforts in others, and the developments in the book-trade will be a fair exposition of the character which literature will assume when it is pressing up amid a toiling and eminently practical people.

Thus, then, for the humble tradesman, or the extensive merchant— for the commercial jurist—the farmer and the planter—for the manufacturer, or him desirous of an extensive acquaintance with the operations of his country; for all of these, and for the mere general reader, there will be matter afforded which will be deeply interesting and instructive.

With party movements and manœuvering and party tactics we have not the most remote connection. We have no cause to chronicle these, nor even to animadvert upon them in any of their intricate and diversified connections. An active *neutrality* is the best position, where all parties are to be benefited, and there is likely to occur little strong enough to move us from it. Whatever may be our individual sentiments upon these questions, and whatever the doctrines we may be called upon to support on other occasions, none of these shall be allowed to give a party character to the work. In discussing questions which incidentally affect and relate to present legislation, a thing that cannot be avoided entirely, there shall be a perfect freedom allowed. If by chance publication should be given to sentiments which may not harmonize with those of particular interests and classes of men, there shall always operate a principle with us to correct the evil. Where truth is the subject, and men are in search of it, fair, honest, and calm discussions are powerful means for its attainment. Let both sides speak then, the better to understand each other and to arrive at legitimate and incontrovertible conclusions.

We solicit, then, generally from all who have made the practical concerns of the country or any department of them their study, who are furnished with facts and statistics whose dissemination is desirable, who sympathize with the motives which actuate us in our journal, and who would aid in carrying them into execution—we solicit an expression of views at any and all times, and cheerfully pledge our pages to the reception and exposition of what may be furnished us. To those who have already volunteered their services in this particular, we make the acknowledgements now.

There are large duties incumbent upon the editorial department of the work, and heavy publishing expenses. These can only be recompensed and sustained in an extended circulation. In the best case the prospects must be small. For a long probation, little more will be done, perhaps than refunding the outlays for printing and publication, if so much. There may be motives enough to continue the work, even without its pecuniary profits, but few can afford to live upon the mere consciousness of benefiting their countrymen. We ask, then, for circulation, and solicit additions to our subscription and advertising lists. We beg our friends, and all to whom we send this number, to act as its friendly agents.

With these remarks, the professions with which we thought it necessary to preface the publication are concluded. As these subjects will not be reverted to again, a reference to them in the opening, though, perhaps, too lengthened a one, will not be considered altogether inappropriate.

II

SLAVERY AND RACE

J. D. B. De Bow described his *Review* as a journal of commerce, agriculture, manufactures, and internal improvements, but almost from the beginning the problems of slavery and race found a prominent place in the pages of the magazine. By the 1850s, when most of the articles below appeared, the questions of slavery and its expansion outside the South had become increasingly divisive in the nation. De Bow chose to confront the issue directly, rather than to skirt it, becoming an ardent advocate of the peculiar institution and of the doctrine of Negro inferiority and opening his journal to contributors who shared his views.

Many of De Bow's contributors to the slavery debate reiterated the familiar themes of Negro inferiority and laziness and the benefits to the slave of the southern plantation system. Occasionally, an author like Samuel A. Cartwright would add a novel twist to the proslavery arguments with his discovery of previously unknown "diseases." Writers like Cartwright and Josiah Nott assumed the inferiority of the Negro race and then bent their talents to proving it through biblical revelation, historical precedent, and quasi-scientific experimentation. They argued that not only were blacks innately inferior and thus particularly suited to slavery, but that slavery was a positive good for the race. Without slavery, the Negroes' natural laziness would dominate and the slave would fall prey to the peculiar diseases that afflicted the race. In America, in competition with white labor, the black man could survive only if compelled to work for his own good—or so the argument went.

The southern readers of *De Bow's Review* were well aware that the system was less than perfect and that the slaves often exhibited obstinate resistance to this benevolent slavery. The institution was, after all, hedged in by a considerable body of laws designed to limit the freedom of the slaves and to detail the responsibilities of the masters. Samuel Cartwright might explain rascality and running away as merely symptoms of "Dysaethesia Aethiopica" or "Drapetomania," but certain restraints were clearly necessary to prevent those symptoms from becoming epidemic. H. W. Walter's essay on the slave laws of Mississippi reveals the practical cast of the southern mind in constructing a legal code that would restrict the slaves' impulses toward freedom, whatever their cause. Mississippi's slave codes reveal, too, the extent to which slavery also bound the master in the web of laws and duties necessary to maintain a repressive system.

Most of the proslavery articles published in the *Review* were well within the mainstream of southern thinking on the subject, for De Bow saw the journal as a voice of the South and, in addition, he wanted to sell magazines. Many pieces, in fact, offered advice on the management of slaves, advice tailored to both planters and small farmers. In one respect, however, several authors, and De Bow himself, diverged from the common view of slavery as best suited to agricultural labor and argued that slaves could profitably be employed in southern factories and in the construction of vital internal improvements. This theme was repeated with increasing frequency as disunion seemed more imminent toward the end of the 1850s and as it appeared likely that the South would have to employ her servile labor force in developing and maintaining a significant industrial sector of the economy to compensate for the absence of northern goods.

The abolition of slavery as a result of the Civil War confronted proslavery writers like Josiah Nott and George Fitzhugh with a dilemma. Before the war, they had argued that blacks were particularly suited to agricultural labor and to their servile status and that without the protection of slavery the black race would be driven to extinction by white competition. The corollary of this argument was that southern agricultural labor was particularly unhealthy for whites who had the good sense to avoid it or to undertake only supervisory tasks. In the labor-short postwar South, writers like Nott and Fitzhugh had to reject their prewar statements in an effort to provide the South with a labor force. Nott took one course by arguing that most of the South was, in fact, quite healthy for white labor, and that the South would prosper even more with white labor because of its greater productivity. Others, however, remained convinced that the Negro would have to remain the primary agricultural laborer and that if black men and women would not work of their own accord, then new means would have to be devised to compel their labor. George Fitzhugh, for example, more accurately forecast the development of southern tenancy and sharecropping, which kept southern blacks tied to the land and maintained white superiority well into this century.

The authors who wrote on slavery and race for *De Bow's Review* were primarily concerned with defending the almost universal belief in Negro inferiority. The arguments might be standard or novel, but there was no questioning the basic assumption of white superiority. Emancipation threatened the maintenance of white superiority, but not the belief in black inferiority. In the few years that the *Review* was published after the war, De Bow's contributors tried to come to terms with the idea and reality of free blacks. Any optimism that blacks would perhaps surmount their inferiority quickly evaporated in the experience of Reconstruction. By 1867–68, the authors of the *Review* were openly calling for the reimposition of some system designed to compel the labor of blacks and to keep them in their "proper" place.

A Mississippi Planter

MANAGEMENT OF NEGROES UPON SOUTHERN ESTATES

The regulation and treatment of the slave labor force on plantations was obviously a subject of considerable interest and importance to many of the readers of De Bow's Review, *and the editor catered to that interest. The selection below, by an anonymous planter, stresses the benefits that accrued to master and slaves when the latter were "treated with humanity," but with an eye to economy of expense.*

[We regard this as a practical and valuable paper for the planters, and hope that those of them who have been experimenting in the matter, will give us the results.]—Editor.

Some very sensible and practical writer in the March No. of "The Review," under the *"Agricultural Department,"* has given us an article upon the *management of negroes*, which entitles him to the gratitude of the planting community, not only for the sound and useful information it contains, but because it has opened up this subject, to be thought of, written about, and improved upon, until the comforts of our black population shall be greatly increased, and their services become more profitable to their owners. Surely there is no subject which demands of the planter more careful consideration than the proper treatment of his slaves, by whose labor he lives, and for whose conduct and happiness he is responsible in the eyes of God. We very often find planters comparing notes and making suggestions as to the most profitable modes of tilling the soil, erecting gates, fences, farm-houses, machinery, and, indeed, everything else conducive to their comfort and prosperity; but how seldom do we find men comparing notes as to their mode of feeding, clothing, nursing, working, and taking care of those human beings intrusted to our charge, whose best condition is slavery, when they are treated with humanity, and their labor properly directed! I have been a reader of agricultural papers for more than

Vol. X (June, 1851), pp. 621–27.

twenty years, and while I have been surfeited, and not unfrequently disgusted, with those chimney-corner theories (that have no practical result, emanating from men who are fonder of using the pen than the plough-handle) upon the subject of raising crops, and preparing them for market, I have seldom met with an article laying down general rules for the management of negroes, by which their condition could be ameliorated, and the master be profited at the same time. One *good article* upon this subject, would be worth more to the master than a hundred theories about "rotations" and "scientific culture;" and infinitely more to the slave than whole volumes dictated by a spurious philanthropy looking to his emancipation. For it is a fact established beyond all controversy, that when the negro is treated with humanity, and subjected to constant employment without the labor of thought, and the cares incident to the necessity of providing for his own support, he is by far happier than he would be if emancipated, and left to think, and act, and provide for himself. And from the vast amount of experience in the management of slaves, can we not deduce some general, practicable rules for their government, that would add to the happiness of both master and servant? I know of no other mode of arriving at this great desideratum, than for planters to give to the public their rules for feeding, clothing, housing and working their slaves, and of taking care of them when sick, together with their plantation discipline. In this way, we shall be continually learning something new upon this vitally interesting question, filled, as it is, with great responsibilities; and while our slaves will be made happier, our profits from their labor will be greater, and our consciences be made easier.

I would gladly avail myself of the privilege of contributing my mite to the accomplishment of this end, by giving my own system of management, not because there is anything novel in it—that it is better, or differs essentially from that of most of my neighbors—but because it may meet the eye of some man of enlarged experience who will necessarily detect its faults, and who may be induced to suggest the proper corrections, and for which I should feel profoundly grateful. To begin, then, I send you my plantation rules, that are printed in the plantation book, which constitute a part of the contract made in the employment of the overseer, and which are observed, so far as my constant and vigilant superintendence can enforce them. My first care has been to select a proper place for my "Quarter," well protected by the shade of forest trees, sufficiently thinned out to admit a free circulation of air, so situated as to be free from the impurities of stagnant water, and to

erect comfortable houses for my negroes. Planters do not always reflect that there is more sickness, and consequently greater loss of life,
from the decaying logs of negro houses, open floors, leaky roofs, and
crowded rooms, than all other causes combined; and if humanity will
not point out the proper remedy, let self-interest for once act as a virtue, and prompt him to save the health and lives of his negroes, by at
once providing comfortable quarters for them. There being upwards of
150 negroes on the plantation, I provide for them 24 houses made
of hewn post oak, covered with cypress, 16 by 18, with close plank
floors and good chimneys, and elevated two feet from the ground. The
ground *under* and around the houses is swept every month, and the
houses, both inside and out, white-washed twice a year. The houses
are situated in a double row from north to south, about 200 feet apart,
the doors facing inwards, and the houses being in a line, about 50 feet
apart. At one end of the street stands the overseer's house, workshops, tool house, and wagon sheds; at the other, the grist and saw-
mill, with good cisterns at each end, providing an ample supply of pure
water. My experience has satisfied me, that spring, well, and lake water are all unhealthy in this climate, and that large under-ground
cisterns, keeping the water pure and cool, are greatly to be preferred.
They are easily and cheaply constructed, very convenient, and save
both doctors' bills and loss of life. The negroes are never permitted to
sleep before the fire, either lying down or sitting up, if it can be
avoided, as they are always prone to sleep with their heads to the fire,
are liable to be burnt, and to contract disease; but beds with ample
clothing are provided for them, and in them they are *made to sleep*. As
to their habits of amalgamation and intercourse, I know of no means
whereby to regulate them, or to restrain them; I attempted it for many
years by preaching virtue and decency, encouraging marriages, and by
punishing, with some severity, departures from marital obligations;
but it was all in vain. I allow for each hand that works out, four pounds
of clear meat and one peck of meal per week. Their dinners are cooked
for them, and carried to the field, always with vegetables, according
to the season. There are two houses set apart at mid-day for resting,
eating, and sleeping, if they desire it, and they retire to one of the
weather-sheds or the grove to pass this time, not being permitted to
remain in the hot sun while at rest. They cook their own suppers and
breakfasts, each family being provided with an oven, skillet, and sifter,
and each one having a coffee-pot (and generally some coffee to put in

it,) with knives and forks, plates, spoons, cups, &c., of their own providing. The wood is regularly furnished them; for, I hold it to be absolutely mean, for a man to require a negro to work until daylight closes in, and then force him to get wood, sometimes half a mile off, before he can get a fire, either to warm himself or cook his supper. Every negro has his hen-house, where he raises poultry, which he is not permitted to sell, and he cooks and eats his chickens and eggs for his evening and morning meals to suit himself; besides, every family has a garden, paled in, where they raise such vegetables and fruits as they take a fancy to. A large house is provided as a nursery for the children, where all are taken at daylight, and placed under the charge of a careful and experienced woman, whose sole occupation is to attend to them, and see that they are properly fed and attended to, and above all things to keep them as dry and as cleanly as possible, under the circumstances. The suckling women come in to nurse their children four times during the day; and it is the duty of the nurse to see that they do not perform this duty until they have become properly cool, after walking from the field. In consequence of these regulations, I have never lost a child from being burnt to death, or, indeed, by accidents of any description; and although I have had more than thirty born within the last five years, yet I have not lost a single one from teething, or the ordinary summer complaints so prevalent amongst the children in this climate.

I give to my negroes four full suits of clothes with two pair of shoes, every year, and to my women and girls a calico dress and two handkerchiefs extra. I do not permit them to have "truck patches" other than their gardens, or to raise anything whatever for market; but in lieu thereof, I give to each head of a family and to every single negro on Christmas day, five dollars, and send them to the county town under the charge of the overseer or driver, to spend their money. In this way, I save my mules from being killed up in summer, and my oxen in winter, by working and hauling off their crops; and more than all, the negroes are prevented from acquiring habits of trading in farm produce, which invariably leads to stealing, followed by whipping, trouble to the master, and discontent on the part of the slave. I permit no spirits to be brought on the plantation, or used by any negro, if I can prevent it; and a violation of this rule, if found out, is always followed by a whipping, and a forfeiture of the five dollars next Christmas.

I have a large and comfortable hospital provided for my negroes

when they are sick; to this is attached a nurse's room; and when a negro complains of being too unwell to work, he is at once sent to the
hospital, and put under the charge of a very experienced and careful
negro woman, who administers the medicine and attends to his diet,
and where they remain until they are able to work again. This woman
is provided with sugar, coffee, molasses, rice, flour and tea, and does
not permit a patient to taste of meat or vegetables until he is restored
to health. Many negroes relapse after the disease is broken, and die, in
consequence of remaining in their houses and stuffing themselves with
coarse food after their appetites return, and both humanity and economy dictate that this should be prevented. From the system I have
pursued, I have not lost a hand since the summer of 1845, (except one
that was killed by accident,) nor has my physician's bill averaged fifty
dollars a year, notwithstanding I live near the edge of the swamp of
Big Black River, where it is thought to be very unhealthy.

I cultivate about ten acres of cotton and six of corn to the hand, not
forgetting the little wheat patch that your correspondent speaks of,
which costs but little trouble, and proves a great comfort to the negroes; and have as few sour looks and as little whipping as almost any
other place of the same size.

I must not omit to mention that I have a good fiddler, and keep him
well supplied with catgut, and I make it his duty to play for the negroes every Saturday night until 12 o'clock. They are exceedingly
punctual in their attendance at the ball, while Charley's fiddle is always accompanied with Ihurod on the triangle, and Sam to "pat."

I also employ a good preacher, who regularly preaches to them on
the Sabbath day, and it is made the duty of every one to come up clean
and decent to the place of worship. As Father Garritt regularly calls on
Brother Abram, (the foreman of the prayer meetings,) to close the exercises, he gives out and sings his hymn with much unction, and always cocks his eye at Charley, the fiddler, as much as to say, "Old fellow, you had your time last night; now it is mine."

I would gladly learn every negro on the place to read the bible, but
for a fanaticism which, while it professes friendship to the negro, is
keeping a cloud over his mental vision, and almost crushing out his
hopes of salvation.

These are some of the leading outlines of my management, so far as
my negroes are concerned. That they are imperfect, and could be
greatly improved, I readily admit; and it is only with the hope that I

shall be able to improve them by the experience of others, that I have given them to the public.

Should you come to the conclusion that these rules would be of any service when made known to others, you will please give them a place in the "Review."

A Mississippi Planter.

Samuel A. Cartwright

DISEASES AND PECULIARITIES
OF THE NEGRO RACE

*Samuel A. Cartwright (1793–1863) was a physician and writer on
medicine, race, and slavery. Born in Virginia, he studied medicine at
the University of Pennsylvania and practiced it in Huntsville, Alabama, Natchez, Mississippi, and, after 1848, in New Orleans. His
medical writings include essays on yellow fever and cholera and won
him some recognition. Between 1851 and 1862, he published fourteen
articles in* De Bow's Review *on such subjects as sugar, education, the
unity of mankind, and the diseases of Negroes. In 1862, he was appointed to improve sanitary conditions for the Confederate Army in
the vicinity of Vicksburg and there contracted the disease that caused
his death in May, 1863.*

*By the 1850s, white southerners needed no convincing that Negroes
were an inferior race, but, prodded by the abolitionist arguments, they
felt compelled to provide scientific evidence to support this belief. Numerous southern physicians such as Cartwright used their medical
experience as the basis for developing quasi-scientific explanations for
Negro inferiority. They believed they could prove that Negroes were
physiologically inferior to whites. Cartwright's "Diseases and Peculiarities of the Negro Race" is a good example of the lengths to which
these defenders of slavery would go in attempting to offer a scientific
rationale for the institution. Cartwright's essay is particularly interesting for his physiological explanations of the tendencies toward rascality and running away so common in the slave population of the
South. Masters found it far more comforting to believe that such behavior was a physiological weakness in the race than to confront the
reality that the slaves were rebelling against the peculiar institution.*

[This interesting subject has never before, we believe, been treated in an independent and philosophical manner, by any of our physiological and medical
writers, although it has a direct and practical bearing upon over three millions

Vol. XI (July, 1851), pp. 64–69, and (September, 1851), pp. 331–36.

of people, and $2,000,000,000 of property! Dr. Cartwright, of New-Orleans, deserves distinguished praise for the able investigations he has conducted in this recondite department, and we believe they will be received among the planters throughout the South as of inappreciable value. They are embodied in a paper, read by him before the late Medical Convention of Louisiana, which we shall present to our readers in two or three parts, according to subjects. It is impossible to occupy the same space with material a tithe part so valuable:]

Although the African race constitutes nearly a moiety of our southern population, it has not been made the subject of much scientific investigation, and is almost entirely unnoticed in medical books and schools. It is only very lately that it has, in large masses, dwelt in juxtaposition with science and mental progress. On the Niger and in the wilds of Africa, it has existed for thousands of years, excluded from the observation of the scientific world. It is only since the revival of learning, that the people of that race have been introduced on this continent. They are located in those parts of it, not prolific in books and medical authors. No medical school was ever established near them until a few years ago; hence, their diseases and physical peculiarities are almost unknown to the learned. The little knowledge that Southern physicians have acquired concerning them, has not been derived from books or medical lectures, but from facts learned from their own observation in the field of experience, or picked up here and there from others.

Before going into the peculiarities of their diseases, it is necessary to glance at the anatomical and physiological differences between the negro and the white man; otherwise their diseases cannot be understood. It is commonly taken for granted, that the color of the skin constitutes the main and essential difference between the black and the white race; but there are other differences more deep, durable and indelible, in their anatomy and physiology, than that of mere color. In the albino the skin is white, yet the organization is that of the negro. Besides, it is not only in the skin that a difference of color exists between the negro and the white man, but in the membranes, the muscles, the tendons, and in all the fluids and secretions. Even the negro's brain and nerves, the chyle and all the humors, are tinctured with a shade of the pervading darkness. His bile is of a deeper color, and his blood is blacker than the white man's. There is the same difference in the flesh of the white and black man, in regard to color, that exists between the flesh of the rabbit and the hare. His bones are whiter and harder than those of the white race, owing to their containing more phosphate of

lime and less gelatine. His head is hung on the atlas differently from
the white man; the face is thrown more upwards, and the neck is
shorter and less oblique; the spine more inwards, and the pelvis more
obliquely outwards; the thigh-bones larger, and flattened from before
backwards; the bones more bent; the legs curved outwards, or bowed;
the feet, flat; the gastrocnemii muscles so long, as to make the ankle
appear as if planted in the middle of the foot; the gait, hopper-hipped,
or what the French call *l'allure dehanchee*, not unlike that of a person
carrying a burden. The projecting mouth, the retreating forehead, the
broad, flat nose, thick lips and woolly hair, are peculiarities that strike
every beholder. According to Sœmmerring and other anatomists, who
have dissected the negro, his brain is a ninth or tenth less than in other
races of men, his facial angle smaller, and all the nerves going from the
brain, as also the ganglionic system of nerves, are larger in proportion
than in the white man. The nerves distributed to the muscles are
an exception, being smaller than in the white race. Sœmmerring remarks, that the negro's brain has in a great measure run into nerves.
One of the most striking differences is found in the much greater size of
the *foramen magnum* in the negro than the white man. The foramen,
or orifice between the brain and the spinal marrow, is not only larger,
but the medulla oblongata, and particularly the nerves supplying the
abdominal and pelvic viscera. Although the nose is flat, the turbinated
bones are more developed, and the pituitary membrane, lining the internal cavities of the nose, more extensive than in the white man, and
causing the sense of smell to be more acute. The negro's hearing is better, his sight is stronger, and he seldom needs spectacles.

The field of vision is not so large in the negro's eye as in the white
man's. He bears the rays of the sun better, because he is provided with
an anatomical peculiarity in the inner canthus, contracting the field of
vision, and excluding the sun's rays,—something like the membrana
nictitans, formed by a preternatural development of the plica lunaris,
like that which is observed in apes. His imitative powers are very
great, and he can agitate every part of the body at the same time, or
what he calls *dancing all over*. From the diffusion of the brain, as it
were, into the various organs of the body, in the shape of nerves to
minister to the senses, everything, from the necessity of such a conformation, partakes of sensuality, at the expense of intellectuality. Thus,
music is a mere sensual pleasure with the negro. There is nothing in
his music addressing the understanding; it has melody, but no harmony; his songs are mere sounds, without sense or meaning—pleasing

the ear, without conveying a single idea to the mind; his ear is gratified by sound, as his stomach is by food. The great development of the nervous system, and the profuse distribution of nervous matter to the stomach, liver and genital organs, would make the Ethiopian race entirely unmanageable, if it were not that this excessive nervous development is associated with a deficiency of red blood in the pulmonary and arterial systems, from a defective atmospherization or arterialization of the blood in the lungs—constituting the best type of what is called the lymphatic temperament, in which lymph, phlegm, mucus, and other humors predominate over the red blood. It is this defective hematosis, or atmospherization of the blood, conjoined with a deficiency of cerebral matter in the cranium, and an excess of nervous matter distributed to the organs of sensation and assimilation, that is the true cause of that debasement of mind, which has rendered the people of Africa unable to take care of themselves. It is the true cause of their indolence and apathy, and why they have chosen, through countless ages, idleness, misery and barbarism, to industry and frugality,—why social industry, or associated labor, so essential to all progress in civilization and improvement, has never made any progress among them, or the arts and sciences taken root on any portion of African soil inhabited by them; as is proved by the fact that no letters, or even hieroglyphics—no buildings, roads or improvements, or monuments of any kind, are anywhere found, to indicate that they have ever been awakened from their apathy and sleepy indolence, to physical or mental exertion. To the same physiological causes, deeply rooted in the organization, we must look for an explanation of the strange facts, why none of the languages of the native tribes of Africa, as proved by ethnographical researches, have risen above common names, standing for things and actions, to abstract terms or generalizations; why no form of government on abstract principles, with divisions of power into separate departments, has ever been instituted by them?—why they have always preferred, as more congenial to their nature, a government combining the legislative, judicial and executive powers in the same individual, in the person of a petty king, a chieftain, or master?— why, in America, if let alone, they always prefer the same kind of government which we call slavery, but which is actually an improvement on the government of their forefathers, as it gives them more tranquillity and sensual enjoyment, expands the mind and improves the morals, by arousing them from that natural indolence so fatal to mental and moral progress. Even if they did not prefer slavery, tranquillity and sensual enjoyment, to liberty, yet their organization of mind is such, that if they had their liberty, they have not the industry, the moral virtue, the courage and vigilance to maintain it, but would relapse into barbarism, or into slavery, as they have done in Hayti. The reason of this is founded in unalterable physiological laws. Under the compulsive power of the white man, they are made to labor or exercise, which makes the lungs perform the duty of vitalizing the blood more perfectly than is done when they are left free to indulge in idleness. It is the red, vital blood, sent to the brain, that liberates their mind when under the white man's control; and it is the want of a sufficiency of red, vital blood, that chains their mind to ignorance and barbarism, when in freedom.

The excess of organic nervous matter, and the deficiency of cerebral—the predominance of the humors over the red blood, from defective atmospherization of the blood in the lungs, impart to the negro a nature not unlike that of a new-born infant of the white race. In children, the nervous system predominates, and the temperament is lymphatic. The liver, and the rest of the glandular system, is out of proportion to the sanguineous and respiratory systems, the white fluids predominating over the red; the lungs consume less oxygen, and the liver separates more carbon, than in the adult age. This constitution, so well marked in infancy, is the type of the Ethiopian constitution, of all ages and sexes. It is well known, that in infancy, full and free respiration of pure fresh air in repose, so far from being required, is hurtful and prejudicial. Half smothered by its mother's bosom, or the cold external air carefully excluded by a warm room or external covering over the face, the infant reposes—re-breathing its own breath, warmed to the same temperature as that of its body, and loaded with carbonic acid and aqueous vapor. The natural effect of this kind of respiration is, imperfect atmospherization of the blood in the lungs, and a hebetude of intellect, from the defective vitalization of the blood distributed to the brain. But it has heretofore escaped the attention of the scientific world, that the defective atmospherization of the blood, known to occur during sleep in infancy, and to be the most congenial to their constitutions, is the identical kind of respiration most congenial to the negro constitution, of all ages and sexes, when in repose. This is proved by the fact of the universal practice among them of covering their head and faces, during sleep, with a blanket, or any kind of covering that they can get hold of. If they have only a part of a blanket, they will cover their faces when about to go to sleep. If they have no covering, they will throw their hands or arms across the mouth and nose, and turn on their faces, as if with an instinctive design to obstruct the entrance of the free external air into the lungs during sleep. As in the case with infants, the air that negroes breathe, with their faces thus smothered with blankets or other covering, is not so much the external air as their own breath, warmed to the same temperature as that of their bodies, by confinement and reinspiration. This instinctive and universal method of breathing, during sleep, proves the similarity of organization and physiological laws existing between negroes and infants, as far as the important function of respiration is concerned. Both are alike in re-breathing their own breath, and in requiring it to be warmed to their own temperature, by confinement which would be insupportable to the white race after passing the age of infancy. The inevitable effect of breathing a heated air, loaded with carbonic acid and aqueous vapor, is defective hematosis and hebetude of intellect.

Negroes, moreover, resemble children in the activity of the liver and in their strong assimilating powers, and in the predominance of the other systems over the sanguineous; hence they are difficult to bleed, owing to the smallness of their veins. On cording the arm of the stoutest negro, the veins will be found scarcely as large as a white boy's of ten years of age. They are liable to all the convulsive diseases, cramps, spasms, colics, etc., that children are so subject to.

Although their skin is very thick, it is as sensitive, when they are in perfect health, as that of children, and like them, they fear the rod. They resemble children in another very important particular: they are very easily governed by love combined with fear, and they are ungovernable, vicious and rude under any form of government whatever, not resting on love and fear as a basis. Like children, it is not necessary that they be kept under the fear of the lash; it is sufficient that they be kept under the fear of offending those who have authority over them. Like children, they are constrained, by unalterable physiological laws, to love those in authority over them, who minister to their wants and immediate necessities, and are not cruel or unmerciful. The defective hematosis, in both cases, and the want of courage and energy of mind as a consequence thereof, produces in both an instinctive feeling of dependence on others, to direct them and to take care of them. Hence, from a law of his nature, the negro can no more help loving a kind master, than the child can help loving her who gives it suck.

Like children, they require government in every thing; food, clothing, exercise, sleep—all require to be prescribed by rule, or they will run into excesses. Like children, they are apt to over-eat themselves, or to confine their diet too much to one favorite article, unless restrained from doing so. They often gorge themselves with fat meat, as children do with sugar.

One of the greatest mysteries to those unacquainted with the negro character, is the facility with which an hundred, even two or three hundred, able-bodied and vigorous negroes are kept in subjection by one white man, who sleeps in perfect security among them, generally, in warm weather, with doors and windows open, with all his people, called slaves, at large around him. But a still greater mystery is the undoubted fact of the love they bear to their masters, similar in all respects to the love that children bear to their parents, which nothing but severity or cruelty in either case can alienate. The physiological laws, on which this instinctive and most mysterious love is founded in the one case, are applicable to the other. Like children, when well-behaved and disposed to do their duty, it is not the arbitrary authority over them that they dread, but the petty tyranny and imposition of one another. The overseer among them, like the school-master among children, has only to be impartial, and to preserve order by strict justice to all, to gain their good will and affection, and to be viewed, not as an object of terror, but as a friend and protector to quiet their fears of one another.

There is a difference between infant negroes and infant white children; the former are born with heads like gourds, the fontinelles being nearly closed, and the sutures between the various bones of the head united,—not open and permitting of overlapping, as in white children. There is no necessity for the overlapping of the bones of the head in infant negroes, as they are smaller, and the pelvis of their mothers larger than in the white race. All negroes are not equally black—the blacker, the healthier and stronger; any deviation from the black color, in the pure race, is a mark of feebleness or ill health. When heated from exercise, the negro's skin is covered with an oily exudation that gives a dark color to white linen, and has a very strong odor. The odor is strongest in the most robust; children and the aged have very little of it.

I have thus hastily and imperfectly noticed some of the more striking anatomical and physiological peculiarities of the negro race. The question may be asked: does he belong to the same race as the white man? Is he a son of Adam? Does his peculiar physical conformation stand in opposition to the Bible, or does it prove its truth? These are important questions, both in a medical, historical and theological point of view. They can better be answered by a comparison of the facts derived from anatomy, physiology, history and theology, to see if they sustain one another. We learn from the Book of Genesis, that Noah had three sons, Shem, Ham and Japheth, and that Canaan, the son of Ham, was doomed to be servant of servants unto his brethren. From history, we learn, that the descendants of Canaan settled in Africa, and are the present Ethiopians, or black race of men; that Shem occupied Asia, and Japheth the north of Europe. In the 9th chapter and 27th verse of Genesis, one of the most authentic books of the Bible, is this remarkable prophecy: "God shall enlarge Japheth, and he shall dwell in the tents of Shem; and Canaan *shall be* his servant." Japheth has been greatly enlarged by the discovery of a new world, the continent of America. He found in it the Indians, whom natural history declares to be of Asiatic origin, in other words, the descendants of Shem: he drove out Shem, and occupied his tents: and now the remaining part of the prophecy is in the process of fulfilment, from the facts everywhere before us, of Canaan having become his servant. The question arises, is the Canaanite, or Ethiopian, qualified for the trying duties of servitude, and unfitted for the enjoyment of freedom? If he be, there is both wisdom, mercy and justice in the decree dooming him to be servant of servants, as the decree is in conformity to his nature. Anatomy and physiology have been interrogated, and the response is, that the Ethiopian, or Canaanite, is unfitted, from his organization and the physiological laws predicated on that organization, for the responsible duties of a free man, but, like the child, is only fitted for a state of dependence and subordination. When history is interrogated, the response is, that the only government under which the negro has made any improvement in mind, morals, religion, and the only government under which he has led a happy, quiet and contented life, is that under which he is subjected to the arbitrary power of Japheth, in obedience to the Divine decree. When the original Hebrew of the Bible is interrogated, we find, in the significant meaning of the original name of the negro, the identical fact set forth, which the knife of the anatomist at the dissecting-table has made appear; as if the revelations of anatomy, physiology and history, were a mere re-writing of what Moses wrote. In the Hebrew word "Canaan," the original name of the Ethiopian, the word *slave by nature*, or language to the same effect, is written by the inspired penman. Hence there is no conflict between the revelations of the science of medicine, history, and the inductions drawn from the

Baconian philosophy and the authority of the Bible; one supports the other.

As an illustration, it is known that all the Hebrew names are derived from verbs, and are significant. The Hebrew verb *Canah*, from which the original name of the negro is derived, literally means *to submit himself—to bend the knee*. Gesenius, the best Hebrew scholar of modern times, renders both the Kal, Hiphil and Niphal form of the verb from which Canaan, the original name of the negro is derived, in the following Latin: *Genu flexit*—he bends the knee; *in genua procidet*— he falls on his knees; *depressus est animus*—his mind is depressed; *submisse se gessit*—he deports himself submissively; *fractus est*—he is crouched or broken; or in other words, *slave by nature*, the same thing which anatomy, physiology, history, and the inductions drawn from philosophical observations, prove him to be.

A knowledge of the great primary truth, that the negro is a slave by nature, and can never be happy, industrious, moral or religious, in any other condition than the one he was intended to fill, is of great importance to the theologian, the statesman, and to all those who are at heart seeking to promote his temporal and future welfare. This great truth, if better known and understood, would go far to prevent the East India Company and British Government from indulging any expectation of seeing their immense possessions in Asia enhanced in value by the overthrow of slave-labor in America, through the instrumentality of northern fanaticism; or of seeing the Union, divided into two or more factions hostile to each other; or of gaining any advantages that civil commotion on this side of the Atlantic would give to the tottering monarchies of Europe. With the subject under this aspect, the science of medicine has nothing to do, further than to uncover its light—to show truth from error.

Drapetomania, or the Disease Causing Negroes to Run Away

Drapetomania is from δραπέτης, a runaway slave, and μανια, *mad or crazy*. It is unknown to our medical authorities, although its diagnostic symptom, the absconding from service, is as well known to our planters and overseers, as it was to the ancient Greeks, who expressed, by the single word δραπέτης, the fact of the absconding, and the relation that the fugitive held to the person he fled from. I have added to the word meaning runaway slave, another Greek term, to express the disease of the mind causing him to abscond. In noticing a disease not heretofore classed among the long list of maladies that man is subject to, it was necessary to have a new term to express it. The cause in the most of cases, that induces the negro to run away from service, is as much a disease of the mind as any other species of mental alienation, and much more curable, as a general rule. With the advantages of proper medical advice, strictly followed, this troublesome practice that many negroes have of running away, can be almost entirely prevented, although the slaves be located on the borders of a free state, within a stone's throw of the abolitionists. I was born in Virginia, east of the Blue Ridge, where negroes were numerous, and studied medicine some years in Maryland, a slave state, separated from Pennsylvania, a free state, by Mason & Dixon's line—a mere air line, without wall or guard. I long ago observed that some persons considered as very good, and others as very bad masters, often lost their negroes by their absconding from service; while the slaves of another class of persons, remarkable for order and good discipline, but not praised or blamed as either good or bad masters, never ran away, although no guard or forcible means were used to prevent them. The same management which prevented them from walking over a mere nominal, unguarded line, will prevent them from running away anywhere.

To ascertain the true method of governing negroes, so as to cure and prevent the disease under consideration, we must go back to the Pentateuch, and learn the true meaning of the untranslated term that represents the negro race. In the name there given to that race, is locked up the true art of governing negroes in such a manner that they cannot run away. The correct translation of that term declares the Creator's will in regard to the negro; it declares him to be the submissive knee-bender. In the anatomical conformation of his knees, we see *"genu flexit"* written in his physical structure, being more flexed or bent, than any other kind of man. If the white man attempts to oppose the Deity's will, by trying to make the negro anything else than *"the submissive knee-bender,"* (which the Almighty declared he should be,) by trying to raise him to a level with himself, or by putting himself on an equality with the negro; or if he abuses the power which God has given him over his fellow-man, by being cruel to him, or punishing him in anger, or by neglecting to protect him from the wanton abuses of his fellow-servants and all others, or by denying him the usual comforts and necessaries of life, the negro will run away; but if he keeps him in the position that we learn from the Scriptures he was intended to occupy, that is, the position of submission; and if his master or overseer be kind and gracious in his bearing towards him, without condescension, and at the same time ministers to his physical wants, and protects him from abuses, the negro is spell-bound, and cannot run away. *"He shall serve Japheth;* he shall be his servant of servants," on the conditions above mentioned—conditions that are clearly implied, though not directly expressed. According to my experience, the "genu flexit"—the awe and reverence, must be exacted from them, or they will despise their masters, become rude and ungovernable, and run away. On Mason and Dixon's line, two classes of persons were apt to lose their negroes: those who made themselves too familiar with them, treating them as equals, and making little or no distinction in regard to color; and, on the other hand, those who treated them cruelly, denied them the common necessaries of life, neglected to protect them against the abuses of others, or frightened them by a blustering manner of approach, when about to punish them for misdemeanors. Before negroes run away, unless they are frightened or panic-struck, they become sulky and dissatisfied. The cause of this sulkiness and dissatisfaction should be inquired into and removed, or they are apt to run away or fall into the negro consumption. When sulky and dissatisfied without cause, the experience of those on the line and elsewhere, was decidedly in favor of whipping them out of it, as a preventive measure against absconding, or other bad conduct. It was called whipping the devil out of them.

If treated kindly, well fed and clothed, with fuel enough to keep a small fire burning all night—separated into families, each family having its own house—not permitted to run about at night to visit their neighbors, to receive visits or to use intoxicating liquors, and not overworked or exposed too much to the weather, they are very easily governed—more so than any other people in the world. When all this is done, if any one or more of them, at any time, are inclined to raise their heads to a level with their master or overseer, humanity and their own good require that they should be punished until they fall into that submissive state which it was intended for them to occupy in all aftertime, when their progenitor received the name of Canaan or "submissive knee-bender." They have only to be kept in that state and treated like children, with care, kindness, attention and humanity, to prevent and cure them from running away.

Dysæsthesia Æthiopica, or Hebetude of Mind, and Obtuse Sensibility of Body—A Disease Peculiar to Negroes— Called by Overseers, "Rascality."

Dysæsthesia Æthiopica is a disease peculiar to negroes, affecting both mind and body in a manner as well expressed by dysæsthesia, the name I have given it, as could be by a single term. There is both mind and sensibility, but both seem to be difficult to reach by impressions from without. There is a partial insensibility of the skin, and so great a hebetude of the intellectual faculties, as to be like a person half asleep, that is with difficulty aroused and kept awake. It differs from every other species of mental disease, as it is accompanied with physical signs or lesions of the body discoverable to the medical observer, which are always present and sufficient to account for the symptoms. It is much more prevalent among free negroes living in clusters by themselves, than among slaves on our plantations, and attacks only such slaves as live like free negroes in regard to diet, drinks, exercise, etc. It is not my purpose to treat of the complaint as it prevails among free negroes, nearly all of whom are more or less afflicted with it, that have not got some white person to direct and to take care of them. To narrate its symptoms and effects among them would be to write a history of the ruins and dilapidation of Hayti, and every spot of earth they have ever had uncontrolled possession over for any length of time. I propose only to describe its symptoms among slaves.

From the careless movements of the individuals affected with the complaint, they are apt to do much mischief, which appears as if intentional, but is mostly owing to the stupidity of mind and insensibility of the nerves induced by the disease. Thus, they break, waste and destroy everything they handle,—abuse horses and cattle,—tear, burn or rend their own clothing, and, paying no attention to the rights of property, steal others, to replace what they have destroyed. They wander about at night, and keep in a half nodding sleep during the day. They slight their work,—cut up corn, cane, cotton or tobacco when hoeing it, as if for pure mischief. They raise disturbances with their overseers and fellow-servants without cause or motive, and seem to be insensible to pain when subjected to punishment. The fact of the existence of such a complaint, making man like a automaton or senseless machine, having the above or similar symptoms, can be clearly established by the most direct and positive testimony. That it should have escaped the attention of the medical profession, can only be accounted for because its attention has not been sufficiently directed to the maladies of the negro race. Otherwise a complaint of so common an occurrence on badly-governed plantations, and so universal among free negroes, or those who are not governed at all,—a disease radicated in physical lesions and having its peculiar and well marked symptoms and its curative indications, would not have escaped the notice of the profession. The northern physicians and people have noticed the symptoms, but not the disease from which they spring. They ignorantly attribute the symptoms to the debasing influence of slavery on the mind, without considering that those who have never been in slavery, or their fathers before them, are the most afflicted, and the latest from the slave-holding South the least. The disease is the natural offspring of negro liberty—the liberty to be idle, to wallow in filth, and to indulge in improper food and drinks.

In treating of the anatomy and physiology of the negro, I showed that his respiratory system was under the same physiological laws as that of an infant child of the white race: that a warm atmosphere, loaded with carbonic acid and aqueous vapor, was the most congenial to his lungs during sleep, as it is to the infant; that, to insure the respiration of such an atmosphere, he invariably, as if moved by instinct, shrouds his head and face in a blanket or some other covering when disposing himself to sleep; that in sleeping by the fire in cold weather he turns his head to it, instead of his feet, evidently to inhale warm air; that when not in active exercise, he always hovers over a fire in comparatively warm weather, as if he took a positive pleasure in inhaling hot air and smoke when his body is quiescent. The natural effect of this practice, it was shown, caused imperfect atmospherization or vitalization of the blood in the lungs, as occurs in infancy, and a hebetude or torpor of intellect—from blood not sufficiently vitalized being distributed to the brain; also a slothfulness, torpor and disinclination to exercise from the same cause—the want of blood sufficiently vitalized in the circulating system.

When left to himself, the negro indulges in his natural disposition to idleness and sloth, and does not take exercise enough to expand his lungs and to vitalize his blood, but dozes out a miserable existence in the midst of filth and uncleanliness, being too indolent, and having too little energy of mind to provide for himself proper food and comfortable lodging and clothing. The consequence is, that the blood becomes so highly carbonized and deprived of oxygen, that it not only becomes unfit to stimulate the brain to energy, but unfit to stimulate the nerves of sensation distributed to the body. A torpor and insensibility pervades the system; the sentient nerves distributed to the skin lose their feeling in so great a degree, that he often burns his skin by the fire he hovers over without knowing it, and frequently has large holes in his clothes, and the shoes on his feet burnt to a crisp, without having been conscious of when it was done. This is the disease called dysæsthesia—a Greek term expressing the dull or obtuse sensation that always attends the complaint. When aroused from his sloth by the stimulus of hunger, he takes anything he can lay his hands on, and tramples on the rights, as well as on the property of others, with perfect indifference as to consequences. When driven to labor by the compulsive power of the white man, he performs the task assigned to him in a headlong, careless manner, treading down with his feet or cutting with his hoe the plants he is put to cultivate—breaking the tools he works with, and spoiling everything he touches that can be injured by careless handling.—Hence the overseers call it "rascality," supposing that the mischief is intentionally done. But there is no premeditated mischief in the case,—the mind is too torpid to meditate mischief, or even to be aroused by any angry passions to deeds of daring. Dysæsthesia, or hebetude of sensation of both mind and body, prevails to so great an extent, that when the unfortunate individual is subjected to punishment, he neither feels pain of any consequence, nor shows any unusual resentment, more than by a stupid sulkiness. In some cases, anæsthesiæ would be a more suitable name for it, as there appears to be an almost total loss of feeling. The term "rascality" given to this disease by overseers, is founded on an erroneous hypothesis, and leads to an incorrect empirical treatment, which seldom or never cures it.

The complaint is easily curable, if treated on sound physiological principles. The skin is dry, thick and harsh to the touch, and the liver inactive. The liver, skin and kidneys should be stimulated to activity and be made to assist in decarbonizing the blood. The best means to stimulate the skin is, first, to have the patient well washed with warm water and soap, then, to anoint it all over with oil, and to slap the oil in with a broad leather strap; then to put the patient to some hard kind of work in the open air and sunshine, that will compel him to expand his lungs, as chopping wood, splitting rails, or sawing with the cross-cut or whip saw. Any kind of labor will do that will cause full and free respiration in its performance, as lifting or carrying heavy weights, or brisk walking; the object being to expand the lungs by full and deep inspiration and expirations, thereby to vitalize the impure circulating blood by introducing oxygen and expelling carbon. This treatment should not be continued too long at a time, because where the circulating fluids are so impure as in this complaint, patients cannot stand protracted exercise without resting frequently and drinking freely of cold water or some cooling beverage, as lemonade, or alternated pepper tea sweetened with molasses. In bad cases, the blood has always the appearance of blood in scurvy, and commonly there is a scorbutic affection to be seen on the gums. After resting until the palpitation of the heart caused by the exercise is allayed, the patient should eat some good wholesome food, well seasoned with spices and mixed with vegetables, as turnip or mustard salad, with vinegar. After a moderate meal, he should resume his work again, resting at intervals, and taking refreshments and supporting the perspiration by partaking freely of liquids. At night he should be lodged in a warm room with a small fire in it, and should have a clean bed with sufficient blanket covering, and be washed clean before going to bed: in the morning, oiled, slapped, and put to work as before. Such treatment will, in a short time, effect a cure in all cases which are not complicated with chronic visceral derangements. The effect of this or a like course of treatment is often like enchantment. No sooner does the blood feel the vivifying influences derived from its full and perfect atmospherization by exercise in the open air and in the sun, than the negro seems to be awakened to a new existence, and to look grateful and thankful to the white man whose compulsory power, by making him inhale vital air, has restored his sensation, and dispelled the mist that clouded his intellect. His intelligence restored and his sensations awakened, he is no longer the *bipedum nequissimus*, or arrant rascal, he was supposed to be, but a good negro that can hoe or plow, and handles things with as much care as his fellow servants.

Contrary to the received opinion, a northern climate is the most favorable to the intellectual development of negroes; those of Missouri, Kentucky and the colder parts of Virginia and Maryland having much more mental energy, being more bold and ungovernable than in the southern lowlands; a dense atmosphere causing a better ventilation of their blood.

Although idleness is the most prolific cause of dysæsthesia, yet there are other ways that the blood gets deteriorated. I said before that negroes are like children, requiring government in everything. If not governed in their diet, they are apt to eat too much salt meat and not enough bread and vegetables, which practice generates a scorbutic state of the fluids and leads to the affection under consideration. This form of the complaint always shows itself in the gums, which become spongy and dark and leave the teeth. Uncleanliness of skin and torpid liver also tend to produce it. A scurvy set of negroes means the same thing, in the South, as a disorderly, worthless set. That the blood, when rendered impure and carbonaceous from any cause, as from idleness, filthy habits, unwholesome food or alcoholic drinks, affects the mind, is not only known to physicians, but was known to the Bard of Avon when he penned the lines—"We are not ourselves when Nature, being oppressed, commands the mind to suffer with the body."

According to unaltered physiological laws, negroes, as a general rule to which there are but few exceptions, can only have their intellectual faculties awakened in a sufficient degree to receive moral culture and to profit by religious or other instructions, when under the compulsatory authority of the white man; because, as a general rule to which there are but few exceptions, they will not take sufficient exercise, when removed from the white man's authority, to vitalize and decarbonize their blood by the process of full and free respiration, that active exercise of some kind alone can effect. A northern climate remedies, in a considerable degree, their naturally indolent disposition; but the dense atmosphere of Boston or Canada can scarcely produce sufficient hematosis and vigor of mind to induce them to labor. From their natural indolence, unless under the stimulus of compulsion, they doze away their lives, with the capacity of their lungs for atmospheric air only half expanded from the want of exercise to superinduce full and deep respiration. The inevitable effect is to prevent a sufficient atmospherization or vitalization of the blood, so essential to the expansion and the freedom of action of the intellectual faculties. The black blood distributed to the brain chains the mind to ignorance, superstition and barbarism, and bolts the door against civilization, moral culture and religious truth. The compulsory power of the white man, by making the slothful negro take active exercise, puts into active play the lungs, through whose agency the vitalized blood is sent to the brain to give liberty to the mind and to open the door to intellectual improvement. The very exercise, so beneficial to the negro, is expended in cultivating those burning fields of cotton, sugar, rice and tobacco, which, but for his labor, would, from the heat of the climate, go uncultivated, and their products be lost to the world. Both parties are benefited—the negro as well as the master—even more. But there is a

third party benefited—the world at large. The three millions of bales
of cotton, made by negro labor, afford a cheap clothing for the civilized
world. The laboring classes of all mankind having less to pay for
clothing, have more money to spend in educating their children, in intellectual, moral and religious progress.

The wisdom, mercy and justice of the decree, that Canaan shall
serve Japheth, is proved by the disease we have been considering, because it proves that his physical organization and the laws of his nature
are in perfect unison with slavery, and in entire discordance with liberty—a discordance so great as to produce the loathsome disease that
we have been considering, as one of its inevitable effects,—a disease
that locks up the understanding, blunts the sensations, and chains the
mind to superstition, ignorance and barbarism. Slaves are not subject
to this disease, unless they are permitted to live like free negroes, in
idleness and filth—to eat improper food or to indulge in spirituous liquors. It is not their masters' interest that they should do so: as they
would not only be unprofitable, but as great a nuisance to the South as
the free negroes were found to be in London, whom the British government, more than half a century ago, colonized in Sierra Leone to
get them out of the way. The mad fanaticism that British writers, lecturers and emissaries, and the East India Company planted in our
Northern states, after it was found by well-tried experiments that free
negroes in England, in Canada, in Sierra Leone and elsewhere were a
perfect nuisance, and would not work as free laborers, but would
retrograde to barbarism, was not planted there in opposition to British
policy. Whatever was the motive of Great Britain in sowing the whirlwind in our Northern states, it is now threatening the disruption of a
mighty empire of the happiest, most progressive and Christian people,
that ever inhabited the earth—and the only empire on the wide earth
that England dreads as a rival, either in arts or in arms.

Our Declaration of Independence, which was drawn up at a time
when negroes were scarcely considered as human beings, "*That all
men are by nature free and equal,*" and only intended to apply to white
men, is often quoted in support of the false dogma that all mankind
possess the same mental, physiological and anatomical organization,
and that the liberty, free institutions, and whatever else would be
a blessing to one portion, would, under the same external circumstances, be to all, without regard to any original or internal differences
inherent in the organization. Although England preaches this doctrine, she practices in opposition to it every where. Instance her treat-

ment of the Gipsies in England, the Hindoos in India, the Hottentots at her Cape Colony, and the aboriginal inhabitants of New-Holland. The dysæsthesia æthiopica adds another to the many ten thousand evidences of the fallacy of the dogma that abolitionism is built on; for here, in a country where two races of men dwell together, both born on the same soil, breathing the same air, and surrounded by the same external agents—liberty, which is elevating the one race of people above all other nations, sinks the other into beastly sloth and torpidity; and the slavery, which the one would prefer death rather than endure, improves the other in body, mind and morals; thus proving the dogma false, and establishing the truth that there is a radical, internal or physical difference between the two races, so great in kind, as to make what is wholesome and beneficial for the white man, as liberty, republican or free institutions, etc., not only unsuitable to the negro race, but actually poisonous to its happiness.

A Small Farmer

MANAGEMENT OF NEGROES

Although similar in some respects to the article by the anonymous Mississippi planter, this letter to De Bow by "A Small Farmer" is especially noteworthy for what it reveals of the differences in approach to slave regulation between the large plantation owner and the small-scale farmer. Near the end of his account, the writer voices his desire, which was no doubt shared by many others like him, to join the ranks of the plantation lords.

J. D. B. De Bow, Esq.—Your number for June contains an article upon this subject, and whilst I agree with the writer in the main, I have also some notions of my own, which you are at liberty to use.

The public may desire to know the age of the writer, the length of time he has been managing negroes, and how long he has tried the mode of management he recommends. It is sufficient to say, I have had control of negroes in and out of the field for thirty years, and have been carrying out my present system, and improving it gradually, for twenty years.

I do not deem it needful to follow "a planter," nor shall I strike a blow at book-farming or theories, as I am an advocate for both, believing that even an error has its advantages, as it will frequently elicit inquiry and a good article in reply, whereas a statement of facts will sometimes pass unnoticed.

Houseing for negroes should be good: each family should have a house, 16 by 18 feet in the clear, plank floor, brick chimney, shingle roof; floor, elevated 2 feet above the earth. There should be no loft, no place to stow away anything, but pins to hang clothes upon. Each house should be provided with a bedstead, cotton mattress, and sufficient bed-clothes for comfort for the heads of the family, and also for the young ones.

Clothing should be sufficient, but of no set quantity, as all will use, or waste what is given, and many be no better clad with four suits than others with two. I know families that never give more than two suits, and their servants are always neater than others with even four.

My rule is, to give for winter a linsey suit, one shirt of best toweling, one hat, one pair of shoes, a good blanket, costing $2 to $2 50, every other year, (or I prefer, after trying three years, a comfort.) In the summer, two shirts, two pair pants, and one straw hat. Several of my negroes will require two pair pants for winter, and occasionally even a third pair, depending mostly upon the material. Others require another shirt and a third pair of pants for summer. I seldom give two pair of shoes.

Food is cooked by a woman, who has the children under her charge. I do not regard it as good economy, to say nothing of any feeling, to require negroes to do any cooking after their day's labor is over.

The food is given out daily, a half pound to each hand that goes to the field, large and small, water carriers and all; bread and vegetables without stint, the latter prepared in my own garden, and dealt out to the best advantage, endeavoring to have something every day in the year. I think four pounds of clear meat is too much. I have negroes here that have had only a half pound each for twenty years, and they bid fair to outlive their master, who occasionally forgets his duty, and will be a gourmand. I practice on the plan, that all of us would be better to be restrained, and that health is best subserved by not over-eating.

My cook would make cotton enough to give the extra one pound. The labor in making vegetables would make another pound. I say this to show I do not dole out a half pound per day from parsimony.

My hours of labor, commencing with pitching my crop, is from daylight until 12 M.; all hands then come in and remain until 2 o'clock, P.M., then back to the field until dark. Some time in May we prolong the rest three hours; and if a very hot day, even four hours. Breakfast is eaten in the field, half an hour to an hour being given; or they eat and go to work without being driven in and out—all stopping when my driver is ready.

I give all females half of every Saturday to wash and clean up, my cook washing for young men and boys through the week. The cabins are scoured once a week, swept out every day, and beds made up at noon in summer, by daylight in winter. In the winter, breakfast is eaten before going to work, and dinner is carried to the hands.

I do not punish often, but I seldom let an offence pass, making a lumping settlement, and then correct for the servant's remembrance. I find it better to whip very little. Young ones being rather treacherous in their memory, pulling an ear, or a sound box, will bring every thing right. I am almost afraid I will subject myself to the "chimney corner theorist's" animadversion, if I say more, but I will risk it. Put up a hewed log-house, with a good substantial door, lock and key, story 12 feet high, logs across above, so as to make a regular built jail. Have air holes near the ceiling well protected by iron bars. The first negro that steals, or runs away, or fights, or who is hard to manage in order to get a day's work, must be locked up every night as soon as he comes in from work, and turned out next morning; kept up every Sunday. Negroes are gregarious; they dread solitariness, and to be deprived from the little weekly dances and chit-chat. They will work to death rather than be shut up. I know the advantage, though I have no jail, my house being a similar one, yet used for other purposes.

I have a fiddle in my quarters, and though some of my good old brethren in the church would think hard of me, yet I allow dancing; ay, I buy the fiddle and encourage it, by giving the boys occasionally a big supper.

I have no overseer, and do not manage so scientifically as those who are able to lay down rules; yet I endeavor to manage so that myself, family and negroes may take pleasure and delight in our relations.

It is not possible in my usual crude way to give my whole plans, but enough is probably said. I permit no night-work, except feeding stock and weighing cotton. No work of any kind at noon, unless to clean out cabins, and bathe the children when nursing, not even washing their clothes.

I require every servant to be present each Sabbath morning and Sabbath evening at family prayers. In the evening the master or sometimes a visiter, if a professor, expounds the chapter read. Thus my servants hear 100 to 200 chapters read each year anyhow. One of my servants, a professor, is sometimes called on to close our exercises with prayer.

Owning but few slaves, I am probably able to do a better part by them than if there were one or two hundred. But I think I could do better if I had enough to permit me to systematize better.

I would keep a cook and a nurse. I would keep a stock feeder, whose whole duty should be to attend to stock in general, to clean out the stable, have troughs filled with food, so that the plow hands would have nothing to do but water, clean down, and tie up the teams. I would build a house large enough, and use it for a dancehouse for the young, and those who wished to dance, as well as for prayer meetings, and for church on Sunday—making it a rule to be present myself occasionally at both, and my overseer always. I know the rebuke in store about dancing, but I cannot help it. I believe negroes will be better disposed this way than any other. I would employ a preacher for every Sabbath. One of my negroes can read the Bible, and he has prayer-meeting every Sabbath at four o'clock, P.M.—all the negroes attend regularly, no compulsion being used.

I have tried faithfully to break up immorality. I have not known an oath to be sworn for a long time. I know of no quarreling, no calling harsh names, and but little stealing. "Habits of amalgamation" I cannot stop; I can check it, but only in the name. I am willing to be taught, for I have tried everything I know. Yours, truly,

A Small Farmer.

P.S.—I endeavor to have regularity on going to bed; forbid sitting or lying by the fire after bed-time. I require fire makers to be up before day in winter, but forbid getting up before day, trotting off to the field, and waiting for daylight, as some persons are said to do. I forbid my driver from keeping hands in the field when there is an appearance of rain.

My negroes get baits of fresh meat occasionally, but always seasoned high with red pepper. At times I give molasses, sugar, coffee and flour, generally laying out about $10 per hand for such luxuries.

Colonel H. W. Walter

SLAVE LAWS OF THE SOUTHERN STATES:
Mississippi

Wherever slavery existed, laws were enacted to proscribe the freedoms of the slave and to outline the duties and responsibilities of the masters. The slave codes of newer states such as Mississippi were often adapted from the older Atlantic seaboard states such as Virginia and South Carolina. The slave codes typically set limits to the acceptable behavior for the slave and attempted to control all aspects of the bondsman's life. Everything, from relations between male and female slaves to the necessity of a pass when off the plantation and the number of whippings for slave offenses, was detailed in the slave codes. The slave codes also regulated the behavior of the masters, requiring them to serve on the slave patrol or to provide certain basic necessities for their slaves. But, as Colonel Walter suggests, these legal proscriptions were not always rigorously enforced. Masters and the government in Mississippi and elsewhere were often forced to choose between their own convictions and convenience and the letter of the law. On isolated plantations, the master rather than the state made the effective laws.

This piece on the slave laws of Mississippi is revealing for the author's awareness of the conflict between law and practice. De Bow hoped to publish a series on the slave laws of all the states, but because of the lack of knowledgeable contributors the project was never completed.

Our legislation in regard to slaves, seems to have been dictated by no *fixed* rule of public policy; constant change seems to have been the only end at which we aimed. Our citizens have scarcely become acquainted with the last laws on bringing slaves into the state, but are already agitating a thorough change. This agitation will result, I trust, in the adoption of a policy which will prohibit forever their further introduction into Mississippi. Our "wild land" is now nearly cleared, and our slave force is fully adequate to its culture; yet our citizens are still pursuing the ruinous policy of expending all their surplus capital in in-

Vol. XI (December, 1851), pp. 617–21.

creasing the number of their slaves. No rest is given to lands, and the soil is daily losing its strength and fertility under an exacting system of culture. A prohibition to the further introduction of slaves, would not only relieve the lands, but compel our citizens to seek new investments for their surplus capital, and avail themselves of the great natural advantages that could be commanded for diversified labor. Our facilities for commerce and manufactures are very great. By clearing out the rivers, we could bring almost every acre of land in the state within thirty miles of steamboat navigation. We listen daily to the murmur of streams that invite us to appropriate them to manufacturing purposes. We have large tracts of country that nature seems to have levelled and graded for the rail-road iron. We have hitherto been blind to all these advantages. In our eagerness to grow more cotton, we have wholly neglected the more important duties of manufacturing our clothing and making our bread-stuffs, and for both food and raiment are dependent on our more sagacious sister states. It is believed by many citizens, that these evils would be removed by prohibiting the further introduction of slaves, and that our surplus capital would be invested in a wise and judicious system of internal improvements and domestic manufactures. In my opinion, there is a still more cogent reason for the adoption of this system of exclusion, not only by Mississippi, but also by most of the extreme southern states. In the northern slaveholding states, slave labor is but little profitable, and a disposition is already manifested by them to sell us their slaves, and eventually abolish the institution within their respective limits. The wild fanaticism of the abolitionist has checked this evil to some extent, but we should also anticipate it by forbidding the introduction of their slaves amongst us, and thus compel them to be our allies, by forcing them to retain their property, and thus possess a common interest with us in its preservation. Texas, Arkansas, and Florida, have yet large quantities of uncultivated land, and are not now prepared to adopt this policy, but it should be adopted by all the other planting states. These reflections have been suggested in part by reviewing the history of our state legislation upon this subject. By the first state constitution, adopted in 1817, the legislature could prevent no emigrant to this state from bringing his slaves with him, but at the same time was empowered to prevent slaves being brought into the state as merchandise. The same provisions were retained in our Revised Constitution of 1832, with this additional proviso, viz.: that the introduction of slaves into the state as merchandise, or for sale, should be prohibited after May, 1833; and fur-

ther providing, that actual settlers should not be prohibited from purchasing slaves out of the state, and bringing them into the state *for
their own use, until the year 1845.* Under this constitution, the legislature passed laws prohibiting the introduction of slaves for merchandise, or for hire, affixing a heavy penalty to the violation of the law, and
declaring all contracts in relation to such slaves null and void. In 1846,
the constitution was again changed, and the legislature empowered
to pass such laws, regulating or prohibiting the introduction of slaves
into the state, as might be deemed proper and expedient. Under this
amended constitution, the legislature, in 1846, abolished all laws prohibiting the introduction of slaves. Such is our present position on this
point.

In regard to the emancipation of slaves, our jurisprudence has been
not only more consistent with itself, but also with sound policy. The
legislature cannot make a forced emancipation of a slave, except for
some great service rendered the state, and upon payment to his master of his full value. A citizen may free his slave by last will and testa-
ment, whenever it can be proven, to the satisfaction of the legislature,
that the slave has performed some meritorious act for the benefit of
the owner or for the state; provided, however, that said will shall be
inoperative until approved by the legislature, (which approval has, I
believe, in no instance been given.) A testator could formerly direct by
his will that his slave should be sent out of the state and freed; but the
legislature, in 1842, forbade this, and annulled all devises theretofore
made, by which slaves, then in the state, were to be carried to a free
state or to Liberia, and there emancipated. Free blacks are not permitted to come into the state or to remain in it. If this law is violated,
forfeiture of freedom is the penalty, and the transgressor is taken
up and sold. No boat or water craft can come within the jurisdiction of
the state, having on board any free black, without incurring a heavy
penalty. The *only* practical mode by which a slave can be emancipated
is, for the master to carry him beyond the limits of the state, there
emancipate and leave him. Should the black be afterwards found in the
state, he forfeits his freedom, and is to be sold. We are thus freed from
the curse of having free blacks in our midst; and as a vast majority of
our citizens very properly regard slavery as a boon to the African, our
policy as to emancipation may be regarded as *settled.*

As to the liability of the master for the acts of his slave, the common
law rules of principal and agent, master and servant, obtain with but a
single exception. The exception is, where the slave steals property, the

master is liable for the full value of the stolen property to the person from whom it was stolen. Under this law, a very singular and exciting case occurred lately in our court, of which I was one of the counsel for the defence. Dr. P. lost a valuable negro girl, and became satisfied that a negro boy of his neighbor M. had stolen her and carried her out of the state. Suit was instituted, and the question was directly presented, "whether a slave could steal a slave, and the master of the thief be rendered liable to the master of the stolen slave for her value." The parties were wealthy and highly respectable citizens; quite a number of counsel were retained for both sides, and the question was examined at great length, and with considerable ability. The court held that the Dr. was in law entitled to recover. The proof, however, was not sufficient to satisfy the jury, and the case stopped at their finding.

Whilst the master is responsible civilly for only this criminal act of his slave, he is nevertheless liable in many instances to pay the costs of criminal prosecutions against the slave when found guilty. He is also liable to punishment for permitting his slave to go at large and trade as a free man—to hire himself out to cultivate cotton for his own use—to keep dogs or stock, or for permitting over six slaves to be quartered beyond one mile from his residence, unless some overseer or white person shall be with them. Whatever may be thought of the policy of these regulations, they are, to some extent, disregarded; and upon some few of our best regulated plantations, slaves keep their dogs, cultivate a small patch of cotton or corn, and at the end of the year their crop is fairly purchased by the master, who sells them in return luxuries that do not often find a place upon the table or about the houses of the poorer classes of citizens, either in the slave or free states. Masters are punished severely for working, or permitting their slaves to work, on the Sabbath-day; and I am pleased to say, that within my observation, this law is universally observed. Masters are not permitted to treat their slaves with cruelty; and if they do not treat them with humanity, and provide them with necessary clothing, provisions, &c., our constitution provides that they may be sold for the benefit of the master.

Severe penalties are inflicted on any person that shall sell a free black into slavery, and the most liberal provisions are made for persons improperly held to service to obtain their freedom. A petition is filed in court, and the person holding the claimant for freedom in his possession, is compelled to give bonds payable to the governor of the state, to have the petitioner forthcoming to answer the judgment of the court.

A competent jury is empanelled, and the issue of freedom is tried, and should it be found in favor of the petitioner, he is entitled not only to his freedom, but damages for the detention in servitude. I will here take occasion to remark, that in a long practice in our courts, I have never known an instance in which the petitioner was not successful. I have known juries, in several cases, climb over a mountain of testimony to find in favor of the claimant, and with them the slightest testimony appears sufficient to warrant a verdict in favor of freedom. Were I an applicant under this law, I would infinitely prefer a jury of Mississippians, to one composed of the abolitionists of the North.

The punishment of slaves for all offences less than capital, is whipping; except in cases of perjury, in which cases the penalty is both whipping and cutting off of the ear. If a slave shall administer poison, with intent to cause death—shall attempt, or commit a rape on a white woman—shall be guilty of burning any dwelling-house, store, cotton-house, gin, out-house, barn, or stable—shall conspire a rebellion or insurrection, or shall consult or advise the same—shall conspire to murder, shall commit murder, shall be guilty of the manslaughter of a white person—shall make an assault and battery on a white person, with intent to kill, with *malice aforethought express*, such slave shall suffer death. Slaves keeping dogs, firearms, or stock, aiding the escape of a slave, harboring a slave, behaving with rudeness to a white man, trading or selling without a pass, assaulting a white person, not in necessary self-defence, assembling in crowds of more than five, except at religious worship, going from home without a pass, committing a riot, selling liquor, committing larceny, and some other offences, are punished with stripes. Slaves may be witnesses for and against each other, but neither for nor against a white man. Slaves are protected against personal injuries. The same punishment is meted to a white man for injuries to a slave, that is meted out between our white citizens. Great moral and religious advantages are given to the slave. Places of public worship are provided for them in almost every community in the state; and upon each Sabbath some white minister of the gospel preaches to them. In many of our towns and villages Sabbath schools are opened for the blacks, and oral instruction freely imparted. They were permitted to learn to read and write, until their abolition allies deprived them of this privilege. Several other ameliorating privileges have been lost to the slave from the same causes, and I have not the least doubt that every effort made by the abolitionist, is but riveting the chain which, in his madness, he is essaying to rend.

There is no chance for a white man to escape punishment for an attempt to steal a slave. The punishment is certain, and the penitentiary inevitable. The same punishment, with the same certainty, falls on any one holding abolition or insurrectionary doctrines in the community or with the slave. Selling liquor to slaves is with us a high misdemeanor, and severely punished. Our legislature has made great efforts to prevent the purchase, by a white from a slave, of any article whatever, without a permit from the owner. All legislation on this subject has heretofore failed to effect this object. In 1850, a law was passed prohibiting any person from purchasing of a slave any corn, fodder, hay, meal, or other produce or commodity whatsoever, under a fine of not less than $50, and not less than one month's imprisonment. The law further provided, that should any slave be found for fifteen minutes in any tippling shop, store, or other house fitted up for trading—or should the slave be seen to carry into those places any article or commodity, and not bring it out—or if he should bring out anything not carried in, each of said acts should be regarded as *presumptive* evidence of improper dealing with the slave, and should be punished as above specified. The same law provides, that upon the trial of any person under the above law, no evidence of the permission of the owner should be received, except the *written* permit. This law is universally disregarded, and is a dead letter upon our statute book. It speaks for our legislators hasty and inconsiderate action on this subject. The penalty is too severe, the mode of proof too contracted.

This article is already spun out to a length not contemplated when it was commenced. It is written without much reference to method, but contains a full, and, it is believed, accurate statement of the present slavery jurisprudence of Mississippi.

THE NIGHT FUNERAL OF A SLAVE

De Bow constantly looked for articles that revealed the genial side of slavery. Viator, a pseudonym meaning wayfarer, *recounts, in this piece taken from the* Home Journal, *a New York magazine, his visit to a plantation during the funeral of a trusted slave. Written with nineteenth-century sentimentality, this essay undoubtedly appealed to De Bow and his readers, who could see in this account by a man who had once opposed slavery additional justification for the peculiar institution.*

[Our southern readers familiar with such scenes as the following will be pleased with the description which is given of one of them in a late number of the Home Journal.]

Travelling recently on business in the interior of Georgia, I reached just at sunset the mansion of the proprietor through whose estate for the last half hour of my journey I had pursued my way. My tired companion pricked his ears, and with a low whinny indicated his pleasure as I turned up the broad avenue leading to the house. Calling to a black boy in view, I bade him inquire of his owner if I could be accommodated with lodgings for the night.

My request brought the proprietor himself to the door, and from thence to the gate, when, after a scrutinizing glance at my person and equipments, he inquired my name, business, and destination. I promptly responded to his questions, and he invited me to alight and enter the house in the true spirit of southern hospitality.

He was apparently thirty years of age, and evidently a man of education and refinement. I soon observed an air of gloomy abstraction about him; he said but little, and even that little seemed the result of an effort to obviate the seeming want of civility to a stranger. At supper the mistress of the mansion appeared, and did the honors of the table in her particular department; she was exceedingly ladylike and

Vol. XX (February, 1856), pp. 218–21.

beautiful, only as southern women are, that is, beyond comparison with those of any other portion of this republic I have ever seen. She retired immediately after supper, and a servant handing some splendid Havanas on a small silver tray, we had just seated ourselves comfortably before the enormous fire of oak wood, when a servant appeared at the end door near my host, hat in hand, and uttered in subdued but distinct tones, to me, the startling words:

"Master, de coffin hab come."

"Very well," was the only reply, and the servant disappeared.

My host remarked my gaze of inquisitive wonder, and replied to it:

"I have been very sad," said he, "to-day. I have had a greater misfortune than I have experienced since my father's death. I lost this morning the truest and most reliable friend I had in the world, one whom I have been accustomed to honor and respect since my earliest recollection; he was the playmate of my father's youth, and the Mentor of mine; a faithful servant, an honest man, and a sincere Christian. I stood by his bedside to-day, and, with his hands clasped in mine, I heard the last words he uttered; they were, "Master, meet me in heaven."

His voice faltered a moment, and he continued, after a pause, with increased excitement:

"His loss is a melancholy one to me. If I left my home, I said to him, 'John, see that all things are taken care of,' and I knew that my wife and child, property and all, were as safe as though they were guarded by an hundred soldiers. I never spoke a harsh word to him in all my life, for he never merited it. I have a hundred others, many of them faithful and true, but his loss is irreparable."

I come from a section of the Union where slavery does not exist, and I brought with me all the prejudices which so generally prevail in the free States in regard to this "institution." I had already seen much to soften these, but the observation of years would have failed to give me so clear an insight into the relation between master and servant as this simple incident. It was not the haughty planter, the lordly tyrant, talking of his dead slave as of his dead horse, but the kind-hearted gentleman, lamenting the loss and eulogizing the virtues of his good old *friend*.

After an interval of silence, my host resumed—

"There are," said he, "many of the old man's relatives and friends who would wish to attend his funeral. To afford them an opportunity, several plantations have been notified that he will be buried to-night;

some, I presume, have already arrived; and desiring to see that all things are properly prepared for his interment, I trust you will excuse my absence for a few moments."

"Most certainly, sir; but," I added, "if there is no impropriety, I would be pleased to accompany you."

"There is none," he replied; and I followed him to a long row of cabins, situated at a distance of some three hundred yards from the mansion. The house was crowded with negroes, who all rose on our entrance, and many of them exchanged greetings with mine host, in tones that convinced me that they felt he was an object of sympathy from them. The corpse was deposited in the coffin, attired in a shroud of the finest cotton materials, and the coffin itself painted black.

The master stopped at its head, and laying his hand upon the cold brow of his faithful bondsman, gazed long and intently upon features with which he had been so long familiar, and which he now looked upon for the last time on earth; raising his eyes at length, and glancing at the serious countenances now bent upon his, he said solemnly and with much feeling—

"He was a faithful servant and a true Christian; if you follow his example, and live as he lived, none of you need fear, when the time comes for you to lay here."

A patriarch, with the snow of eighty winters on his head answered—

"Master, it is true, and we will try to live like him."

There was a murmur of general assent, and after giving some instructions relative to the burial we returned to the dwelling.

About nine o'clock, a servant appeared with the notice that they were ready to move and to know if further instructions were necessary. My host remarked to me, that by stepping into the piazza, I would probably witness, to me, a novel scene. The procession had moved and its route led within a few yards of the mansion. There were at least one hundred and fifty negroes, arranged four deep, and following a wagon in which was placed the coffin; down the entire length of the line, at intervals of a few feet, on each side were carried torches of the resinous pine, and here called lightwood. About the centre was stationed the black preacher, a man of gigantic frame and stentorian lungs, who gave out from memory the words of a hymn suitable for the occasion. The southern negroes are proverbial for the melody and compass of their voices, and I thought that hymn, mellowed by distance, the most solemn and yet the sweetest music that had ever fallen upon my ear. The stillness of the night and strength of their voices enabled me to distinguish the air at the distance of half a mile.

It was to me a strange and solemn scene, and no incident of my life has impressed me with more powerful emotions than the night funeral of the poor negro. For this reason I have hastily and most imperfectly sketched its leading features. Previous to retiring to my room, I saw in the hands of a daughter of the lady at whose house I stopped for the night a number of the Home Journal, and it occurred to me to send this to your paper, perfectly indifferent whether it be published or not. I am but a brief sojourner here. I hail from a colder clime, where it is our proud boast that all men *are* free and equal. I shall return to my northern home, deeply impressed with the belief that, dispensing with the *name* of freedom, the negroes of the south are the happiest and most contented people on the face of the earth.

Josiah C. Nott

CLIMATES OF THE SOUTH IN THEIR
RELATIONS TO WHITE LABOR

Josiah C. Nott (1804–1873), a Mobile, Alabama, physician, was one of the best-known writers on race and slavery in the antebellum South. Born in South Carolina, where he attended college, he received his medical training at the University of Pennsylvania. After additional training in Europe, Nott took up practice in Mobile, where he began his medical research. He investigated the causes of yellow fever, and he was one of the first to suggest that it might be spread by an intermediate host such as the mosquito. Beginning in the 1840s, Nott turned his attention to the anthropology, ethnology, and physiology of the blacks. His observations convinced him that the Negro and the Caucasian races had been created separately, contrary to the biblical account. In 1854, Nott and George R. Gliddon published Types of Mankind, *an eight-hundred-page treatise defending the plural origins of man as well as finding biblical justifications for slavery. During the Civil War, Nott served as a medical inspector of the Confederate Army. Afterward, he moved to New York, where he concentrated on his private practice, returning to Mobile shortly before his death.*

Before the Civil War, Nott and other racists like Samuel Cartwright had repeatedly argued that blacks were particularly suited to work in the hot and steamy cane and cotton fields of the South. Conversely, the southern climate was debilitating to Caucasians, who could, however, withstand the rigors of overseeing the physical labor of the slaves. The end of slavery posed a problem for men of Nott's persuasion. They were convinced that abolition would quickly lead to the natural extermination of blacks, thus denuding the South of its primary labor force. Where Nott had once argued that whites could not survive physical labor in the South, by 1866 he had changed his mind. With the possible exception of the rice fields, he discovered that Caucasians could indeed labor in the South with no ill effects. In spite of the racist bias to Nott's arguments, he had unwittingly hit upon a physiological difference that increased black resistance to malaria. Twentieth-century

Vol. I, After War Series (February, 1866), pp. 166–73.

science has uncovered a defective gene, found predominately among blacks, that can cause sickle-cell anemia and can also confer greater immunity to malaria. Only in this respect have Nott's speculations on adaptability to climate been proven to have some validity.

[The following contribution to our pages is made by Dr. J. C. Nott, of Mobile, a most distinguished physician, medical statistician and scientific writer, the author in conjunction with Gliddon of the celebrated work entitled, "Types of Mankind." Dr. Nott has resided a third of a century at Mobile, and is profoundly familiar with all the laws relating to the sanitary condition, mortality and longevity of the white and black races of the South, and his authority on such matters is paramount. We referred to his investigation in a letter addressed by us in the January number of the Review to Governor Perry, of South Carolina. The position which we took in that letter is amply sustained by him, and we commend this letter to thoughtful men in every part of the Union. We then said and repeat:

"By far the larger portion of each of the Southern States is well adapted to white labor, and actual mortuary returns indicate a much higher degree of physical health in these localities than in the New England and Northwestern States. . . . The region referred to embraces nearly the whole of the great States of Virginia, North Carolina, Tennessee, Kentucky and Texas, threefourths of Georgia and Arkansas, one-half of South Carolina, Alabama, Mississippi, Louisiana and Florida."—Editor.]

To J. D. B. De Bow, Esq.:

Sir,—The question of labor, for the production of the great staples of the Southern States is now the all-absorbing one with us, and you ask for my views on the subject, particularly the results of my professional observation, in regard to the adaptability of the white race to field labor in our cotton and sugar regions.

Every reflecting man that has studied the past history of the negro, and spent as I have, half a century in daily contact with the race, must apprehend that freed blacks cannot be relied upon as an agricultural population, and that emancipation must ultimately result in their extermination.

In order to show that I have no cherished theory to maintain, or no prejudices of education to combat, I will here repeat what I have been saying and publishing for twenty years past. I have always been an emancipationist at heart—have been utterly opposed to the slave trade—have maintained that every people capable of self-government had a right to liberty, and have again and again said to the few slaves that I have owned, "Whenever you think you can do better without me than with me I will pay your expenses to Boston or Liberia."

Nevertheless I have not been an abolitionist; for the reason that I looked upon emancipation of our Southern slaves as a measure leading only to misery, and the ultimate destruction of the race in this country. But the United States Government has done the deed, has assumed all the responsibility, which frees my conscience of the offense, and I rejoice that the institution is gone.

The physical and civil history of the negro proves that he never has lived, and never can live, in any other condition than that in which he has been placed. In Africa, he has had nearly a whole Continent to himself for ages, and been in constant contact with Egypt, the mother of European civilization, and yet, unlike the Jews, the Phoenicians, the Assyrians, the Greeks, the Romans and other white races, he has not made a step forward in the march of civilization for five thousand years! There is not a relic of art or science to be found, from the Great Desert of Sahara to the Cape of Good Hope, (the land of the true negro,) to show that civilization ever had a local habitation on that Continent. The negro has never invented an alphabet, nor founded or maintained a constitutional government. He has reached his nearest approximation to civilization in our country. He has never, in his own or any other country, from the time of Moses to the present, except under the direction of the white races, *been an agricultural laborer*, and every well-informed Southern man knows, both from history and personal observation, that, as a class, he will not work unless under restraint. Like the Indian and other inferior races, he may expect to be driven out by the superior intelligence, energy and perseverance of the whites.

The negro rarely thinks of the future, and learns little from experience. There are now thousands of the race scattered over our country, with starvation staring them in the face, unless fed by the Government, and yet, as a general thing, they are making no contracts with employers, or arrangements of any kind for the coming year, though I am now writing in the last days of December. In my professional rounds, every day, persons are asking me, "Where can I get a cook, a washwoman, a house servant?" and though willing to pay twenty dollars a month or more, the want cannot be supplied. The negroes are dying in idleness around this city from disease and starvation.

There is but one thing which saves the South from utter ruin for the next half century, and that is the enormous price of our great staple, cotton. One-fourth of the ordinary number of bales will bring as much money as a full crop in former years, and there is good reason to believe that there will not be more than one-fourth of a crop made in 1866. It is probable that negro labor, the year after that will be better organized, and something like one-third to half a crop of cotton will be made. After that negro labor will gradually decline, and, as it disappears, white labor will infiltrate into the country, and not only supply the labor of the disappearing negroes, but gradually bring up the cotton product not only to its original figures, but carry it far beyond what it has ever been. How many years this will require no one can foresee; but there is every reason to believe, that the cotton crop will continue to bring, quite as large an income from the present time forward, as it did before the war. Fifty cents a pound is too tempting a bait for the whites to overlook, and there is nothing in our climate potent enough to keep them from it.

With white population too, will come wealth, power and national greatness to the South. With the increase of white population will come increase of intellect, energy, the mechanic arts, etc., and development and progression will be the order of the day. The South has all the elements of greatness, and all she needs is a thorough system of practical education, and a population capable of receiving it.

But let us leave this digression and come to the question before us, viz: that of *Race in connection with climate.*

To comprehend it fully, *climate* must be viewed under two very distinct aspects, first, that of simple *temperature*—second, temperature and malaria combined.

Without touching at all on the vexed question of original Unity or Diversity of Races, we may assert, without fear of contradiction, that the races of men, as we now see them, scattered over the face of the globe, if not so in the beginning, have become peculiarly adapted to certain climates. The negro for example is not only a native of tropical Africa, and maintains his highest physique in hot climates, but is proverbially unsuited to cold latitudes. In New England and Canada, the deaths among the blacks there is every reason to believe, exceed the births, and the race in a few generations would be exterminated by the climate if not renewed by constant immigration.

On the other hand, the Anglo-Saxon and Teutonic race generally, flourish in the middle temperate zone, and deteriorate in the Tropic and Arctic regions. The native land of the negro is death to the white man, and the negro race would be exterminated in Russia.

That these idiosyncracies of the two races can be changed, we have no evidence from history to prove, but on the contrary, we have positive evidence in abundance to prove that the white and black races stood face to face around the Mediterranean sea five thousand years ago, and that there has been no example from that time to this to show that one race can be transformed into another by anything short of a direct miracle. Climate certainly will never do it.

Official statistics establish conclusively that, in the full acceptation of the term, the French cannot colonize Algeria, nor the English, India. The deaths in those countries, among European colonists steadily exceed the births, and were it not for the constant supply of fresh victims, these colonies would long since have died out. It should be remembered too, that the English in India are engaged in commercial and other pursuits that keep them much within doors and protected from the burning sun of the climate. They have not tilled the soil and been exposed to the intense heat and its malarial creations, as the natives are. Very few scores of years would be sufficient to exterminate one hundred thousand Englishmen in India, if they had to earn their bread at the tail of the plough.

I have not for several years examined any official French statistics in connection with Algeria on this point, but Mons. Boudin, chief surgeon of the department, some years ago proved by figures that more than one hundred thousand Frenchmen had died in Algeria during their attempt at colonization—that the deaths exceeded the births, and that the country could not be colonized by Frenchmen.

It is useless in the present day to multiply facts on this point, and the same reasoning applies with equal force to all the races intermediate between the whites and blacks. Every climate has its Fauna and Flora, and every Fauna has a type of Man peculiarly adapted to it.

Each race of mankind, however, has a certain degree of *pliability* of constitution, a certain degree of *adaptability* to other climates, approximating that of its own Fauna; but there are limits to this *pliability*, which cannot be transcended with impunity.

The negro belongs properly to the tropic, but yet has flourished in full vigor in our Southern States. When, however, you cross the Potomac going northward, his power of endurance begins to yield, and every degree north cuts deeper and deeper into his constitution.

It is estimated that in all, about 400,000 negroes have been imported into the United States from Africa, and our census returns show that they have increased to upwards of 4,000,000; or more than ten-fold—an increase, unparalleled in any agricultural population in the world. All the facts show that they have thriven well, and that too, when exposed in open fields to all the influences of climate.

The white race enjoys a higher degree of *pliability* of constitution than the black. A native of the middle temperate zone, where there are considerable extremes of heat and cold, he is by nature habituated and adapted to much wider range of temperature than the negro. The negro is a native of the tropic, one extreme of climate, and cannot go very far beyond the tropic before he begins to deteriorate. While the white man, the native of a land of cold winters and warm summers, can migrate to the verge of the arctic, and to many parts of the tropic with impunity.

But the question next comes as to *how far* this pliability of the white race extends? In plain English, Can white emigrants be brought to our Southern States, and be made to live, prosper and cultivate cotton, sugar, tobacco and rice? With regard to *Rice* I must enter a strong doubt, but with regard to the other staples I feel *no doubt*. Even rice will be cultivated by white labor at some future day, when the drainage of rice lands becomes more perfect, and, I may add, when there comes a struggle for bread in a crowded population.

I have already remarked that climate must be considered under two heads—1st, that of simple temperature; 2d, temperature and malaria combined. They do not necessarily go together—we have many localities where there is a hot climate without malaria, or the causes of intermittent and bilious fevers; but on the other hand we do not have marsh malaria, except in warm climates, or at least where there are warm summers.

The climate of our cotton region cannot properly be called *hot*, though a *warm* climate. It is not the mere *heat* of our region that makes it unfriendly to European constitutions, but it is the diseases which the sun eliminates from the soil we cultivate. The hilly pine lands, for example, of the Southern States, forming an immense tract, extending from Virginia to the Mississippi, and even far beyond, under the same temperature as other neighboring lands, are *exempt from the*

influence of marsh malaria, and are universally regarded as salubri-
ous, and resorted to by the better class of society as summer residences with perfect safety.

Not so with really *hot* climates. In India, for example, the Anglo-
Saxon is killed outright by high temperature independently of atmospheric poisons. The frame is attenuated by the exhausting effects of
heat and profuse perspiration—the muscles are relaxed and debili-
tated, the nervous system is exhausted, the liver inflames and becomes corroded with abscesses, and the whole machine is worn out by
the wear and tear of *heat*, and the want of exercise which the climate
does not permit. All this, I say, may and does occur independently of
malaria, from high temperature alone.

It will be readily admitted that when the Germanic, or Anglo-Saxon
people come into our cotton region, they leave their normal position,
and subject themselves to an unaccustomed test of climatic influence.
The system is called upon for a certain amount of resistance to a foreign climate, and the struggle results in a certain amount of physical
deterioration. The descendants of the Anglo-Saxon and German are no
longer exact models of the original prototypes, though the race is still
essentially the same—modified, but not changed in type. The complexion is less clear and florid; the body is less plump and vascular; the
marks of age appear earlier. An English man or woman is as youthful
in appearance at the age of fifty as ours ten years younger; their
statesmen and literary men wear longer than ours; the value of life,
even in the healthiest parts of the South, is a grade less than in Great
Britain and other temperate parts of Europe.

Although more favorable, perhaps, as a whole to European constitutions than our cotton States of the South, I do not regard the climate
and population of New England as at all comparable to those of the better parts of Europe. Certainly the population of New England does not
compare with that of old England, nor do I think it by any means certain that there is more health or more longevity in New England than
in the non-malarious districts of the Southern States.

I recollect hearing Henry Clay say, that the finest population in the
world is seen walking in Regent Street, London; and in this opinion I
fully concur.

It must be confessed, however, that the climate of the Gulf States
particularly is unfavorable to mental cultivation and high intellectual
development. The people are full of genius, courage, chivalry, and all
the high qualities that adorn humanity. Such characters as General

Washington, Patrick Henry, Stonewall Jackson, General Lee, the Lowndes, the Rutledges, the Pinckneys, and many others of the South, can no more be grown in extreme Northern latitudes than cotton, sugar, pineapples and oranges, and yet the heat of the climate for four months of the year puts a stop to steady, plodding, intellectual labor, and the South, in my opinion, will never equal the North in profound learning and general literary attainment. Too much time is lost out of each year to keep up in the race.

But, as we have said, the mere matter of temperature at the South is no serious impediment to the introduction of white labor, and the next question is, What are the difficulties arising from the influence of marsh malaria, with its fevers and other diseases of our climate?

We have said that the pine hills are healthy, and that the whites can and do live there with health. We have on the other hand said, that the white man cannot cultivate the rice fields, and a considerable portion of the *alluvial* cotton lands. *But on the other hand there is an immense proportion of our cotton lands, on which white laborers can and will live with a reasonable degree of health—perhaps (when we take into consideration the many diseases incident to dense populations) with as much health as in most parts of Europe from which our emigrants come.*

A very large portion of our cotton lands are to a great degree exempt from malarial diseases, and making an average of the whole year, and thus including diseases of cold as well as heat, it may be well doubted whether these portions are not as favorable to health and longevity as either our New England or Western States. For example, the lime or prairie lands of Mississippi and Alabama, and the uplands generally of the Carolina's, Georgia and other cotton States—even the fertile lands on the banks of the Mississippi, when thoroughly drained and cultivated, may be considered as quite healthy, and if a good system of drainage and culture was generally adopted, the proportion of land unsuited to white labor would be small.

Laying aside all speculation on the subject, there are facts in abundance to prove that whites can live, labor and make cotton in our climate, and the bait is too tempting to be resisted. At fifty cents a pound, one industrious laborer can make his food and clothing, and put besides yearly a thousand dollars of good money in his pocket, and the white man will do it at a much greater risk of life or health than he is called upon to make in well-selected cotton-fields of the South.

Even now, every where through the Carolinas, Georgia and the Gulf

States, you see little farms worked successfully by white laborers, both male and female. We should, too, have seen a great deal more of this kind of labor had it not been for the proximity of slave labor. Not only have these small farmers been driven off by the monopoly of the rich, in buying up their little farms to get them out of the way, but agricultural labor has scarcely been considered honorable at the South. The poor white man was put on a footing with the slave that he despised.

Another proof of the availability of white labor is seen around our towns—nearly all the market gardens around Mobile and New Orleans (and so with other towns) are cultivated by white laborers, although these localities are among the most insalubrious in the South. The towns themselves are healthy to the acclimated, but the marshy suburbs are very sickly.

Who, let us ask, have built our Southern towns. Is it not almost exclusively Northern and foreign carpenters and bricklayers, who labor in the full blaze of a Southern sun?

Although Germans, Irish and Northerners can and will live and prosper in the Southern States, there is no doubt that emigrants from France, Spain and Italy would be most readily and perfectly adapted to our climate. The elegance and robustness of the Creole population, male and female, of Louisiana, is proverbial. They are one of the finest-looking people in the world, and the most healthy ever seen. I doubt whether even the population of Great Britain possesses more health, vigor and longevity than the creole population of Louisiana, but it is all physique. They are generally deficient in energy and entertainment, and rarely attain intellectual excellence.

This physique of the creoles is easily accounted for. The population of France, including that of Normandy (which is mostly of German descent) is like all the population bordering the Mediterranean Sea, essentially *Southern*. The American traveller, after leaving Paris *en route* for Marseilles, does not go far before he is struck by the Southern look of the people—short stature, dark complexion, black hair and eyes—in short, a physique contrasting strongly with the inhabitants of Germany and Britain.

Having prepared this paper at your request, and upon short notice, I can only regret its deficiencies. The subject is a vast one, and might very well occupy a volume. All I can hope by this hasty sketch is to induce thought in others.

III

AGRICULTURAL AND INDUSTRIAL DEVELOPMENT

When the *Commercial Review* first appeared in January, 1846, De Bow announced in the lead article that his journal's chief purpose was to promote the economic progress of the South and Southwest. To that end, he promised, the *Review* would address all matters touching on commerce, agriculture, internal improvements, and invention in a spirit of vigorous, but nationally patriotic, regional pride. Although the tension over slavery in the 1850s increasingly diverted De Bow from his initial course and eroded his commitment to fostering southern progress within the Union, the *Review* never entirely abandoned its commercial orientation or its concern for southern economic development. The articles reprinted below are representative of those that addressed this broad subject and fall into four categories: internal improvements, agriculture, industrialization and technological change, and what might be called "the other side of progress."

The chapter opens with De Bow's 1846 essay on the then-novel Morse electric telegraph, which De Bow correctly predicted would soon significantly affect commerce as well as every other facet of society. De Bow's calls for action on internal improvements found a more somber, but also more informed, echo in the admonitory article by Albert Stein, published in 1850. Unlike many of the *Review*'s contributors, whose concern for internal improvements revolved around the railroad and largely ignored the region's waterways, Stein believed that the Mississippi River should not be taken so lightly. The hydrologist, whose professional judgment De Bow greatly respected, urged Louisianians to improve the river's channel, lest the river abandon it and them.

Because of the *Review*'s initial mercantile orientation, De Bow was at first not disposed to consider essays on agricultural matters. By mid-1846, however, this policy had changed to one of actively encouraging planters to send in articles, notes, and, of course, agricultural statistics. De Bow's aim in this was twofold: first, to accumulate the necessary body of information with which to assess the state of southern agriculture; and second, to campaign relentlessly for the abandonment of traditional but wasteful practices and for the adoption of modern methods of cultivation and husbandry. No doubt responsible, in part, for De Bow's new-found interest in agriculture was his early difficulty in attracting a sufficient number of subscribers and contributors from among the mercantile communities of New Orleans and other southern cities. His expedient decision to address the interests of planters and farmers, however, was probably reinforced by his realization that hopes for southern commercial and industrial development ultimately rested on the South's extensive agricultural base.

Cotton, by far the most important southern cash crop, was always a subject of great interest for De Bow's contributors, but seldom in and of itself. Instead, writers on King Cotton, particularly in the 1850s, tied the staple's importance to northern and British textile production and to sectional politics. The absence from this chapter of an article on cotton culture and the inclusion of four dealing with the commercial and manufacturing aspects of the commodity reflect this practice. Similarly, the article on the cultivation of rice, reprinted below, accurately mirrors what De Bow and many of his contributors considered of interest and importance under the general subject of agriculture and under the specific one of improvements in agricultural practices.

When De Bow's contributors took up the subject of southern industrialization, they were concerned, first and foremost, with the application of machinery and power to produce textiles from the South's enormous cotton crop. The 1849 essay by the Kentucky manufacturer, Hamilton Smith, is one of the earliest, and also one of the best, articles on the subject that appeared in the *Review*. Smith proposed a concerted effort by planters and investors to make the cotton South a manufacturer of coarse textiles as a means of sustaining the price of the raw fiber at a time when the supply was rapidly increasing.

William Gregg had anticipated some parts of Smith's program for southern manufacturing in a volume published a few years before Smith's article appeared. In 1850, Gregg returned to his favorite theme in an article for the *Review*, emphasizing the importance of removing hindrances to industry in the South. Unless southerners disposed of obstructive laws and destructive prejudices against manufacturing, he warned, their region's great industrial potential and its promise of economic freedom from northern economic domination were little more than chimera.

By 1860, Gregg had moved from advocating southern industrial self-sufficiency within the Union to urging southern economic *and* political independence from the North. But, after ten years, the persistence of a familiar problem worried him. Although, as he realized, a southern industrial base would be vital to the success of an independent southern nation, southerners themselves seemed not to realize that, without their support, the South's manufacturers could not succeed. Instead of patronizing local industry, southerners looked to the North to supply their needs—a practice that Gregg opposed.

Even within the Union, economic development was by no means a steady process, free from blemish. Progress had its other, uglier side. De Bow's article in 1853 on railroad accidents and an anonymous author's sharp characterization of the "tight times" of the business cycle of the mid-1850s reveal two facets of commercial and industrial advance from which we are still not free today. More hopeful in outlook is Edwin Q. Bell's article. Published after De Bow's death in 1867, Bell's essay proposed to southerners that they introduce farm machinery in place of agricultural labor—a suggestion that, before the war, most had considered inconceivable, not to say in bad taste. Bell was concerned about a shortage of labor arising from the movement of freedmen to the cities, and he offered his proposal as a solution to the problem. The South eventually adopted labor-saving farm machinery, but long after Bell had written. At about the time his article appeared, southern planters began to introduce their own solution to the problem presented by emancipated slaves: the sharecropping system.

J. D. B. De Bow

MORSE'S ELECTRO-MAGNETIC TELEGRAPH

Ever the advocate of the innovative in commerce, manufacturing, and technology, De Bow embraced the still-crude telegraph invented by Samuel F. B. Morse in the 1830s. Failure to obtain financial support from private backers for experiments to perfect the instrument had led Morse in 1837 to apply to Congress, which, in 1843, advanced $30,000 for the construction of a telegraph line from Washington, D.C., to Baltimore, Maryland. On May 1, 1844, the first messages passed over this line between Annapolis Junction and Washington, thereby demonstrating the invention's practicability and utility. Private capital, now convinced of the telegraph's potential, rushed in where it had once feared to tread. In 1846, the year in which De Bow wrote this essay, about 40 miles of telegraph lines were in operation; two years later, 2,000 miles had been strung, and by 1854 more than 30,000 miles had been constructed.

Although no telegraph service existed in the South in 1846, De Bow's hope that this deficiency would soon be remedied was realized in 1848, when six companies competed for the distinction and profits awaiting the first to reach New Orleans. On the eve of the Civil War, well over 2,000 miles of telegraph lines operated within the South. In the following essay, De Bow predicts this rapid growth in service and suggests that the federal government operate the telegraph as a public monopoly. At the time, Congress was debating the very question—a debate quickly made moot by the proliferation and progress of private companies.

"Vanquished nature yields,
Her secrets are extorted."
—Young

. . . Had we searched throughout the whole domain of the arts and sciences, and made each particular achievement the object of severe in-

Vol. I (February, 1846), pp. 132–41.

vestigation, there would have occurred, we think, no object more justly and naturally calculated to excite the emotions which have been passing through our mind, than the *Electro-Magnetic Telegraph*. This extraordinary victory over the powers of nature has not a parallel in the archives of discovery. It stands alone in its brilliancy, and reflects more of honor upon the age and country which gave it origin, than has been derived from any other of the results of physical science. The steam engine, which has been so long the wonder of mankind, and which is hailed as the miracle of human skill and genius, is after all but the application to useful purposes of those powers which have been applied to humbler ones in every age. The steam engine appears to be a wonderful result of combined art and science; we consider it such, and honor its projectors; but there is nothing in it which refuses to accord with our preconceived notions of the possible, and of the powers and resources with which the intellect of man is endowed. We have endeavored in vain to regard the electric battery in its adaptation to the conveyance of intelligence in a similar point of view. There is something so gigantic and stupendous in its results, something so far beyond all the conceptions which had ever entered into the brain of philosophy before, something so infinitely higher even than the achievement which was thought worthy to appear in the epitaph of Franklin, *"eripuit cælo fulmen,"* he snatched the thunderbolt from heaven! The Electro-Magnetic Telegraph seizes upon the lightning itself and endows its flashes with intelligence. It bids the terrible slave toil in the empire of a master. It harnesses the last conquered rebel in the car of mind, and seizing upon the reins, bids it execute high purposes ten thousand miles away at the very moment they are conceived. The speaking lightning has no limit—it has no time. It flashes from either pole of the earth to the other, in an interval which a superior being only could compute!

We have essayed to describe this extraordinary invention which Professor Morse has the honor of having presented to America and to the world. We shall endeavor to trace its progress and show the extent of its present application in this country and in Europe, and also the destinies which are likely to attend it in the future.

The Electro-Magnetic Telegraph, whether we consider it as it came from the hands of Mr. Morse, or as its improvement has been suggested by Mr. Page, depends upon the power of different substances when brought into contact, to develop electricity. In this it is as simple as the principle of the steam engine, which is resolvable into the power

of contraction and expansion which water possesses at a high temperature. The science of galvanism, which is but yet in its earliest infancy,
furnishes the ground-work and the essential condition of the telegraph. The property of the galvanic current which induces it to travel
over iron wire, is an indispensable condition. Discovery has not paused,
however, with the mere use of wire. The galvanic current will, to a certain extent, admit even the earth as a substitute. Galvanic currents—
and here amazement is the natural feeling—galvanic currents will
travel from each extremity of a wire, meet and pass each other in their
opposite progress, without sustaining any interruption. But more than
all, and the most extraordinary phenomenon, galvanic currents leap
from bank to bank of a river without the intervention of cord or con-
ductor. Upon these facts and principles depend the brilliant application
of the Telegraph.

The principles of this instrument are so simple, that they may be
comprehended by any one who will give a moment to the subject. A
common galvanic battery is a thing familiar enough to most persons,
and is capable of sending electrical currents through wires, whatever
may be their length. These wires are made to terminate at the ex-
tremities of a bar of iron, which then becomes, of course, as it is technically termed, "charged." A bar of iron charged with electricity or
magnetism in this way, it is also common knowledge, will attract another bar, and continue its grasp upon it while the electrical influence
continues. Disturb the influence, and the attracted bar is at once released, and falls. This second bar performs the work of the Telegraph.
Attracted or repelled, as the electricity operates or ceases to operate
upon the wires, it produces a motion which may be applied to practical
purposes. The individual who has command of the electrical fluid or
current, whatever may be his distance, has command, as a matter of
course then, of the bar with which it communicates, and may regulate
all its motions to suit his pleasure. If this bar were connected with a
steel point and a sheet of paper, he might make such impressions upon
the sheet of paper as suited him. He might puncture it in one point, or
two, or three, or any number of points; he might inscribe it with lines,
and all of this by his control of the electrical battery before him. He
could attribute to these points, set of points, or lines, alphabetical values which would render them capable of translation into intelligible
language in a moment. This is the whole mystery of what Professor
Morse has done; but simple as it is, we repeat our observation, it is the
most magnificent effort of the mind of man.

One of the earliest practical applications of the Telegraph was made in May, 1844, when the Democratic Convention was in session in Baltimore, and its proceedings were reported, as they occurred, at Washington. The same line, we are told by Mr. Morse, in a letter to the Secretary of the Treasury, operated during eight months, day and night, and at all hours of the day and night, without being interrupted altogether as much as twenty-four hours. The two principal disturbances were a fire in Baltimore, which destroyed one of the posts, and the fall of a tree across the wires. These accidents were remedied soon enough for the Telegraph to give the first notice of them.

Mr. Morse mentions the following instance of the practicability of his Telegraph:

"In October, a deserter from the United States ship Pennsylvania, lying at Norfolk, who had also defrauded the purser of the ship of some $600 or $700, was supposed to have gone to Baltimore. The purser called at the telegraph office in Washington, stated his case, and wished to give notice in Baltimore, at the same time offering a reward for the apprehension of the culprit. The name and description of the offender's person, with the offer of the reward, were sent to Baltimore, and in ten minutes the warrant was in the hands of the officers of justice for his arrest; and, in half an hour from the time that the purser preferred his request at Washington, it was announced from Baltimore by the telegraph, 'The deserter is arrested; he is in jail. What shall be done with him!'"

A game of drafts was played upon the instrument by two individuals at Washington and Baltimore, with the facility of players at the same table. So independent, too, was the telegraph of all questions of storm and darkness, that on an intensely dark night in December, with torrents of rain and storms of wind, "it seemed more than ordinarily mysterious, to see a company around a table in a warm, retired chamber, on such a night in Washington, playing a game of chess with another company similarly situated in Baltimore—the darkness, the rain and the wind, being no impediment to instantaneous communication."

With respect to the capacity of the wonderful influence to overleap rivers, without the intervention of artificial conductors, Professor Morse tells us that in 1842, having to make some experiments between Governor's island and Castle Garden, near New York, a vessel accidentally spoiled his experiment, by drawing up on her anchor part of his wire. In the mortification of failure, sleep fled from his eyelids; and while tossing upon his pillow, the thought was suggested, that even water might be made the vehicle of communication. It was the Eureka of Archimedes; the experiment succeeded beyond all expectation; and the Susquehanna river, at Havre de Grace, a mile wide, furnished the means of deciding it.

Preparations are now being extensively made to introduce the telegraph into every part of the United States. A company was organized last spring to construct a continuous line from Washington to New York. The part of it between Philadelphia and New York is completed, with the exception of a very few miles, on which the posts only are yet put up. The remaining portion from Philadelphia to Baltimore, will be prosecuted with all possible dispatch.

Another company charged itself with a line from New York to Buffalo, and the whole distance from Albany to that place is nearly completed with two wires. . . .

In the summer of the same year, a line was projected from Philadelphia to Pittsburgh and St. Louis, with a branch to Lake Erie. Money to extend it to Pittsburgh has been raised. From Harrisburg to Lancaster is finished, and the rest of the distance to Philadelphia is in rapid progress.

From Buffalo to Lockport, thirty-eight miles, are in successful operation.

From Boston to Lowell, twenty-five miles, a line is nearly completed. Various lines are in course of construction in the States of Massachusetts and New York, of which we may particularly mention those leading down to the offing from the harbors of the cities of New York and Boston.

A grand route is contemplated from Washington to New Orleans, operations upon which will soon be undertaken. A writer upon the subject, however, remarks:

"The arrangement for sending an agent South, to push forward the Magnetic Telegraph extension from Washington to New Orleans has not yet been consummated, and there is some doubt if it will be done at once. There is a strong disposition here among the telegraph people to make the line, but still the parties seem disposed to hold back until the New York and Boston, and New York and Philadelphia lines are in operation, and the practical results of a long line between important cities are ascertained. To what extent the commercial interests are going to use this method of communication is still a matter of theory, and although the stockholders of those lines are very sanguine of the profits of their enterprise, yet they can approach Southern capitalists with

more confidence, if they can show them a large and profitable employment of the northern lines. The New York and Philadelphia line is completed from this city to Somerville, about seventy miles, and has been
tested. From Philadelphia this way a portion is also in operation. The
gap is about thirty miles, which has the posts and wires up, but which
has not yet been tried. By the first of February the New York and
Boston line will be connected by the magnetic wires."

"We encounter," says Amos Kendall, Esq., to whom we are indebted
for some of our information upon the subject, "some unforeseen difficulties, and have been much disappointed by erroneous estimates as to
the time requisite to build these lines; but nothing has occurred to
shake the perfect confidence entertained as to the practicability and
profit of this great enterprise."

In illustration of the capacity of the telegraph to convey "a given
amount of information in a given time," it has been stated, that nearly
a whole column of a large newspaper was transmitted in thirty minutes, more rapidly than it could be transcribed by the reporter. . . .

We cannot conclude this paper without expressing the hope that the
magnetic telegraph will, to a large extent, be taken under the patronage of the American government, and that so powerful an instrument
for the conveyance of intelligence to every portion of an immense country, will meet with the favor it so richly merits. We are not sure if the
government has the right to establish the mail monopoly, that it has
not the right to establish the telegraphic. Whether or not, however, it
is most expedient for this course to be adopted, or whether it would
not be better to leave it to the control of private enterprise, we are
unprepared at this moment to pronounce an opinion. The subject will
no doubt be acted on by Congress, as it has been suggested in the late
report of the Postmaster-General, and Mr. Morse has not been wanting
in urging it upon their attention.

There is one view of the subject, however, which has not been sufficiently attended to, and that is its connection with the national defenses. Mr. Morse makes a remark upon this head, with which we shall
conclude our sheet:

"But when all that transpires of public interest at New Orleans,
at St. Louis, at Pittsburgh, at Cincinnati, at Buffalo, at Utica, at Albany, at Portland, at Portsmouth, at Boston, at New York, at Philadelphia, at· Baltimore, at Washington, at Norfolk, at Richmond, at
Charleston, at Savannah, and at all desired intermediate points, shall
be *simultaneously* known in each and all these places together—when

all the agents of the government in every part of the country are in instantaneous communication with head-quarters—when the several departments can at once learn the actual existing condition of their remotest agencies, and transmit at the moment their necessary orders to meet any exigency—then will some estimate be formed both of the powers and advantages of the Magnetic Telegraph."

R. A. Wilkinson

PRODUCTION OF RICE IN LOUISIANA

De Bow's somewhat belated recognition of the significance of agricultural matters for his readers led him to advocate innovative farming methods and the cultivation of new or underexploited crops. Consistent with this latter goal was De Bow's call for the diversification of southern agriculture; to this end, the Review *accorded considerable space to articles that offered practical advice on the cultivation of familiar as well as underexploited crops. This essay on rice-growing in Louisiana by R. A. Wilkinson, a planter in Plaquemines Parish, is a case in point.*

In 1849, Louisiana ranked fourth behind South Carolina, Georgia, and North Carolina in the production of rice. The state's crop that year was only 2,425,000 pounds, compared with South Carolina's almost 160,000,000 pounds. Thus, Wilkinson's query: "Why is not more attention paid to . . . this valuable and lucrative staple?"

Sir,—It was with much pleasure that I perused an article upon the subject of Rice, in one of your numbers; a product that has latterly been diminishing, I think, in this state, the lands being bought up for the perhaps more lucrative crop of sugar. Though not quite so heavy in its gross amount as our two great staples, yet not an inconsiderable portion of our large parish (Plaquemines,) and other parts of the state, are devoted to its production. This crop is more to be valued, as it is within the reach of the middling and poorer classes, giving to them a neat and comfortable support, and to many, a handsome revenue. But little capital is required in its cultivation, and it constitutes a particularly healthy food in damp southern latitudes. The consumption of it is immense; and from having been used a short time past in this county as a luxury, it is now to be found on all well-arranged tables in the Union.

In regarding the expensive and laborious works of a South Carolina rice plantation, one accustomed to the manner of its cultivation here, cannot but be struck with the very small difference in the yield, and

Vol. VI (July, 1848), pp. 53–57.

the vast difference in labor. The quality, however, is different. South Carolina rice commands from one-half to three-fourths of a cent here more than Louisiana. This arises from two causes—the Louisiana rice not being as white, and the grains being more broken than the Carolina. Both of these faults, I believe, can be remedied by cultivation and improvements of machinery. I hoped to have seen in your article on the subject, the reason that some rice breaks more in cleaning than others. The difference in whiteness, I am aware, proceeds from the inferior manner of preparing it for market. Can you not point out the means of remedying the former defect, which must proceed from the *culture*? These are the two objectionable things against Creole or Louisiana rice. It is, however, much sweeter, and not so apt to get musty as the imported. I have heard exactly opposite reasons given by the planters here for the first of these faults. Certainly the improvement of a crop so important to a large number of the inhabitants of our state, tending to the division of our farming labors, a result most anxiously to be desired, from the low prices of both sugar and cotton, should occupy most particular attention.

The rice crop, from the great care with which it is made here, the extreme richness of the land, the adaptation of the climate to it, and perhaps it may be, the enervated habits of the people generally, has never been fostered or reduced to a science, as in other countries, where the soils are poorer and climate worse. I have conversed with many intelligent South Carolina planters and managers of plantations, and they all agree, that the land is suitable and climate proper, to vie here with Carolina, in both quantity and quality. There is this difference in favor of the cultivation of rice in Louisiana, on the borders of our rivers and tributaries:—It is well known that in Carolina, on the rice plantations, the water used is tide water, with little or no current, and the swamps large; that the water lies on large districts, sometimes drawn off, at others let on, leaving great fields, subject to the influence of a burning sun, creating malaria, and engendering the worst kind of disease, insomuch, that the planters yearly leave the country for the cities, where smoke and fires, or some other causes, seem to dispel the evil.

Such is not the case here. It is a well-known fact, that the rice plantations, both as regards whites and blacks, are more healthy than the sugar and cotton. From what cause does this arise, has been often asked by many? With the same hot sun and climate, and occupying a district of thirty to forty miles on both sides of the river, with but two or three sugar plantations, at long distances, there exists almost one undivided rice-field, making on an average about thirty thousand barrels of clean rice yearly, and overflowing the whole country around them, except a few front acres, generally appropriated to corn and potatoes. There can be but one cause for its health. The fall of the land is abrupt to the bayous and lakes behind, and the sea being near, at the time the Mississippi is high the rice is at the watering stage, and the water here not being taken off at all, is kept constantly running from the river back, preventing the back water from ever becoming stagnant, and carrying off, with the rapidity of its current, the vegetable matter that in decomposing causes malaria. The water, too, being drawn off at so late a date, the land does not dry sufficiently early to cause decomposition, before the cooler and stormy months come on and disperse it. Most certain it is, that no country so thickly settled in southern latitudes as the rice planting part of the Parish of Plaquemines, has a greater amount of healthy people and fine children. Why is not more attention paid to the improvement of the cultivation and manufacture of this valuable and lucrative staple?

The rice planters, as a body, generally consist of those who have but small farms, not wealthy, and hitherto almost entirely uneducated, and unable, from the smallness of their means, to vary their crops from their general routine; and not having the capital to put up sufficiently valuable machinery, and to properly prepare their crops for market, nor yet to get out more than ten to twelve barrels a day, they have never progressed since their commencement. This, too, while our other staples have advanced beyond the most sanguine expectations; having, at this present moment, we may say, stocked the whole world.

The common system of rice-planting here, is to begin in February to dig out the ditches, which, in a farm of four acres front on the river, consists of one ditch, four feet wide or more, four to five feet deep, running from the river to the swamp, with a dam or gate behind, at right angles, to this main ditch. At every half-acre is a two-foot cross ditch, with a bank behind it to confine the water about a foot high, or more. At the back of the field is a four-foot ditch running parallel with the river, with a high bank on the outside to completely dam in the field, with a flood-gate opening behind to gauge the height of water. When March arrives, all the ditches having been opened, they commence ploughing, mud or not, rain or sunshine, if the oxen can go through it. There are generally six oxen, two drivers, and one to guide the plough. The work is, generally, where the land is dry, well and neatly done, with the old Roman plough, by us called the French sock plough, the best in the world for stiff land. I have tried such land successively with the centre draft of Jacob's, Cary, and others, none of which could equal this with the same team.

The planters sow and harrow in the rice in succession, as they can generally water the back cuts first, being lower than the front; and in the early part of the season, the river is not high enough to water any but the back, which covers up first, and is ready sooner for the water. The rice is sown broad-cast, about three-fourths of a barrel to an acre. I have often seen the planters harrow it in with oxen, knee-deep in mud. As soon as the back rice comes up, they put on a little water, just leaving the heads out, to check the weeds and grass; and from this time out it is kept in water, always leaving the heads out until ripe for cutting, at which time all the water is drawn off, or a little before. When the rice comes up, the weeds and grass also appear; the grass is kept under by water, but not so the weeds, and a kind of grass having a thousand seeds, that sometimes takes almost entire possession of the fields. These have to be carefully eradicated with the hand, pulling them up frequently, knee-deep in water. The process produces disagreeable effects on the legs, but is avoided by greasing them before going in, in the morning. The hands weed about one quarter to one-third of an acre per day, and sometimes one-half or more, as the weeds are more or less bad, thick pulling them up by the roots, which readily yield. So quick is the vegetation of rice, that one weeding is enough; but from the slowness of the operation, the last part of the crop is very full of weeds before they can get to it, and sometimes should the water fall too soon, it is much injured by being choked by them. Here is, I think, one of the faults of the cultivation by the present mode. I will presently point out the mode of avoiding this disaster. The crop being finished, and the weeds taken out from the rice, they spend a short time preparing latania strips from the woods, to tie up the bundles, which they do in the field as it is dried. This is generally in July or August, when a man or two is hired to assist, and then, with the cycle, the rice is cut down very neatly, about one-half to three-quarters of an acre a day, as it may be, better or worse, standing or blown down. It dries one day in the sun. It is then tied in bundles, and put in small stacks in the field convenient to the cutters, without stack-poles. The grain is turned inside and the stem outside. When all is cut down and stacked in three small stacks, they arrange their grain-yards and begin hauling in; the first cut being hauled first, and so on, until all is stacked at the house. The blocks are about three feet from the ground, and the stacks are made regular to hold about twenty barrels clean rice. They are well pointed, without poles, and topped with latania. By stacking first in the field in small stacks, the first sweat is passed through, and when it is opened and hauled, it is stacked a second time; it then becomes aired, and dries perfectly, and keeps for years without mould or mildew.

When rice is wanted for the mill, eight or ten tackeys, or small horses, are tied one to another to a post; the rice is placed on the ground about three feet deep, the heads up, and the animals are made to trot around, occasionally shaking up the rice. In this way about twenty barrels per day are usually trodden out. It is then turned in a small hand-mill of wood, like a common corn-mill, and partially hulled; then placed in a mortar, or four mortars in a row, where the like number of pestles pound it till the balance of the hull, and a skin that has a yellow appearance, is taken off. When it is fanned and freed from the chaff by this process, about seven to eight barrels a day is cleaned and prepared for market. This is, as yet, the largest amount averaged, I believe, in a day, except by a small steam-mill once started here by an engineer, which got out about twenty barrels a day; but the prejudice was so strong against that mode of cleaning, that the mill could at last neither buy, nor get rice upon toll, and was abandoned.

It is by preventing the weeds in the rice that its more extensive cultivation can be conducted, a better article produced, and the worst part of the labor avoided, allowing the worker to make more to the hand by a considerable quantity. It is here, generally, the rice planter fails; the weeds and grass catch him, and he loses much of his yields. He has also a worse quality of rice. I have recommended the following cultivation to several planters, but have been told that enough is made by the present process, and why should our alteration be adopted? The reason the weeds are so bad and the grass so troublesome, preventing the cultivation of so many acres properly, is that the ground is broken up in the spring after all the grass begins to grow, and the rice being planted immediately in succession, the roots of the grass and weeds never lose their life, but go on growing immediately, and gets ahead of the rice, which has to sprout, and is at first delicate and slow in starting. These roots can be killed by starting the ox plough in October and November, and ploughing all the land deeply during those months, the roots of the grass being turned up and exposed to the frosts of winter. Ditch in December and February, and then, with three horse ploughs in March, the already pulverized ground can be turned up and knocked to pieces, and harrowed over with a light horse harrow; then sow the rice and harrow it in lightly keeping the ground as dry as you can; now you may moisten it with water slightly, and the rice will all come up and require little or no weeding. The quality will be better, and the quantity certainly considerably increased. By this process also, the old residuum on the ground will, being ploughed in early, be well rotted, and assist the vegetation of the crop. The consequence of this fall and winter ploughing would save the like amount of work in the water at our most unhealthy season, and in the most valuable time to the planter. The weeding being light and early over, the preparations for cutting can be sooner made, the crop gathered in in good time, and I have no doubt, that instead of seven and eight barrels, ten and twelve can be made to the acre, and a much easier crop.

If the Carolina mode of working by drill were tried properly, I have no doubt it would be found advantageous here as it has been there. I have tried fifteen or twenty acres many years ago in that manner, and found it do well, yield well, and the rice was of good quality. I had no difficulty, with a good canal, in taking the water off and on when wanted. I hoed it the same as corn, and then let on water again. It is said that water had better be kept on until the rice is nearly ready to be cut, as it makes the stalk tender, and prevents it from breaking. In case of blowing down, many say if they make very heavy crops they cannot take them off. This is applicable to all southern crops; more hands have always to be hired in harvest, and it is a poor excuse.

There is no reason why Louisiana rice should not be as good as any other, and yield as much, except bad cultivation and worse manufacture. There is an immense amount of valuable rice land in the lower part of this parish, near the sea shore, on the river, very cheap, and far more valuable in proportion to their quantity than any other lands in the state. They have the advantage of climate for sugar, rice, or cotton. The net product of a common acre of land in rice, ready for sale, is eight to ten barrels. The common price is seven to eight dollars, sometimes five and ten dollars per barrel. The acres planted per hand are eight to ten, and as many as fifteen, sometimes, by the inhabitants of this neighborhood.

Trusting that these hasty lines will be followed by more elaborate contributions from experienced pens, and that an interest will be given in Louisiana to the important subject of rice,

I am, your ob't serv't,
R. A. Wilkinson.

Parish of Plaquemines, La.

Hamilton Smith

COTTON, AND THE ONLY PRACTICAL METHODS PRESENTED TO ITS PRODUCERS OF ADVANCING AND CONTROLLING ITS PRICE

Born in Durham, New Hampshire, Hamilton Smith studied law and, as a young man, moved to Louisville, Kentucky, where he founded a highly successful law practice. Shortly after the death of his wife in 1840, Smith established a cotton factory and a coal company, both of which proved profitable. Evidently meticulous in his regard for the details of cotton manufacturing and cost accounting, Smith's advocacy of southern cotton textile production using the surplus capital of planters was buttressed by hard figures on employment, wages, and capital. His goal was the achievement of an integrated economic unit: the plantation on which cotton was not only cultivated but also manufactured into coarse textiles. In pursuit of this object, Smith also proposed a constitutional amendment to permit the imposition of an export duty on raw cotton "to ensure the fabrication of all coarse cotton goods at home."

Although De Bow's Review published numerous articles that addressed the question of how best to stimulate southern manufacturing, Smith's essay is of particular interest because of its specificity and his obvious understanding of the state of national and international economic affairs, particularly the joint problems of overproduction and declining prices of raw cotton. In 1849, the year in which Smith wrote, the cotton crop of the South exceeded 2,000,000 bales, or more than 766,000,000 pounds. And, as Smith intimated, the trend in production was rising. At the same time, the price of raw cotton had, with only short-lived interruptions, dramatically declined. Hence, the dilemma of the cotton planter, a dilemma Smith proposed to relieve.

That this country does now, and probably for ever will, possess the monopoly of raw cotton, is assumed. Great Britain has in vain endeavored

Vol. VII (July, 1849), pp. 48–53.

to become independent of us, and has made fruitless experiments after experiments to encourage the growth of this staple in every part of her empire most favorable to its cultivation; the field of experiment has been unlimited, and the means used have been fully adequate to the object in view.

As long as children come into the world naked, so long is the cotton fabric likely to be of more extensive use than any other covering; until the iron hands of machinery are palsied, so long will civilized man put down all competition of bark, grass, furs, and even of wool, with his cotton garments.

Have we clothed all the shivering people of the north? Have we covered the nakedness of all who dwell within the tropics? By no means: a small proportion of mankind have just begun to rely on us, and the residue of our race have markets for us yet to be opened.

We alone, then, have a great staple, which may be made of universal use, and to the consumption of which no limit can be fixed.

But how shall we enlarge its consumption, and how regulate its value? *To do this effectually we must control its fabrication as well as its production.*

So long as we rely on cotton spinners and weavers, who are starving this year, fighting next year, and in all years are trodden to the earth by the tax gatherer and police officer, it is very clear that we cannot effect the end in view. Neither shall we be more successful while we waste our substance and exhaust our energies in and about the costly machinery of exchange.

To undersell the *tapa* of the Pacific, and the fabrics made of grass and the fibres of the cocoanut and agave, we must sell cheap. The rich will buy the lawns at any price, but the masses require cheap sheetings. How shall the cost of these be lessened? What says the cotton planter? Is he willing to grow the material at rates cheaper than now? The starving operative of Europe declares that he can barely live on what he now receives as wages; the Manchester, Glasgow, and Lille mill owners, show a balance sheet indicative of a most unprofitable business; the sailor refuses to work at lower rates, and the shipyards of the country are now comparatively silent, because capital invested in ships does not pay.

Turn the glass whichsoever way he will around the present horizon, the cotton planter sees over-production and the fall in value of his staple. Even if he grows less cotton and more food and hemp, the food and hemp growers of Kentucky, Missouri, and Tennessee, deprived of a market for their staples, will send their slaves to compete with his in the cotton fields of the South. He has but one mode of relief. *His staple must be fabricated nearer home.* The profits of making the cloth must not be absorbed in the support of kings, queens, bishops, field-marshals, the paupers, soldiers and sailors, the mistresses of nobles, and the pensioners of the state in Europe. And how shall these expensive instruments be discarded? Perhaps the salvation of England depends on the present state of things. *The cheaper she can buy the raw cotton, the higher taxes she can impose on her people who work it up.* Her policy is always the same. The power of her government and of her monster bank has ever been, is now, and for ever will be, exerted to their utmost limit, that her imported raw materials shall be laid in at the cheapest, and that her manufactured commodities shall be sold at the highest rates.

Can the cotton planters, scattered over nine large states, ever expect to fix a uniform and satisfactory price on their staple by individual association. The history of individual combinations, formed to effect pecuniary interests, shows clearly the futility of any such movement.

There are but two methods now presented to the cotton planter for achieving his independence, and securing reasonable profits on his capital and a fair remuneration for his labor. Both are equally certain. The one would effect the result almost immediately, and the other in time. The one by legislation, and the other by the force of circumstances.

At the formation of our constitution, the South insisted on a positive prohibition of export duties. It was then evident that she was to be chiefly dependent on agricultural products, and she wisely provided that these products should be burthened with no domestic shackles, but be left free to seek the best markets of the world. But *then* the supply of these products was far less than the demand; *then* the South had no knowledge of her capacity to fabricate her own products; *then* she did not expect the settlement and cultivation of the country west of her for centuries; *then* human labor did the work now performed by machinery; and *then* we did not, as now, control the whole cotton district of North America.

But circumstances have changed; we do now over produce, we can now manufacture. We are, in respect to industrial pursuits, situated as older countries have been, and we need not be ashamed to examine the lessons of national policy taught in foreign schools.

The general policy, the common usages of civilized nations, are generally based on the principles of equity and common sense. Now, if there is one principle that more than another has been acted on by every government, civilized and uncivilized, it has been that of making every possible profit out of any and every material and commodity over which it possessed the control.

Holland monopolized spices—Spain, quicksilver—France, silk fabrics; England put a prohibitive export duty on raw wool for a long series of years, and she even interdicted, under the most severe penal enactments, the exportation of mind until it had expended all its profitable results at home. For years the English inventor of labor-saving machinery was under a closer surveillance of the police than the felon; he could not leave home, nor could he send abroad the slightest description of his improvements.

But the instances of this policy are so numerous and well known, that it is needless labor to cite more of them. The policy remains the same in this as in preceding centuries, and is strictly followed by every country except our own. Our cotton planters could afford to be liberal, while their profits were ample, and until they had the means of realizing the profits of the mill, as well as those of the field.

The first method then proposed for consideration, is the calling for such an amendment of the constitution as will authorize the imposition of export duties, and, when this is obtained, the imposition of such an export duty on raw cotton as will ensure the fabrication of all *coarse* cotton goods at home; laces are for the rich, and, as they are more the product of human hands than of machinery, their material will bear almost any duty.

If the cotton planter asks for such a change, and such a law, both can be obtained. The food and hemp growers of the West, and the manufacturers and carriers of the East, would interpose no difficulties, but, on the contrary, aid the movement, when they understood its object.

Can any one doubt the result? Let the year 1865 be fixed as the period when the law advocated should take effect; will any one deny that, within the period named, cotton mills would start up, as if by magic, all over the country, and sufficient for the working up of the entire cotton crop, whatever its increase may be? Our own surplus labor would direct its attention to this employment and to its auxiliary branches of industry. The English, French, Belgium, Swiss, Prussian and Saxon cotton mills, would be gradually closed, and their spinners and weavers, by hundreds of thousands, would bring their tools of trade where they would be of use. Capital would follow this labor; we should have a home market for whatever is produced by our fertile soil, and the rich ores that now lie undisturbed beneath that soil; money would accumulate, because we should have ceased to send it abroad in large quantities for the necessaries of life. Our exports of cotton fabrics would be exchanged with China for tea, with Brazil for coffee, with Southern Asia and the Islands of the Indian Ocean for spices, with the West Indies for inter-tropical fruits, with Chili, Peru, Mexico and California for the precious metals. Our land would appreciate, our labor would be better paid, and our capital would yield larger returns up to the point at which the supply of the cotton fabric—the product of the combined surplus labor of the country—would reach the demand.

The South has but to will this thing and it is done. The result *can* be accomplished by ourselves in half the time named. The machine shops already in operation in the country, have the capacity of duplicating our own cotton machinery in five years; we now have the best teachers and in abundance, and we have spare labor enough for twice the number of mills required for our purpose.

But, although I believe the constitution and laws will eventually be so modified and framed, as to protect our home industry from the legislation and preponderating capital of foreign nations, I do not look for such a change of opinion among southern men as would result in affording us immediately relief by law.

I present, therefore, the other method, and append to it such statistics and calculations as may best commend it to the attention of the cotton planters, who are now investing their surplus capital in lands and negroes to make more cotton and a superabundance of that which is now superabundant.

Let the cotton planter look into the *modus operandi* of manufacturing cotton. An examination of the subject will show him, that less labor, capital, and care, is required in the fabrication than in the production of his staple; and that one bale of cloth will bring him more money, or more exchangeable commodities than five bales of his material. Let him employ the cheap and inexhaustible power and ores of the West; let him use cheap labor and skill at home, and invite both from abroad; let him encourage the building of ships out of our cheap timber, with fastenings of our tenacious iron, with rigging from our cheap hemp— to be provisioned with our cheap food, and to carry our own fabrics of cotton to the most remote consumers; let the cotton planter of the South, and the food and hemp producer of the West, unite in developing all the home resources that will tend to cheapen the production, the fabrication, and the transportation of the materials which should naturally be combined at home.

That the cotton planter may see the relative cost of producing and manufacturing the cotton, I give the following estimates. Of the fairness of the first, the planter is fully competent to decide. Of the correctness of the last, I have to say that it shows *actual results*. The mill, from whose books the items were taken, is of modern construction and has been running twelve months. Its operatives are chiefly new to the business, and its position is remote from machine shops, founderies, and other auxiliaries, and it is seventy miles by railroad from the city where its material is purchased and its goods are sold.

The cloth is the finished product of the labor and capital of the planter, the carrier, and the manufacturer and their respective adjuncts.

For convenience I take a mill of 10,000 spindles, making No. 14 sheetings, averaging 2–30/100 yards to the lb. The cloth sells in the markets of the central West at 7½ cents per yard. I allow 6 cents per lb. for the cotton, good middling, and middling fair, which is higher than its present value.

The mill will employ 275 operatives, chiefly girls, and produce per annum 4,500,000 yards, at 7½ cents		$337,500
Cost of cotton 1,800,000 lbs. at 6 cents	$108,000	
50,000 bushels of coal, at 3 cents	1,500	
Carding (less waste) 1,650,000 lbs. at 0.804 cents per lb.	13,266	
Spinning (less waste) 1,650,000 lbs. at 0.893 cents per lb.	14,734	
Dressing including starch at 0.564 cents ...	9,306	
Weaving including all expenses at 1.612 cents	26,598	
Repairs, including machinists, or wear and tear at 0.788 cents	17,002	
General expenses, including all officers, insurance, transportation, taxes, &c., at 1.251 cents	20,642	211,048
		$126,452

We may now deduct further expenses attending the operations of the mill owned by distant stockholders, and managed by paid agents.

Say salary of Treasurer	500	
Say 5 per cent on sales, and guarantee	16,875	
Salary of local manager	3,000	20,375

Net profits, $106,077

The cost of mill	$25,000
The cost of manager's house	3,000
The cost of tenements for 275 operatives ..	20,000
The cost of warehouse and store	2,000
The cost of 10,000 spindles and machinery complete	160,000
Working capital for over 4 months stock ...	40,000

Capital invested, $250,000 yields $106,077

Cost of Producing 1,800,000 lbs. of Cotton

The fixed capital is the land, improvements and negroes. Sixty working hands are as many as can be profitably managed by an overseer. There will require 900 acres of good land. Let us take a model plantation on the Mississippi river, between latitudes 32° and 34°.

600 acres of land in cotton, at $32 per acre .	$19,200
150 acres of land in corn, at $32 per acre ...	4,800
150 acres of land in pasture and wood, at $12 per acre	1,800
60 working hands averaging $650 each	39,000
Cost of gin, mill, dwelling and cabins	5,000
Cost of mules, oxen, carts and tools	4,000

Fixed capital in the model plantation $73,800

Annual cost of operation—

Overseer	$600
Clothing $15 per hand	900
Deficiency of meat, sugar, coffee, &c.	650
Medicine and attendance	200

$2,350

The accretion of slaves is about balanced by deterioration of stock and improvements, abrasion of the river and renewal of levees.

There is an average loss on bagging and rope. $20 per acre will be regarded as a low cost of clearing land, and $12 per acre for wild land is below its present rate.

The average produce per hand is not over 7½ bales of 400 lbs. each.

Then the model plantation will yield per annum 180,000 lbs. of cotton, and ten plantations will be required to supply the mill with 1,800,000 lbs.

The aggregate of slaves to produce the cotton is	600	
The amount of fixed capital is	$738,000	
The aggregate cost of operating the plantation is	23,500	

Summary

The gross product of the joint operations per annum is			$337,500
Of this the fixed capital of the planter receives		$108,000	
Less cost of operating	$23,500		
Less carriage $1 per bale	4,500		
		28,000	
Or $738,000 yields		$80,000	
The fixed capital of the manufacturer receives		$337,500	
Less cost of materials and of operating or $211,048 plus 20.375		231,423	
Or $250,000 yields		$106,077	

The capital of the planter is nearly three times that of the manufacturer, and yet he receives the least portion of the profits. The 600 laborers get less than the 275. The planter has to look after ten overseers, on whom there can be but few checks. The manufacturer has but five overseers and these are checks on each other. The manufacturer is charged with the cost of a treasurer, who gives bonds for the faithful disbursements of the money he receives and of a manager whose high salary ensures the exertion of all his energies. They who are responsible to the planter may assign floods, winds, the worm, sickness of the hands, &c., as the reason of short crops; they who are accountable to the manufacturer can find few excuses.

Your readers will bear in mind that these estimates of the results of manufacturing cotton, are based on the supposition that the mill is located at a coal field on the northern bank of the lower Ohio, where power, food, and lands are cheap; where the climate will allow full work, to which eastern and foreign skilled labor can be attracted, and where a large part of the expenses of transportation can be saved.

William Gregg

DOMESTIC INDUSTRY—
MANUFACTURES AT THE SOUTH

Perhaps the most forceful and articulate advocate of southern indus-
trialization, William Gregg (1800–1867) ridiculed those of his fellow
southerners who condemned northern industrial society and at the
same time complained that unscrupulous Yankee manufacturers were
taking advantage of the South. Gregg's convictions in this matter were
grounded in his own extensive experience as a cotton textile manufac-
turer in South Carolina.

Born in what is now West Virginia, Gregg began his career as a
manufacturer of watches in Columbia, South Carolina, in the mid-
1820s. About ten years later, he retired from business because of poor
health. Unable to remain inactive for long, Gregg acquired part own-
ership of a failing cotton factory and quickly reorganized it, thereby
making it a profitable concern. This marked the beginning of Gregg's
increasingly intimate and successful involvement in the textile indus-
try of the South. In 1846, he founded the Graniteville Manufacturing
Company to produce cotton textiles. De Bow frequently cited this ven-
ture as a model after which southern industrial enterprise should be
patterned. In the mid-1840s Gregg published Essays on Domestic Industry, *which urged the South to emulate rather than criticize the fac-*
tory system and industry of the North. Particularly disturbing to
Gregg, however, was the inevitable dependency of a stubbornly agrar-
ian South on northern manufactures, especially when southern re-
sources were more than adequate to enable the South to meet her own
needs.

In this selection written for De Bow's Review, *Gregg addresses*
many of his remarks to the institutional obstacles to industrialization
that he found in Charleston, South Carolina, including the city's re-
strictive ordinances governing the numbers and use of steam engines.
For Gregg, southern industrial self-sufficiency was the means to a va-
riety of desirable ends, not the least of which was the assurance of con-
tinued prosperity for the South, and South Carolina particularly, in
the face of a rapidly changing world economy. He pursued this theme

Vol. VIII (February, 1850), pp. 134–46.

still more vigorously after December 17, 1860, when South Carolina issued its ordinance of secession, which Gregg signed.

[Several years ago William Gregg, Esq., of South Carolina, published a series of essays upon the industry of the South, which afterward appeared in pamphlet form. We expressed at the time our objection to the manner in which Mr. Gregg saw fit to introduce some of our most distinguished political men, although the general views of the author interested and instructed us. We have been lately re-perusing the essays, and at this period, when the South would seem to be aroused in every quarter with regard to home or domestic manufactures, their republication in the Review may subserve a useful purpose. We therefore offer them to the reader for preservation in this and our next number, omitting some parts which relate more particularly to Carolina, and some again now unimportant. Since Mr. Gregg wrote, the South has greatly improved in many respects, and his picture of South Carolina and Charleston, always highly colored, varies at the present time, we are gratified to state, very far from the reality.—Ed.]

It must be apparent to all men of discernment that, whether a tariff for protection is continued or not, our only safety, in this State, lies in a change of our industrial pursuits. The United States is destined to be a great manufacturing country, and a few years, even without a protective tariff, will place her on a footing with, if not ahead of, the most skillful nations, and all who have any knowledge of the subject admit that South Carolina and Georgia possess advantages, which only need to be fostered to lead to success in cotton manufacturing. We already see North Carolina on the one side, and Georgia on the other, making rapid strides in these pursuits, and shall we stand with our arms folded, crying save us from our oppressors, until we are awakened to compete with those neighboring States, skilled in the arts! It is only necessary for us to turn our faces to the South-west to behold the people who are to take the very bread from our mouths, if we continue to place our reliance on the culture of cotton, and the time is at hand when we shall set about, in good earnest, changing our pursuits. It would indeed be well for us, if we were not so refined in politics—if the talent, which has been, for years past, and is now engaged in embittering our indolent people against their industrious neighbors of the North, had been with the same zeal engaged in promoting domestic industry and the encouragement of the mechanical arts. If so, we should now see a far different state of things in South Carolina. It is only necessary to travel over the sterile mountains of Connecticut, Massachusetts, Vermont, and New Hampshire, to learn the true secret of our difficulties, to learn the difference between indolence and industry, extravagance and economy. We there see the scenery which would take the place of our unpainted mansions; dilapidated cabins with mud chimneys and no windows; broken down rail fences; fields overgrown with weeds, and thrown away, half exhausted, to be taken up by pine thickets; beef cattle unprotected from the inclemency of winter, and so poor as barely to preserve life. In fact, every evidence that can possibly be exhibited to satisfy a stranger, that we are, to say the least, destitute of every feature which characterizes an industrious people, may be seen among us. Laying aside the vexed question of a tariff for protection, which I don't pretend to advocate, I cannot see how we are to look with a reasonable hope for relief, even from its abandonment, without a total change of our habits. My recent visit to the northern States has fully satisfied me that the true secret of our difficulties, lies in the want of energy on the part of our capitalists, and ignorance and laziness on the part of those who *ought* to labor. We need never look for thrift while we permit our immense timber forests, granite quarries and mines, to lie idle, and supply ourselves with hewn granite, pine boards, lath and shingles, &c., furnished by the *lazy* dogs at the North—all, worse than this, we see our back country farmers, many of whom are too lazy to mend a broken gate, or repair the fences to protect their crops from the neighboring stock, actually supplied with their ax, hoe and broom handles, pitchforks, rakes, &c., by the *indolent* mountaineers of New Hampshire and Massachusetts. The time was, when every old woman in the country had her gourd, from which the country gardens were supplied with seeds. We now find it more convenient to permit this duty to devolve on our careful friends, the yankees. Even our boat-oars, and handspikes for rolling logs, are furnished, ready made, to our hand, and what jim-crack can possibly be invented of which we are not the purchasers? These are the drains which are impoverishing the South—these are the true sources of all our difficulties. Need I add, to further exemplify our excessive indolence, that the Charleston market is supplied with fish and wild game by northern men, who come out here, as regularly as the winter comes, for this purpose, and from our own waters and forests often realize, in the course of one winter, a sufficiency to purchase a small farm in New England.

A change in our habits and industrial pursuits is a far greater desideratum than any change in the laws of our government, which the most clamorous opponents of the tariff could devise. He who has possessed himself of the notion that we have the industry, and are wronged out of our hard earnings by a lazy set of scheming yankees, to get rid of this delusion, needs only seat himself on the Charleston wharves for a few days, and behold ship after ship arrive, laden down with the various articles produced by yankee industry. Let him behold these vessels discharging their cargoes and count the cost to South Carolina. From the month of September till May, our wharves are crowded, not only with the articles manufactured by the handicrafts-men of the North, but vast quantities of dairy articles, and all kinds of culinary vegetables, which are far better adapted to the soil of South Carolina, than to those places where they are grown. Here may be seen a picture that ought to bring a blush on the face of the statesman who would advocate legislative resistance as the remedy for our State. It ought to make every citizen who feels an interest in his country, ashamed to visit the clothing stores of Charleston, and see the vast ex-hibition of ready made clothing, manufactured mostly by the women of Philadelphia, New York, Boston, and other northern cities, to the det-riment and starvation of our own countrywomen, hundreds of whom may be found in our own good city in wretched poverty, unable to pro-cure work by which they would be glad to earn a decent living.

One would not suppose that the South was laboring under embar-rassment, if he were to see the crowds that are continually thronging the northern cities and places of amusement. I have heard the number variously estimated at from forty to sixty thousand in one summer. Taking the lower estimate of the two, and allowing for the expenses of each individual $300 (and this is certainly below the mark), we shall have $12,000,000 transferred yearly from the South to the North, by absenteeism. As bad off as we know South Carolina to be, yet we are certain she furnishes her full *quota* of this immense sum. Go where you may, in the city or out of it—in what direction you please, and you can scarcely set your foot into a railroad car, in which you will not find some half dozen persons from this State. The register book of every fashionable hotel that I visited, exhibited a large share of names, with South Carolina attached to them. Nor are our people remarkable for their economical habits, as the bar-keepers will inform you, that their wine bills exhibit liberality even to wastefulness. You may see them too, flying around cities, in the finest and most costly equipages that money can procure, and while a *millionaire* of New York is content to ride in an *omnibus*, from Wall street to the upper part of the city, many of these persons, not worth ten thousand dollars, would be ashamed to be seen in such vehicles. With tailors, milliners, mantua-makers, &c., these persons are considered to have gold without measure, and it is a perfect *windfall* for them to meet occasionally with one. You cannot step into a furniture store, carpet warehouse, or dry goods establishment, where fine silks and laces are sold, without meeting persons from our State, making lavish expenditures and purchasing thousands of articles of wearing apparel, which are not worn until they return home, where the same articles can be obtained in the stores of our own tradesmen, at cheaper rates than those at which they were purchased at the North.

At one tailor's establishment in Boston, I was informed by the proprietor, that his sales for the last year, to Charleston alone, amounted to upwards of $50,000, and this year he expected they would reach $80,000. How much trade others in Boston in the same business receive from Charleston, and what amount falls to the lot of the fashionable clothiers of New York and Philadelphia, cannot be estimated, but there is little doubt, that the amount would be found quite sufficient to support three or four fashionable establishments in our own city.

Let South Carolina be true to herself, let her go to work with a determination to resist the northern tariffites, by resolving not to purchase or use their articles of manufacture. This will cure the evil, and bring us to the point we desire to arrive at, by an easier and much shorter road than legislative action. Limited as our manufactures are in South Carolina, we can now more than supply the State with coarse cotton fabrics. Many of the fabrics now manufactured here are exported to New York, and, for aught I know, find their way to the East Indies. We can most assuredly make our own ax-handles, raise our own cabbages, beets, potatoes and onions; our boys, as in olden times, may be taught to make their own toy-wagons and wheel-barrows; our wives and sisters can hem our handkerchiefs and bake our bread. If we continue in our present habits, it would not be unreasonable to predict, that, when the Raleigh Railroad is extended to Columbia, our members of the Legislature will be fed on Yankee bakers' bread. Pardon me for repeating the call on South Carolina to go to work. God speed the

day when her politicians will be exhorting the people to domestic industry, instead of State resistance; when our Clay clubs and Democratic associations will be turned into societies for the advancement
of scientific agriculture and the promotion of mechanic art; when our
capitalists will be found following the example of Boston and other
northern cities, in making such investments of their capital as will give
employment to the poor, and make them producers, instead of bur-
thensome consumers; when our city council may become so enlightened as to see the propriety of following the example of every other
city in the civilized world, in removing the restrictions on the use of
the steam-engine, now indispensable in every department of manufacturing, and to be found by hundreds, from the cellars to the garrets of
houses, in the most densely peopled parts of Philadelphia, New York,
Boston, and other cities.

We want no laws for the protection of those that embark in the manufacture of such cotton fabrics as we propose to make in South Carolina; nor does it follow, as a matter of course, that because we advocate a system which will diversify the pursuits of our people, and
enable them to export a portion of one of our valuable staples, in a
manufactured state, that we wish manufactures to predominate over
other employments. All must admit that, to a certain extent, the system we advocate could not operate otherwise than to produce beneficial results, by regulating prices—by insuring a certain reward to labor—a profitable income to capital, and by infusing health, vigor and
durability into every department of industry. It is a well established
fact, that capital employed in this State, in the culture of cotton, does
not, with ordinary management, yield more than 3 or 4, and in some
instances, 2 per cent; this being the only mode of employing our capital, except in the culture of rice, how can we expect to retain men of
capital and *enterprise* among us? Those having the first, must be
wholly wanting in the last—or they must possess an extraordinary at-
tachment to the land of their nativity, to remain with us under such a
state of affairs.

With this fact before us, is it surprising that South Carolina should
remain stationary in population? And let it be remembered that the
same cause which has produced this result, will continue to operate
hurtfully, in the same ratio, as the price of our great staple declines. In
all probability, an additional outlet will soon be opened to drain us of
our people and our capital. How much this is to take from us, remains
to be seen. Unless we betake ourselves to some more profitable em-

ployment than the planting of cotton, what is to prevent our most enterprising planters from moving, with their negro capital, to the South-west? What is to keep our business men and moneyed capital in South Carolina? Capital will find its way to places that afford the greatest remuneration, and, in leaving our State, it will carry with it its enterprising owner. These are truly unpleasant reflections, but they force themselves upon us. Who can look forward to the future destiny of our State, persisting, as she does, with such pertinacity, in the exclusive and exhausting system of agriculture, without dark forebodings? If we listen much longer to the *ultras* in agriculture and *croakers* against mechanical enterprise, it is feared that they will be the only class left, to stir up the indolent sleepers that are indisposed to action, and that are willing to let each day provide for itself.

Since the discovery that cotton would mature in South Carolina, she has reaped a golden harvest; but it is feared it has proved a curse rather than a blessing, and I believe that she would at this day be in a far better condition, had the discovery never been made. Cotton has been to South Carolina what the mines of Mexico were to Spain—it has produced us such an abundant supply of all the luxuries and elegances of life, with so little exertion on our part, that we have become enervated, unfitted for other and more laborious pursuits, and unprepared to meet the state of things, which sooner or later must come about. Is it out of place here to predict, that the day is not far distant, yea, is close at hand, when we shall find that we can no longer *live* by that, which has heretofore yielded us, not only a bountiful and sumptuous living, at home, but has furnished the means for carrying thousands and tens of thousands of our citizens abroad, to squander their gold in other countries—that we have wasted the fruits of a rich, virgin soil, in ease and luxury—that those who have practiced sufficient industry and economy to accumulate capital, have left, or are leaving us, to populate other States.

We shall indeed soon be awakened to look about us for other pursuits, and we shall find that our soil has to be renovated—our houses and workshops have to be built—our roads and bridges have to be made, all of which ought to have been done with the rich treasures that have been transferred to other States. Let us begin at once, before it is too late, to bring about a change in our industrial pursuits—let us set about it before the capital and enterprise of our State has entirely left us—let croakers against enterprise be silenced—let the working men of our State who have, by their industry, accumulated capital, turn out and give a practical lesson to our political leaders, that are opposed to this scheme.

If we look at this subject in the abstract only, we shall very naturally come to the above conclusions; it is, however, often the case, that practical results contradict the plainest abstract propositions, and it is hoped, that in the course of these remarks, it will be proved to the satisfaction of at least some of our men of capital and enterprise, that the spinning of cotton may be undertaken with a certainty of success, in the two Carolinas and Georgia, and that the failures which have taken place, ought not to deter others from embarking in the business, they being the result of unpardonable ignorance, and just such management on the part of those interested, as would prove ruinous in any other undertaking.

Surely there is nothing in cotton spinning that can poison the atmosphere of South Carolina. Why not spin as well as plant cotton? The same hand that attends the gin may work a carding machine. The girl who is capable of making thread on a country spinning wheel, may do the same, with equal facility, on the *throstle frame*. The woman who can warp the thread and weave it, on a common loom, may soon be taught to do the same on the *power loom*; and so with all the departments, from the raw cotton to the cloth, experience has proved that any child, white or black, of ordinary capacity, may be taught, in a few weeks, to be expert in any part of a cotton factory; moreover, all overseers who have experience in the matter, give a decided preference to blacks as operatives.

There are many reasons why blacks should be preferred; two of which may be adduced. First—You are not under the necessity of educating them, and have, therefore, their uninterrupted services from the age of eight years. The second is, that when you have your mill filled with expert hands, you are not subjected to the change which is constantly taking place with whites. In the northern States, these are inconveniences of no small moment. In Massachusetts, the laws forbid the employment of persons under *fourteen* years of age, unless the employer can show a certificate from a school-master, stating that the individual has been at school three months in the year. The teaching of new hands and the constant change of operatives, are evils seriously felt; and in the summer season, when it is desirable to ramble in the country, many eastern factories have one-third of their machinery standing idle for want of hands. While on this part of my subject, I would ask, shall we stop at the effort to prove the capacity of blacks for

manufacturing? Shall we pass unnoticed the thousands of poor, ignorant, degraded white people among us, who, in this land of plenty, live
in comparative nakedness and starvation? Many a one is reared in
proud South Carolina, from birth to manhood, who has never passed a
month, in which he has not some part of the time, been stinted for
meat. Many a mother is there, who will tell you that her children are
but scantily supplied with bread, and much more scantily with meat,
and if they be clad with comfortable raiment, it is at the expense of
their scanty allowance of food. These may be startling statements, but
they are nevertheless true, and if not believed in Charleston, the members of our Legislature, who have traversed the State, in electioneering campaigns, can attest their truth.

It is only necessary to build a manufacturing village of shanties, in a
healthy location, in any part of the State, to have crowds of these poor
people around you, seeking employment at half the compensation
given to operatives at the North. It is indeed painful to be brought in
contact with such ignorance and degradation; but on the other hand, it
is pleasant to witness the change, which soon takes place in the condition of those who obtain employment. The emaciated, pale-faced children, soon assume the appearance of robust health, and their tattered
garments are exchanged for those suited to a better condition; if you
visit their dwellings, you will find their tables supplied with wholesome food; and on the Sabbath, when the females turn out in their gay
colored gowns, you will imagine yourself surrounded by groups of city
belles. How easy would it be for the proprietors of such establishments, with only a small share of philanthropy, to make good use of the
school-funding in ameliorating the condition of this class of our population, now but little elevated above the Indian of the forest. The cause
of this degradation and poverty will hereafter be noticed; it is an interesting subject, and one that ought to engage the attention of every phi-
lanthropist and Christian. It is, perhaps, not generally known, that
there are *twenty-nine thousand* white persons in this State, above the
age of twelve years, who can neither read nor write—this is about one
in every five of the white population.

That we are behind the age in agriculture, the mechanic arts, industry and enterprise, is apparent to all who pass through our State; our
good city of Charleston speaks a language on this subject not to be mistaken; she has lost 1000 of her population, according to the census of
1840, while her sister cities have doubled and quadrupled theirs; she
has had, for thirteen years, the advantage of the South Carolina Rail-

road, which, under ordinary circumstances, should have doubled the number of her population. How does she now stand? Precisely where she stood twenty years ago, and, but for the two conflagrations which swept off many of her old houses, she would present at this moment the same appearance that she did in 1824. Where is the city in this age of improvement, except Charleston, that a book-binder, or job-printer is prohibited the use of a small steam-engine, to enable him to carry on his business with more facility, and to cheapen the price of those articles that we are purchasing from other cities more liberal to their artizans? and where a carpenter is not allowed the use of the same, to turn a circular saw or drive a mortising chisel, to enable him to compete with others in supplying us with ready made doors, blinds, sashes, shutters, &c.? Even the boxes in which our merchandise is packed, are made in the city of New York, by steam-power, and brought to our very doors. The book-binder, tanner, currier, hatter, wagon-maker, carriage-maker, carpenter, turner, tinner, and, in fact, persons engaged in every branch of mechanism, find steam-power indispensable; and knowing, as we do, that they are unrestricted in its use in other cities, why are our mechanics forbid to use it in this city? There is a strong disposition manifested by this class of our citizens to elevate and improve their several trades, and if they are properly encouraged, there is no doubt that a great change would soon be brought about; but the labor of negroes and blind horses can never supply the place of *steam*, and this power is withheld lest the smoke of an engine should disturb the delicate nerves of an agriculturist; or the noise of the mechanic's hammer should break in upon the slumber of a real estate holder, or importing merchant, while he is indulging in fanciful dreams, or building on paper, *the Queen City of the South*—the *paragon* of the age. No reflections on the members of the city council are here intended—they are, no doubt, fairly representing public opinion on this subject; some of that body are known to be in favor of a modification of these restrictions, which certainly are behind the age, and a reproach to our city. Our mechanics ought to rise in their strength, and procure the signature of every liberal minded man, to a *petition* to the city authorities, asking that they may be placed on the same footing, in this respect, as the tradesmen of other cities.

These restrictions are but in character with many other things; and while we are on this subject, permit me to ask, whether any other town of the same size, would have allowed the greatest work of the age—the Hamburg Railroad—to come into the city and find its terminus in a mud hole, scarcely passable in the winter season for a family carriage, much less for a loaded wagon. It cannot be denied that it is a disgrace to the City and Neck, that this great work, which will immortalize its projectors, should not have been met by a stone road leading from it to our wharves. That the hundreds of thousands of bales of produce and merchandise that have entered into, and departed from our city, during the last thirteen years, should have been dragged through the sand and mud of King and Meeting streets, demonstrates a fact, about which there can be no mistake—the hand of enterprise is not among us. And shall we continue in our downward course? Is it not time that a warning voice were raised, to proclaim to the good people of Charleston, that in these times of enterprise, no city need expect to thrive that does not encourage and foster the mechanic arts and artizans? It is this class of men that gives life, strength and vigor to all branches of trade, and every department of life, and if they were properly encouraged, our city authorities would no longer have to resort to dram shop licenses for revenue; money would soon be found to pay her debts and pave her streets. Let our city council begin, by removing the restrictions on the use of the steam-engine. Who would not rather have an occasional whiff of smoke from a steam-engine, than the scent of an odious grog shop? The former a benefit, the latter a curse to the community. So far as fire risks are concerned, it would be safer to have three engines; than one such magazine of mischief and corruption, licensed by our city council, under the title of "retailers of ardent spirits."

Need any thing be said about the amount of capital required for embarking in these pursuits? It is only necessary to revert to the fact, that lands and negroes pay but *three* per cent when engaged in the culture of cotton, and to name the price of 5 and 6 per cent. State stocks. Need a word be said as to the men who are to carry on these enterprises? It is only necessary to point you to the bone and sinew that are leaving our city and State, to enrich and populate others. Any one that has visited Mississippi and Alabama, can soon point out the *maelstrom* that has swallowed up so much of the capital and enterprise of South Carolina.

The period is fast approaching in South Carolina, which shall produce a great change in these matters. Many persons are now looking to the subject of manufactures with intense interest, and it is believed that many men of capital would at once embark in this business, could this field for profitable enterprise be laid open before our wealthy business men of Charleston, a host of whom can be found, with nerves that never tire, and with as much forecast and shrewdness as the merchant manufacturers of Boston, and these latter gentlemen see that it is only necessary that Georgia and the two Carolinas shall engage in the manufactory of *coarse* cotton fabrics, in order to monopolize the trade in these articles. What is to prevent such a result? Have we not the raw material on the spot, thus saving the freight of a double transportation? Is not labor cheaper with us than with our northern brethren? and if we believe that they are reaping such golden harvests, what shall prevent our participation in the spoils? Let the ball be set in motion, then will our miserably poor white population at once rise from their ignorance and degradation, and we shall no longer hear the complaint, that planting capital will pay no more than 3 per cent. The commerce and trade of our State would at once receive a fresh impulse— our city would become a mart for domestic goods—railroad stocks would increase in value—our city would disrobe herself of her old fashioned, rusty, tattered and torn garments, to be clad in the fashionable clothing of the day—her whitened walls and improved suburbs would remind the stranger as he passed through, that the hand of industry and enterprise was at work among us. Our retired merchants would find it no longer necessary or desirable to invest their capital, or look for rural retirement in other States. They would find that we have in our upcountry, within a few hours ride of Charleston, all the advantages that we can desire for such purposes; and, besides spending our money among ourselves, they would also find that there is no better country for the profitable employment of capital, or rural retirement, than in our own State. . . .

Albert Stein

MISSISSIPPI VALLEY
Remarks on the Improvement of the River Mississippi

Albert Stein, an engineer from Mobile, Alabama, contributed more than twenty articles to De Bow's Review *between 1849 and 1867. His subject was almost always the physical geography of the Mississippi River and the removal of natural obstacles and hazards to river navigation. The selection below is one of Stein's less technical essays on the great river and focuses on the peril presented by the increased rate of sedimentation of the river's bed. Flooding of riverside plantations and even of New Orleans was, of course, one disastrous possibility. But even worse, Stein warns, was the real danger that a shallower, more sluggishly flowing Mississippi River would eventually find a new route to the Gulf of Mexico via one of the smaller but deeper lateral water courses. The economic results would be catastrophic and, to prevent these from ever coming to pass, Stein proposes a program of river improvements that included the deepening and straightening of the established channel.*

Long after Stein wrote, the U.S. Army Corps of Engineers and the various state authorities with direct interests along the Mississippi began to pursue most of Stein's suggestions with an eye to preventing disastrous flooding and an equally disastrous change of course by the river. Today, both dangers still threaten.

The river Mississippi is one of the largest rivers on the earth, and, certainly, the most important. Its past and present condition are interesting, not only because they afford to the student of physical laws an inexhaustible source of information as to their operation, but also, because, with its future condition, are inseparably connected the commercial interests of the inhabitants of the many cities along its banks, and the agricultural prosperity of an immense and rapidly increasing population in the interior. It is remarkable for the length and winding character of its course, its large tributaries, the immense volume of

Vol. IX (December, 1850), pp. 594–601.

water it discharges into the gulf, and the vast amount of sedimentary matter which it brings down from above.

Formerly, before the banks along the lower part of the river and adjacent country became subject to cultivation, there were no levees, and the river, in time of flood, inundated the vast extent of low grounds, and deposited a large portion of its sedimentary matter beyond its channel; since the adjacent country, however, has come more into cultivation, and levees have become more necessary and more used, the entire sedimentary matter has been confined to the channel; while, at the same time, the quantity of it has been vastly increased, by the increased cultivation of the lands in the interior, adjacent to its banks and those of its tributaries. Notwithstanding the increase and confinement of the sedimentary matter within its channel, the increased velocity gained by preventing the water, in time of flood, from spreading over all the low grounds, and confining it to its legitimate channel, would have been sufficient to enable the current to keep that channel open and deep, had not other causes been at work which prevented that result. As the interior of Louisiana began to fill up with population, and her lands came into cultivation, the planters along the banks of the Atchafalya, Plaquemine, La Fouche, &c., in order that they might be able to carry their produce to market by water—the cheapest mode of conveyance—cleared out and opened the steamboat navigation to these outlets of the Mississippi. Being cleared of rafts and other impediments that had previously contributed to stop up their channels, and having a more direct channel and a shorter course to the gulf, and, therefore, a greater fall, which caused a greater velocity in their currents and a greater scouring power at their bottom than in that of the main river, they drew off a much larger quantity of water from it than they had done before. The consequence is, that these outlets continue to deepen their channels, while the main river is elevating its bed more and more, and its ability to keep its channel open and clear is evidently diminishing every year.

There can be no doubt that the bed of the main river is gradually being elevated by the deposit of sedimentary matter, which the decreased velocity of the current, in consequence of the heavy drafts made upon its volume of water by the outlets already mentioned, is no longer able to transport to the gulf. Some years ago, if a levee gave way in high water, it did but little damage and excited no alarm; the breach was easily repaired. The services of an engineer were not thought necessary. An overseer, with the labor of a few negroes, was fully able to repair the damage. Now, formidable crevasses take place every year, and are becoming more frequent, and, with the elevation of the river's bed, more dangerous. Whole plantations are swept over, and even the city of New-Orleans, at times, does not seem altogether beyond the reach of danger. That this increased danger does not arise from any increase in the volume of water in the main river, is evident. The average quantity of rain that annually falls in the valley of the Mississippi, if not less, is certainly not greater than formerly, while the increased cultivation of the valley admits of such an increase of evaporation, as must rather diminish than increase the quantity of water that the valley empties into the gulf. Besides, the clearing out of those outlets already mentioned, and their increased depths consequent upon their increased velocity, has drawn off from the main river as much, at least, as it has gained by the confinement of its waters within the levees, if not more.

Should this condition of the river continue progressing, as it certainly has done for some years, the future affords but a gloomy prospect for those who reside near its banks. The steady elevation of the bed of the river, and consequent elevation of its surface above the adjacent banks, will cause the fertility of the plantations near the river to be gradually destroyed, by the slow but certain process of filtration; while the crevasses will continue to become more frequent and destructive, until the plantations along its banks, or within a certain distance of its course, will be rendered either utterly unfit for cultivation, or considerably depreciated in value, as their cultivation will be attended with too much risk and too little profit.

But this is not the worst danger to be feared from its present condition. If the river should be permitted to continue thus elevating its bed, the consequence must be, that the quantity of water that passes into the lateral outlets, which, having more fall and greater velocity at the bottom, will also have deeper channels, will continue to increase; while the volume of water in the main river, its velocity and consequent transporting power decreasing, the deposit of sedimentary matter will increase, and the bed become more rapidly elevated every year. The result of this progressive change must necessarily be, that the present main river will cease to discharge the same volume of water it now does, cease to be the main river, and finally cease to be navigable; while one of the now lateral outlets, having a shorter course and a greater fall to the gulf, and consequently greater velocity at the bottom, and a constant tendency to enlarge its channel, will receive a continually increasing proportion of the water descending from the interior, and ultimately become the main stream. This is a question of too much importance to be treated lightly, or overlooked, until the mischief is irreparable. In it is involved the interest of every man who lives or owns property on the lands adjacent to the present course of the river, but more particularly of the owners of real estate in New-Orleans, and thousands who now live by its commerce, and expect to leave it as a legacy to their children. For, if the river be permitted to fill up its bed until its elevation begins to interfere with its navigation, some new city will start up on the new channel, a commercial rival to New-Orleans, while real estate in the latter will become comparatively worthless, and its commercial reputation sink far more rapidly than it rose.

But it may be asked, what should be done? What course should be adopted to remedy the evils which are becoming every year more formidable, and remove the dangers which are becoming more threatening? Let me first consider what are the principal defects of the river, and then suggest the best, and, as I believe, the only means by which these defects can be remedied and these dangers removed.

The principal defects of the Mississippi are—1st. The winding character of its course, which causes alteration in its banks, and which causes the greatest depth and force of the water to be always nearer to one bank than the other, also increases its length in the same distance proportionally, diminishes the fall, increases the resistance, and, consequently, by lessening the velocity, weakens the scouring power.

2d. The great number of lateral outlets, which, by diminishing the volume of water, lessen the velocity of the current, and consequently its power to keep its channel open and clear.

3d. The bar at the mouth, which, by offering the resistance of a vast accumulation of sedimentary matter, retards, and thereby diminishes the velocity of the water above, which will produce a greater rise of the surface of the river, and consequent overflow of the banks in time of a flood.

If the course of the river were more direct, there would be less abrasion of the banks, the fall would be greater, the velocity would also be greater, and the power of the current, acting with more force upon the middle of the bed of the river, the channel would necessarily be deeper, and the height of surface of the river be reduced. A winding channel diminishes the velocity of a river, not only by increasing the length of its course, but also by the increased resistance which the current meets in the channel, and produces the effect of damming back the stream.

As the channel of a river is made by its currents, its depth depends, all other things being equal, upon the volume and velocity of the water. Therefore, every lateral outlet which, by discharging a portion of the water, diminishes its volume and velocity, and thereby lessens its weight and scouring power, inevitably lessens the depth of the channel; for when the current is no longer powerful enough to carry seaward the immense quantity of sedimentary matter that comes down from above, the bed of the river is elevated by the settling of that sediment along the bottom. The more the bed of the river is elevated, the more the surface of the water is also elevated, and consequently the danger of overflow is increased.

A bar at the mouth of a river, by the resistance which it offers to the free discharge, will dam back the water until it acquires a sufficient height to enable it to overcome the impediment, and thus may produce inundations in the upper reach of the river.

All these defects are attended with injurious consequences to the permanent importance of the river, and the prosperity of the inhabitants along its banks, from the fact that whatever checks the current, or diminishes its velocity, causes sedimentary matter to be deposited in the channel. It is necessary, therefore, that these defects should be removed, otherwise the continued elevation of the bed will render crevasses more frequent and destructive every year, and the final result will be the filling up of the present channel.

To prevent the dangers which the present condition of the river seems to threaten, all that is necessary is to assist nature, or, in other words, to remove the obstacles that prevent nature from working to accomplish our desired end. Nature sends water enough from the interior to make a channel for itself, but before it reaches the gulf, instead of having its united strength concentrated in one channel, it is permitted to dissipate it by dividing itself into many channels, thus diminishing its volume in the main river, increasing its velocity, and destroying its power of relieving itself. Therefore it is that we see, where the water is united, the channel is deep, and sufficiently large to answer all the purposes of a river; and where it is divided and wasted among innumerable branches or outlets, as it is before reaching the gulf, nature is no longer able to relieve itself, and the mouth remains choked up with an accumulation of sedimentary deposit, upwards of 100 feet higher than the bottom of the bed opposite New-Orleans. Had the volume of water which flows down from above been prevented from wasting its strength among so many outlets, its weight and velocity would have been sufficient to have swept away long ago this great mass of deposit; and the water above, no longer kept back by the retarded velocity of the water in front, would flow down with such an increased velocity, as would not only serve to keep the channel always open, but by lowering the surface of the river, render the recurrence of a crevasse no longer possible.

The only remedy, therefore, is to deepen the channel; and this work may be commenced at the mouth. Let one of the passes which at present is the deepest, be selected. Let the volume of water which enters the upper end of the pass, be prevented from dividing, thereby decreasing its velocity and dissipating its strength, until it reaches the gulf. Let all the outlets on either side of the pass be closed, so that the water may be able to bring its whole and undivided weight and velocity to bear on the vast accumulation of soft mud at the mouth. The immediate and necessary result must be, the deepening of the bar.

In proportion as the mouth deepens, the resistance will diminish, and the velocity increase, by which means the acting power of the current being increased, the removal of the bar, and the deepening of the mouth, will progress still more rapidly. The water, being thus relieved by the deepening of the mouth in front, will not only flow more rapidly through the pass, but will make way for the water above, which is now retarded by the weight of the water in front kept back by the resistance of the bar. This, again, will then flow with an increased velocity, and in turn make more rapid way for the accumulated water still higher up. Thus, an increased velocity extending far up the river, will give a more immediate relief in time of flood, and also an increased power to render the continuation of the relief steady and permanent. Having commenced the work at one pass, the same principle could be applied to another, which I have no doubt could be opened to an improved navigation also; for enough of water passes by New-Orleans to keep both channels open, and navigable for all ships, if it could be kept from distributing its volume, and thereby wasting its strength into any other outlets than these two. The same principle also could be carried as far up the river as might be thought necessary.

It would be, however, entirely unnecessary to attempt to carry this principle so far up the river as to apply it to the La Fouche, Plaquemine, and Atchafalaya, for there is below the lowest of these outlets enough of water to keep the two mouths open and clear, and, if properly confined to its normal channels, to preserve their depths. Besides, those outlets being navigable, there are vested rights interested in keeping them open, that could not now be disturbed. But I do think it would be advisable that every outlet, not navigable, should be closed, as every addition to the volume of water in the river will increase its velocity, and consequently its power, to deepen its channel, and thereby relieve itself.

Having thus deepened the mouth and given relief to the water below, and also increased velocity to the water above, something might be done to make the channel in some places more direct, and the banks, wherever it was possible, more uniform.

Where there was a bend that could be cut through, without any extravagant expenditure of labor or money, whereby the course of the river would be made materially shorter and more direct, it should be done. This would increase the fall, and consequently the velocity and power of the current.

Where the channel is contracted into a space narrower than the required breadth of the river, by any obstructions, geological or accidental, these obstructions should be removed, and the channel opened to its proper breadth. Where the channel, on the other hand, has been permitted to spread itself over a space wider than usual, it should be confined to the normal breadth.

All islands and sand-banks in front of a projecting bank, or in the middle of the river, should be removed, and those situated in front of a concave bank, and partly outside of the proper channel, should be joined to the continent.

The object of such changes must be obvious. It is that, by removing the irregularities of the channel, the least resistance may be opposed to the current, and an uniform velocity be given to it, so as to aid it as far as possible, in establishing and preserving a permanent uniformity in the channel itself.

Having thus improved the mouth, channel and course of the river as far as may be necessary to the permanent interests of those who live upon its banks, which are intimately connected with those improvements, the next to be attended to would be the levees;—though there is, in reality, no good reason why all these several improvements may not go hand in hand, and be carried on as near as may be necessary at the same time. The construction of levees, as it is, in fact, a matter of general interest, so it should be made an object of public care. They should be constructed in accordance with some regular and uniform plan, recommended by competent skill, after careful examination, and with a due regard to solidity. A batture of — feet ought to be left between the channel and levees on each side.

These battures, in time of flood, would be subject to a considerable deposit of sedimentary matter, and thus would continue to rise higher, and become every year a better protection to the levees, and may furnish materials enough for their repairs. The height, and other dimensions of the levee, its mode of construction, distance from the main channel, &c., &c., might be made subject to legislative enactments, and a state officer appointed to see that their provisions are properly enforced. In this way only can the public expect that levees will be constructed of such uniformity, solidity and durability, as will not only ensure their ability to resist the action of the river in high floods, but will inspire with confidence every man whose interest, perhaps safety, is involved in the security they promise. Where they are left to the construction of individual planters, and the supervision of overseers, there can be no security.

But in order to carry out the improvements here suggested, in the manner they ought to be carried out, that is, with a view to permanent effect, it is necessary that proper steps should be taken to place within the reach of those persons to whom the direction and supervision of such works as may be undertaken, shall be entrusted with full and accurate information, in every respect, regarding the river and its outlets. The Mississippi should be surveyed from such points on the river as may be judged necessary to the mouth; not a mere topographical survey, but such an one as would be both geometrical and hydrometrical; and would give the most complete information with regard to the channel and bed of the river, the depth of the one and the character of the other, the height of the water in the channel at its ordinary stage and in time of flood as shown by the water-meter, the degree of velocity at various points, the quantity of sediment brought down, and the degree of velocity necessary to keep it from settling,—all such information, in fine, arising from a thorough examination of the river's channel, accompanied with correct special levels, maps and profiles, as a competent and experienced hydrotect, thoroughly acquainted with the principles on which river works should be carried on, must know to be requisite, in order to authorize him to undertake such works with any prospect of success. The outlets, Atchafalaya, Plaquemine, and La Fouche, from their commencement to their mouth, should be surveyed in the same accurate and complete manner. The effect upon them of a rise in the main river, the quantity of water they draw from the Mississippi at different stages of the river, and the velocity of their currents compared with that of the river, should be particularly noted. This information should be embodied in a complete and accurate report, accompanied by suitable maps and profiles, on which should be displayed the result of the actual measurements and examinations made.

Permanent water-meters should, previously to the commencement of these operations, be erected at various points on the river, and on each of its outlets, so that accurate information could always be obtained as to every change that takes place in the elevation of the surface or bed of the river, and its outlets. These are absolutely necessary to give complete accuracy to the hydrometrical measurements, &c.

In this way a mass of information could be obtained, which would enable a competent engineer to proceed with accuracy, despatch and certain success. Without this information, he would be working in the dark, without reliable *data* on which to base his plans, or enable him to carry out his views. Without it, no engineer, who has a reputation, will risk it in undertaking works, the effect of which he cannot calculate with any approach to certainty, and the success of which he cannot guaranty. Without it, no works that may be undertaken can be looked forward to, by the public, with any degree of confidence in their future security, or even present success. But with this valuable and necessary information before the public, there can be no difficulty in carrying out the suggestions previously made, provided engineers of competent skill and experience in hydrotechnics be selected to superintend and direct the improvements.

The bars at the mouth of the passes can be removed sufficiently to admit ships of any size to New-Orleans, the bed of the river can be deepened, the channel made in some degree more regular, uniform and direct, and the levees subjected to a regular system of construction, which, accompanied by the other improvements, can promise safety for the present and security for the future.

Mobile, January, 1850.

J. D. B. De Bow

RAILROAD SLAUGHTER;
HOW IT CAN BE REMEDIED

Generally an uncritical proponent of technology and industrialization, De Bow departs here from his customary enthusiasm for American railroads to castigate the railroad companies for their greed and wanton disregard for the safety of the traveling public. At a time when no federal railroad legislation existed and most state legislation was, as De Bow notes, "lamentably defective," the problem of railroad safety was generally ignored in the law. His solution was the passage of legislation that would subject the railroads to stiff financial penalties for accidents. Otherwise, he warns, the public would take matters into its own hands to ensure its safety. De Bow's ultimate solution to the problem of forcing the owners of the railroad companies to remedy the unsafe conditions on their lines reflects his anger and frustration. His hopes for effective federal safety legislation were not realized until the early twentieth century.

Before entering upon our usual monthly summary of internal improvements, we wish to say a few words regarding the frightful disregard of human life which has been exhibited on some of our most important rail-roads during the past summer. We say disregard of human life, for it can certainly be nothing else! We need not enumerate the accidents that have happened, and the number of lives that have been lost, for these are matters of general notoriety; but we cannot avoid a few words of censure applicable to those roads which have stained their tracks with human blood. Steamboats had long been dreaded for their destructiveness of human life, and people cherished the hope, when rail-road cars came to take the place of them, that these were to afford better security to the lives of travelers; but how sad is the disappointment; instead of greater security there is greater destruction.

But why, we ask, should these frightful rail-road accidents so often

Vol. XV (October, 1853), pp. 425–30.

occur? We answer, because men are, in these times, and in this country at least, more heedful of money than of human life. They care more about high speed than human safety. To save a minute, or a dollar, they are often ready to jeopardize the lives of a whole train of passengers. We do not say that rail-road men deliberately sit down and premeditate rail-road slaughter; but we do say, that they sit down daily and premeditate the ways and means of saving time and dollars, *without thinking* that their plans involve the *possibility* of a frightful slaughter of human beings. And here is where they are to blame. They are to blame, and ought to be severely punished, for suffering even the *possibility* of an accident to travelers; because, unlike steamboats, it is possible on rail-roads to prevent all accidents by using proper care, and incurring the necessary expenses. The evil of this latter item—the necessary expenses—these rail-road men do not like to incur.

What are these necessary expenses, which, if incurred, would prevent rail-road accidents? This question could easily be answered by rail-road directors, if they felt disposed; but they always prefer being entirely silent on the subject, and endeavor to make it appear that they have done all they can to prevent the destruction of human life. Who believes them?

What they could do is this: they could have double tracks, in the first place; 2d, they could, by being a little more liberal with their money, employ intelligent, faithful and respectable "switch-tenders;" 3d, they could employ trusty and industrious men to walk the entire track, daily and hourly, in order to keep it clear, and see that the track is in order; 4th, they could have telegraphs to communicate information from post to post along the line; and 5th, they could have such rules and regulations regarding "turn-outs," as would effectually prevent the possibility of collisions.

Passing over the requirement of a double track, let us examine all the other requirements which we have laid down above. Why are there so many accidents through the carelessness, or something worse, of "switch-tenders?" It is because, to save a few cents a day, rail-road directors entrust the important care of a "switch" to some miserable, careless, drunken vagabond, who cannot be relied on—who, because his employers are careless about rewarding his services with a salary that would command an intelligent and faithful man, thinks that he too may be careless about his duty, and about the lives depending on his care. He gets nothing for his services worth an honest man's notice, and he labors according to what he gets. His pay is small, very small, and he makes his labors as light as possible as an offset. All this is very natural. It grows out of the pitiful, penurious, nay, murderous parsimony of rail-road directors. It is all to save a few cents a day. The traveling public and their friends suffer the dreadful consequences.

Again, men could be employed, at short intervals, along rail-road tracks, to keep them in perfect order and free from all obstruction. This is done in England, and in Europe generally; and this prevents the possibility of accidents from obstructions. Why is it not done in this country? Because, again, rail-road directors love money too well to incur such an expense. They think that, on the whole, it is better to let travelers take their chance of losing their lives from obstructions on the tracks; as although a few lives—which are nothing—might be occasionally lost, the rail-road company would save money by it, and have a greater dividend to distribute. In this matter, we say, again, rail-road directors are *criminally* to blame; for if they do not take all possible precaution for keeping the tracks clear of obstructions, they are guilty of suffering the *possibility* of fatal accidents.

Again, some of the principal roads have no telegraphs to indicate the movement of trains, &c., along the tracks, or to give other information necessary for the safety of trains and passengers. Is not this a criminal neglect? We think it is—and one highly criminal, too. The late awful destruction of human life, on the Amboy line, would not have taken place if this means of communicating information along the line had existed. And yet we are told by the *intelligent* (one of them could not write his own name) committee of investigation, that nobody was to blame except one of the engineers, who was censurable for carelessness. The poor engineer, we have no doubt, did as well as the miserable arrangements of the rail-road company would admit. They had neglected to provide means of communication along the line, and all the engineers could do was to "go ahead," as directed by the conductors.— The blame lay with the company, and they ought to be severely punished for it.

Lastly, it appears that, on some of the roads, there are no definite and positive regulations regarding the management of trains at "turn-outs." Where there is but one track, the simple regulation of requiring a train to stop at a "turn-out," until the other train arrives and passes, would prevent even the possibility of a collision. How, then, do collisions happen? By such regulations being entirely disregarded.

The fact is, that all our legislation regarding the management of rail-roads is lamentably defective. Such legislation should extend to the minutest particulars regarding rail-road management. It should positively forbid the running of a single car on a road, that has not all those safe-guards against accidents which we have pointed out above, with the exception of a double track, and even that should be required on certain routes.

The only way to make rail-road directors decently careful of human life, and less penurious, is not to threaten them with indictments for manslaughter, &c., that only creating legal proceedings for the benefit of lawyers—but to enact laws compelling rail-road companies to forfeit the sum of at least $10,000 for every life lost by any accident whatever of the train—it being proved that the train, at the time of the accident, was in the charge of the agents of the company; and $5,000 for every passenger wounded not fatally; and that the company's charter be considered as forfeited, and no train be allowed to run, until the above fines for loss of life and for wounded be paid.

Such legislation would bring rail-road companies to their senses. It would teach them that human life was worth something, and that the granting of a rail-road charter was not a license to commit wholesale murder.

The terrible destruction of human life on rail-roads in this country—while in Europe it is a thing almost unknown—is becoming so common, that public indignation is beginning to be aroused. The laws afford no relief. Every verdict of a committee of investigation declares that no one is guilty. The present laws on the subject, such as they are, afford every facility for escaping punishment. If something is not done in the way of legislation, to punish the gross and criminal carelessness of the agents of rail-road companies, the public will take the matter into their own hands, and Lynch law will inflict its awful and summary punishments upon them. We would regret to see things come to this pass; but the public cannot, will not, quietly see men, women and children, made the sport of a few rail-road conductors and engineers, who, through sheer carelessness, and the bad regulation of rail-road companies, so often make wholesale slaughter of passengers entrusted to their charge. Some symptoms of a lynching propensity manifested themselves at the Amboy slaughter; and if legislation does not soon come to the aid of the public, we may expect to hear of the awful and summary chastisements of rail-road agents without the aid of judge or jury.

To show the frightful extent to which rail-road slaughter has prevailed, since the commencement of the present year, we present the following table from the New-York Herald:

Number of Rail-road accidents, with the killed and wounded, during each month of the present year

Months	No. of Accidents	Killed	Wounded
January,	12	25	40
February,	6	6	11
March,	14	24	62
April,	4	25	54
May,	8	54	49
June,	5	6	19
July,	11	8	22
August,	5	29	76
Total to Aug. 12	65	177	333

Sixty-five casualties, a hundred and seventy-six deaths, and three hundred and thirty-three persons injured! There is a total which should put our civilization to the blush, and almost make men forswear the progress of the age.

Can it be believed that in a country like this, where we make our civilization a boast, there is no legislation adequate to prevent the monthly commission of human slaughter on our rail-roads? And yet such is the fact. Who ever heard of rail-road agents or steamboat agents being punished for the destruction of human life, through their gross negligence of duty; or of rail-road or steam-boat companies being punished for a laxity of caution and regulation which resulted in the most awful destruction of human life? Murder after murder is committed on our rail-roads, and all that is heard of them afterwards is, that the verdict of a committee of investigation declared that no one was to blame! Will the world believe it? Will they not just as soon believe, that such verdicts are bought with the money of rail-road companies?

In the name of justice, of humanity, and of civilization, we call upon the legislatures of our States to legislate more effectually for the preservation of human life on rail-roads. It needs no lengthened statutes to effect the desired object. To prevent effectually these horrid slaughters, our legislatures have only to enact *that rail-road companies shall pay the sum of $10,000 for every life lost, and $5,000 for every passenger wounded, and shall not run their trains until such fines are paid—it being proved that the accidents of the trains were not caused by the passengers.* The regulations of trains should also be fixed by law, and any violation of them, or neglect of them, should be punished by a fine of not less than $10,000.

If any one should think this is not sufficient, we would adopt the suggestion, in all seriousness, that the law should require, that *every train should be provided with a small private car, to be placed immediately behind the locomotive engine, in which, at least, one of the Directors of a company should always be found during the movement of the train*—a fine of $10,000 being forfeited by the company, in case that the car should cease to be occupied for a single moment during a transit.

The progress of rail-road enterprise in this country is truly astonishing. Road after road follows in rapid succession, and new roads are projected every day. It is difficult for any journal, except one devoted exclusively to rail-roads, to keep pace with them.

TIGHT TIMES

An obviously whimsical piece, but one with an edge and a point to make, "Tight Times" gives anthropomorphic identity to the frequent financial and commercial panics that plagued the antebellum American economy. The essay, curiously enough, appeared at a time when general business conditions had improved and some two years before the disastrous plunge of the Panic of 1857. Because the author chose to remain anonymous, there can be no certainty about when the article was written. February, 1855, marked the tail end of a very modest drop in wholesale commodity prices that had begun in mid-1854, and this slight decline may have been enough to worry the author of "Tight Times." A more likely explanation of the article's origins is that the record of speculation in railroads and public lands haunted the thoughts of bankers, merchants, and manufacturers of the period very much as did the roving specter who prowled the wharves, counting-houses, and workshops of the essay.

"The times are out of joint."

Tight Times is around again. He has been in town for a week. He may be seen on 'change every day. He is over on the pier, along Quay street, up Broadway, stalks up State street, looks in at the banks, and lounges in the hotels. He bores our merchants, and seats himself cozily in lawyers' offices. He is everywhere.

A great disturber of the public quiet, a pestilent fellow is this same Tight Times. Everybody talks about him, everybody looks out for him, everybody hates him, and a great many hard words and no little profane epithets are bestowed upon him. Everybody would avoid him if they could, everybody would hiss him from 'change, hoot him from the pier, chase him from Quay street, hustle him out of Broadway, kick him out of the banks, throw him out of the stores, out of the hotels, but they can't. Tight Times is a bore. A burr, he will stick. Hints are

Vol. XVIII (February, 1855), pp. 228–30.

thrown away on him, abuse lavished in vain, kicks, cuffs, profanity are all thrown away on him. He is impervious to them all.

An impudent fellow is Tight Times. Ask for a discount, and he looks over your shoulder, winks at the cashier, and your note is thrown out. Ask a loan of the usurers at one per cent a month, he looks over your securities and marks two and a half. Present a bill to your debtor, Tight Times shrugs his shoulders, rolls up his eyes, and you must call again. A wife asks for a fashionable brocade, a daughter for a new bonnet, he puts in his caveat, and the brocade and bonnet are postponed.

A great depreciator of stocks is Tight Times. He steps in among the brokers and down goes Central to par, to ninety-five, ninety, eighty-five. He plays the deuce with Michigan Central, with Michigan Southern, with Hudson River, with New York and Erie. He goes along the railroads in process of construction, and the Irishmen throw down their shovels and walk away. He puts his mark upon railroad bonds, and they find no purchasers, are hissed out of market, become obsolete, absolutely dead.

A great exploder of bubbles is Tight Times. He looks into the affairs of gold companies, and they fly to pieces; into kiting banks, and they stop payment; into rickety insurance companies, and they vanish away. He walks around corner lots, draws a line across lithographic cities, and they disappear. He leaves his foot-print among mines, and the rich metal becomes dross. He breathes upon the cunningest schemes of speculation, and they burst like a torpedo.

A hard master for the poor, a cruel enemy to the laboring masses is Tight Times. He takes the mechanic from his bench, the laborer from his work, the hod-carrier from his ladder. He runs up the prices of provisions, and he runs down the wages of labor. He runs up the price of fuel, and he runs down the ability to purchase it at any price. He makes little children hungry and cry for food—cold, and cry for fire and clothing. He makes poor women sad, makes mothers weep, discourages the hearts of fathers, carries care and anxiety into families, and sits a crouching desolation in the corner and on the hearth-stones of the poor. A hard master to the poor is Tight Times.

A curious fellow is Tight Times, full of idiosyncracies and crotchets. A cosmopolite—a wanderer too. Where he comes from nobody knows, and where he goes nobody knows. He flashes along the telegraph wires, he takes a free passage in the cars, he seats himself in the stages, or goes along the turnpikes on foot. He is a gentleman on Wall street to-day, and a back settler on the borders of civilization to-morrow. We hear of him in London, in Paris, in St. Petersburg, at Vienna, Berlin, at Constantinople, at Calcutta, in China, all over the commercial world, in every great city, in every rural district—everywhere.

There is one way to avoid being bored by this troublesome fellow, Tight Times. It is the only way for a country, a city, a town, as well as individual men to keep shut out of his presence always. Let the country that would banish him beware of extravagance, of speculation, of over-trading, of embarking in visionary schemes of aggrandizement. Let it keep out of wars, avoid internal commotions, and go right along, taking care of its own interests and husbanding its resources. Let the city that would exclude him be economical in its expenditures, indulging in no schemes of speculation, making no useless improvements, building no railroads that it cannot pay for, withholding its credit from mushroom corporations, keeping down its taxes, and going right along, taking care of its own interests and husbanding its own resources. Let the individual man who would exclude him from his domestic circle be industrious, frugal, keeping out of the whirlpool of politics, indulging no taste for office, holding up his dish when pudding falls from the clouds, laying by something when the sun shines to make up for the dark days, for

"Some days must be dark and dreary;"

working on always with a heart full of confidence in the good providence of God, and cheerful in the hope of "the good time coming."

William Gregg

SOUTHERN PATRONAGE TO SOUTHERN IMPORTS AND DOMESTIC INDUSTRY

In this article, William Gregg returns to a subject that he had actively pursued a decade earlier, but now with a special urgency. By July, 1860, talk of secession had become both more open and more insistent throughout the South and especially in Gregg's own state, South Carolina. His essay reflects this militancy and warns of the coming clash of arms between the "gallant young men of the South" and the "Yankee crusaders" for abolition. Not one to shrink from this prospect, Gregg advocates southern political independence, which, he says, must ultimately rest on a firm foundation of southern commercial and industrial self-sufficiency. Surveying the state of the southern economy, Gregg finds the section's industry weak, but not for want of initiative by southern manufacturers. The fault lay instead with the galling habit of southerners of purchasing machinery and other industrial goods from the North. So long as this long-standing practice continued and southern industry languished, an independent southern nation had little chance of survival.

Chapter I

There is no subject that ought to excite more general interest with us, than that of home patronage of Southern importations direct from Europe, and manufacturing at the South the commonest articles to supply the substantial necessaries of domestic consumption.

Our long experience as a merchant, our opportunities of intercourse for many years with the manufacturers of the Southern States, as well as all other parts of the Union, together with Great Britain and France, has enabled us to gather facts which may be of interest to the public at this juncture, when all the men of the South have their minds directed to the necessity of self-reliance and Southern independence, whether in the Union or out of it.

However ardently we may have cherished the union of the States in

Vol. XXIX (July, 1860), pp. 77–83.

bygone days, and however confidently we may have relied on the good sense of the Northern people, their enlightened commercial spirit, their industrious enterprise, and proverbial desire for the accumulation of wealth, as a sure protection to us of peace, and the enjoyment of our rights in the Union, we have been forced to the conclusion that the time has come when the Southern people should begin in earnest to prepare for self-defence and self-reliance. Abolition of Southern slavery was, but a few years ago, nothing more than an insignificant sectional political hobby. It has now become a religious sentiment. Children have been educated to look on negro slavery as a horrible and intolerable evil. Ministers of the gospel have been educated and placed in the pulpit to disseminate these doctrines, and they, connected with dishonest politicians have so poisoned the public mind, that the moderate, conservative, talented, good men of the North, who ought to rule, have lost their influence and power of control. Even Daniel Webster, if now living, would be trodden under foot, for the body politic is no longer directed by the good and the wise men, but by the intriguing politicians and fanatical madmen, for the lower ten thousand have suffered themselves to be carried away by an irreligious fanaticism, which pays no regard to the dictates of reason, and may be led to do anything which physical power can accomplish, even to trampling under foot the laws which secure their self-protection and the enjoyment of civil liberty.

Who would not step out of the way of a madman? Where is the Southern man who can feel safe under a government which is to be controlled by men who are imbued with abolition fanaticism, and who profess to be governed by a higher law than the Bible and the Constitution of the United States? If things go on as they have, it will not be long before we will lose sight of the word "filibuster," and that of "crusader" will take its place; our gallant young men of the South, who are seeking employment in filibustering expeditions, will find vent for their patriotism in defending the slave States against the Yankee crusaders who may invade us with fire and sword, in the cause of negro freedom and equal rights of all men.

Is it not strange that a people, such as compose New-England (Massachusetts in particular), proverbial for its good sense—I say, is it not passing strange that such a people should seek to destroy the institution and the customers from whom its wealth has been obtained? Since the establishment of manufactures in New-England, the Southern people have been the main customers and the best patrons to Yankee industry and Yankee enterprise—enjoying all the advantages of the wealth they have drawn from confiding Southern patronage. They quarrelled with us because we would not grant them an exorbitant tariff, and thus commenced a strife which has brought us at points, and they are now ready to wage a war on us and our system of labor. It is quite as strange that a State like New-York should do likewise. Her great city is the emporium of Southern commerce. That city is the intermediate agent between New-England and the South, besides being our factor for all European trade, and yet the politicians of New-York are willing to lay aside the Constitution and be governed by a higher law, and wage an extermination war on an institution which is not only the basis of our wealth, but of our existence as a community.

Recent developments have led the South, almost to a man, to the conclusion, that we should separate from the North; and this brings us to the question: Are we prepared for separate nationality? There is no dependence in man, and nations are equally as unreliable. The nation that may be our friend and great customer to-day, may make war on us to-morrow. Hence the necessity of the South becoming more self-reliant, by the encouragement of direct Southern commerce, and, as far as possible, diversified home industry. It is not necessary that we should have any intermediate agents in exchanging our cotton for the articles of Southern consumption, but it is absolutely necessary that we should make, within ourselves, all the prime necessaries of life, in order to secure independence.

Every article that a negro wears and everything necessary to his health and comfort can be made at the South, without trenching on the labor now employed in the culture of cotton. With a little attention directed to the growth of sheep, we would soon have domestic wool enough to make our negro blankets and negro woollen cloths. We can manufacture all the woollen and all the cotton goods necessary to clothe our negroes. We can easily make our leather, and a proper degree of home patronage would soon bring about large shoe manufactories, all of which can be carried on to an extent which will fully supply the demand, and be done by the white people of the South, who could be brought into that service, thus giving them employment and the means of education and of becoming better citizens and of adding strength to the body politic. Rather than have any difficulty in supplying shoes, how easy it would be for the large planters each to have a small shoe shop, where one or two negroes could make brogans so honestly and faithfully as to render one pair equal, in point of durability, to two pairs of polished up flimsy Yankee brogans, with inner soles of brown paper or thin boards.

We can make our own ploughs, our own wagons, buggies, and carriages. We can make our own railroad locomotives, passenger and burden cars.

If a line were drawn which would be a barrier to the importation of Northern locomotives, two years would not elapse before Charleston, Columbia, Augusta, Atlanta, Macon, Columbus, Chattanooga, Nashville, and other Southern railroad towns would be stirred up, and busily employed in those branches of business. The puffing of stationary engines, the noise of the trip-hammer would be heard, and those comparatively stagnant towns would feel the cheering influence of a busy throng of mechanical engine-builders. The absence of patronage to home industry is an evil that cannot be overcome by political agitation or conventional platforms, but must be worked out by the people themselves. One man ardently engaged in such a work will be worth far more to the South than a thousand noisy politicians.

Who could have dreamed, twenty-five years ago, that so large a number of artisans would be so soon reared among us, as we now witness in all the Southern towns, employed on railroad machinery, steam-engines and various other iron works? Notwithstanding the great lack of Southern patronage which has been so indifferent to Southern enterprise, that it has effected not only this, but every other branch of industry. Professing as we do to be a highly intelligent people, it is strange, nevertheless true, that we are in a great measure indebted to the Northern people for teachers to instruct our children in the elements of education. We surely ought to make our own school-books, and teach our children; but it is known to everybody, that this is a duty we employ foreigners to perform. The recent move among the medical students at the North is one of the proofs of the vast patronage which has been given by the South to that department of education at the North. If we have not now, we can have as good schools of learning, in every department, as may be found at the North; and to secure it in future, it will be only necessary to have our mind's eye, in all our movements, on Southern patronage to home institutions; and to secure our perfect independence, it will only be necessary to extend Southern patronage to home industry in all its departments.

We propose, in the course of these numbers, to notice the meeting of the merchants of Chester, in this State, and to demonstrate the change which the efforts of that class of men can bring about in promoting the success of Southern importations, Southern manufactures, and Southern independence. They, and the country merchants in general, are the agents who stand between the importer and manufacturer and the consumer, and have the power to work, in a short time, a complete revolution in such matters. We will endeavor to show, also, that the consumers in general have the power in their own hands, if the merchants should neglect their duty, to work out the change which the prosperity of the country so imperatively demands.

We will endeavor to show, too, that all the failures of manufacturing establishments at the South have been mainly the result of the absence of Southern patronage; that thousands and hundreds of thousands, and we might say millions, of Southern capital have been sunk, from the fact that Yankee goods have been purchased, and Yankee establishments patronized, to the great detriment of Southern consumers, all resulting from an absence of that spirit which should prompt a Southerner to patronize Southern importation and Southern domestic industry.

Chapter II

We promised to set forth the fact, that the failure of Southern manufacturing establishments have been mainly caused by a want of Southern patronage, and the same may be said to Southern imports. It is a heavy and ruinous tax on a Southern manufacturer to be under the necessity of sending his goods to New-York to find Southern customers. Yet this has been the course of things from the earliest dawn of manufacturing at the South; even the first small establishments that were put up, and which could not make cloth enough to half supply the country for twenty miles around them, the proprietors were forced to submit to this ruinous taxation. We well recollect having heard people, for twenty-five years past, exulting in the idea that Southern goods would command a market in the Northern cities.

Years ago it was the generally-received opinion that, as our Southern products were able to stand side by side with New-England goods of a similar kind, and command customers in Boston, New-York, and Philadelphia, that it was unmistakable evidence that Southern factories were bound to succeed.

It speaks well for Southern manufacturers that their goods can hold a fair competition with New-England products, or take a premium at the World's Fair in London, as has been the case with Graniteville sheetings and drills. But that they should be habitually in the hands of New-York commission merchants for sale, and, at times, forced on the markets of the world at ruinous losses, shows that there is a canker-worm at work, that will, ultimately, undermine the best efforts at success—the absence of Southern patronage—an evil which cannot be overcome except by herculean enterprise, and in nine cases out of ten will blight the fairest hopes of the Southern manufacturer. This is a subject of vast importance to the South, and ought to enlist the strenuous efforts of all patriotic Southerners.

Everybody knows that it is a common complaint against Southern manufacturers that their goods are sold cheaper at New-York than at the factory. It is a lamentable truth, for nine tenths of our Southern spinners begin without the requisite capital to hold their goods under a limit when they are sent to the North to be sold, and are forced to let them go when the drafts mature that have been drawn on the consignment.

It is a matter of serious moment to inquire why it is (with our limited power to supply Southern consumption) that thousands of bales of honestly made Southern domestics, composed of a sounder material than is used anywhere else in the world for the manufacture of such—we say it is a matter of interest to know why thousands of bales of our substantial goods should be sold in New-York, to supply the great West, while the same ships which carry our goods north, bring back as many more of Yankee make of inferior quality to enter into Southern consumption.

These are matters that we will endeavor to explain in the course of these pages.

That there is a ruinous absence of Southern patronage to all branches of mechanical industry, no man can question. No manufacturer can live unless he receives a fair proportion of home patronage. In order to illustrate this matter, we will cite the operations of the Graniteville Company, who have been compelled at times to send large quantities of their fabrics to Northern markets. They have, however, been happily situated as regards cash capital, and have never been under the necessity of making forced sales. Long experience has proven to that company, that goods sold in New-York or Philadelphia, at the same price which they bring in Charleston, will not produce a net sum equal to the Charleston prices by half a cent a yard, so that the cloth sold in Charleston at eight cents, will produce a net sum equal to a similar sale in New-York at eight and a half cents.

The Graniteville factory turns out fifteen thousand yards of cloth per day. They are principally sold in Charleston and the south-western towns. If the entire product had to go to New-York to find a market, at the rate of half a cent a yard, the loss would cost that company seventy five dollars per day, or twenty two thousand five hundred dollars a year, and if the goods had to be forced off at half a cent below their value, as is frequently the case, the loss would be one hundred and fifty dollars a day, or forty five thousand dollars a year.

It is a difficult matter for even the best merchants to realize the above stated fact. It is, nevertheless, the truth, and I state the simple fact, leaving those who doubt to figure the matter out for themselves. Figures will not always tell the truth, but facts are stubborn things, and when you draw conclusions from a regular series of transactions, year after year, the results you arrive at become a sound basis for conclusions.

It is inconceivable how a large city, containing a million of people, can live and grow rich; yes, live in the most gorgeous splendor, and amass millions of capital. They produce nothing, and yet they live on the fat of the land; live by their wits in exchanging luxuries produced in other nations for the products of the labor of the country which is tributary to their trade. Every man who handles an axe or drives a hoe into the ground, is a contributor. Every child that toils at the factory spindle in the United States, contributes its mite toward the support and wealth of that great city, New-York. Southern toil and labor has furnished its full quota toward supplying the means to rear that immensely wealthy city. Unsuspecting Southern liberality has been showering down gold for fifty years into her lap, amounting to countless millions. The patronage of the South has gone there to feed and pamper that monster city, while our Southern importing cities have been left to stagnate and die out.

It is a hopeless task to undertake to even approximate to the vast sums of wealth which have been transferred from the South to the North by allowing the Northern cities to import and export for us. The figures above set forth, in relation to the sale of goods from one Southern factory, give a little insight into the matter, and may, at least, open the eyes of some who have not reflected on the subject.

We will, however, drop these speculations, and proceed with that branch of our subject which relates to Southern manufactures, the products of which is becoming an important branch of our internal commerce at the South.

The manufacture of wagons, carriages, and buggies, has been struggling to obtain a foothold among us for thirty years; much capital has been sunk in that way, and many enterprising, industrious proprietors have been starved out by the floods of Yankee work which has been made up for sale by workmen far away from us, from whom we cannot look for redress if the vehicle prove to be defective, and, as sometimes has been the case, almost worthless. We do not pretend to say good carriages have not been made in the Northern States and sent to the South, or that such are not now offered and sold here, by many worthy men engaged in that trade, but we hazard nothing in asserting that millions of dollars have been lost to the South, by the purchase of what we may call trash in that line of trade. We have not for the last fifteen years purchased a carriage or a buggy which has been made at the North. Yet we have kept up a liberal family supply of vehicles made at the South, and feel fully satisfied that we have been honestly and faithfully served, and that we have not paid a greater average cost than would have been expended had we purchased Northern-made carriages and buggies.

We have been a careful observer of the embarrassments that have attended our Southern carriage-makers, from the vast quantity of cheap Northern carriages with which the South has been flooded, and the perfect indifference that Southern consumers have manifested with regard to where a carriage was made; a large majority of purchasers seem to forget that it is important to have the maker of any article near at hand, where redress can easily be obtained for any defect in the article purchased. A carriage must of necessity be well made, if it is to be warranted and worn out in the immediate vicinity of the builder.

This is a branch of mechanism that is rapidly gaining a foothold at the South; fine, and we may say, splendid carriages may be purchased of Charleston make. No finer or better carriages, buggies, and wagons, can be purchased anywhere than in Greenville, S. C. There is scarcely a village in the South now that has not its buggy or carriage shop, besides many country places where wagons and all wheel carriages are made and repaired—and if the South would only be true to herself, and by strictly adhering to the system of extending home patronage to all branches of Southern industry, Northern carriages would soon be entirely excluded from the commerce between the North and the South, and we would see the trade of every town and village in our country stimulated by a busy throng of handicraftmen in the carriage and wagon-making line.

It was asserted by a gentleman in a speech before the legislature of

South Carolina, in December last, that Southern manufacturers had been embarrassed and had failed for the want of laborers, and that what the South needed more than anything else, was laborers; hence the necessity of re-opening the African slave-trade. Let us assure that gentleman of his error, and beg him to follow us until we prove that manufacturing has not fagged, sickened, and died, for the want of laborers, but for the want of Southern patronage to domestic industry.

Edwin Q. Bell

IN LIEU OF LABOR

The irony of a southern writer advocating the adoption of labor-saving machinery in the once slave-labor South could not have been lost on readers of De Bow's Review. *The Civil War seemed, in 1867, to have altered radically the traditional relationship of an abundant agricultural labor supply to landed capital, and the once inconceivable possibility of labor scarcity in the South loomed ominously. Bell correctly, if only briefly, notes the sources of the problem: the movement of many freedmen to southern cities and a variety of institutional changes in southern society. Rejecting the notion that either northern or foreign immigration would be sufficient to compensate for the loss of skilled black fieldhands, he urges his fellow southerners to emulate the people of midwestern states, whose agricultural output greatly exceeded the level warranted by their numbers by virtue of their ready substitution of capital, in the form of farm machinery, for labor.*

The great question which has agitated the South this season, has been the supply of food; and this matter has assumed such alarming proportions and has borne so instantly upon the attention of the planter, that another and scarcely less important subject for reflection—the rapidly diminishing supply of skilled labor—has been comparatively lost sight of. The magnetic attraction which, since the close of the war, has drawn tens of thousands of our best hands from the plantation to the cities and towns throughout the South; the indulgences from which the heedfulness and the interest of their late owners carefully guarded them, but into which they now plunge recklessly; the fearful effects, both moral and physical, of the license which, in their ignorance, they look upon as liberty; the drafts upon the younger portions of the laboring classes for educational purposes; the withdrawal of very many of the women from the field, and the disinclination among these to be burdened with families, a newly developed mania which hesitates not to adopt criminal measures to attain its object; these are but a few of the

Vol. IV, After War Series (July/August, 1867), pp. 69–74.

many causes which might be mentioned as bearing directly and destructively upon the system of freed labor, and which renders it imperative that we should at once look about us for such measures of relief as may be practicable.

These measures are—

1st. Foreign Immigration.

2d. Northern Immigration.

3d. Improved Labor-Saving Implements and Machinery.

With regard to foreign immigration, while we strongly advocate its encouragement in every possible way, and look hopefully forward to the time when the tide now flowing toward the west may be diverted from its accustomed channel by the allurements of our superior soil and climate, yet, it cannot be denied that any relief from this quarter for many years to come will be sadly disproportionate to the losses which the census returns of 1870 will we confidently predict show to have been frightful. From the North, in the present disturbed condition of political affairs, there will be little or no emigration to the South. Vicious and untruthful correspondents have so convinced the public mind that there is no safety for the Yankee within the borders of Dixie, that for once the native acquisitiveness of the race has yielded to its fears, and the land from which they formerly contended they were wrongfully excluded by slavery, remains simply a land of promise, available in some uncertain but golden future.

Turning, then, from these precarious, or, at all events, tardy sources of relief, we come now to consider what merit there may be in the adoption and use of improved labor-saving implements and machinery. Here the experience of the great West in the absence of any knowledge or skill of our own, must be accepted as a true test of the economy and the simplicity in the use of, and the advantages derived from, the many valuable and reliable machines for the multiplication of manpower, which the inventive genius of the country has perfected during the last decade. Without encumbering this article with the statistics, we will simply state, that the increase in the agricultural products of any of the Western States—Illinois, for example—is so out of proportion to the increase in farming population, that no other reasonable explanation is afforded than that found in the universal demand for, and use of labor saving implements. A machine costing five hundred dollars, and doing the work of twenty men, is just so much a saving as the difference between the interest on the cost of the machine and its wear and tear, and the annual wages of the twenty men, less the time of the one or two hands necessary to its guidance. All over the North and West, labor-saving tools are eagerly sought after, and inventors offering real improvements, rapidly amass prodigious fortunes, a sure proof by the way, that the farmer finds it profitable to buy and use such implements. For the cultivation of cereals, it would seem that labor-saving machinery had reached the outside limits of inventive genius, and as the South is now devoting much more attention than formerly to this class of crops, it is to be hoped that our intelligent planters will inaugurate a new era by the free use of such improved implements as we shall, from time to time, bring to his notice. During the past month we have visited many parts of New York, and watched with interest the harvesting of a portion of the wheat and hay crops, and we do not hesitate to admit, that the celerity with which the work was accomplished by the aid of horse-power reapers, rakes, etc., filled us with profound astonishment and admiration. To this particular branch of the subject we shall have occasion to revert in a future article.

But the great staple of the South, and that upon which, after all, she must depend for recuperative resources in those States adapted to its production, is cotton. It enriched her in the past, it will be to her a source of wealth in the future. In nearly all the territory comprised in the Southern States, all the elements most favorable to its growth in unequalled perfection and yield are admirably combined. A soil naturally rich in the constituents of the cotton plant, and easily kept in the best producing condition by proper culture and the judicious use of such well-known fertilizers as will restore those elements annually drawn from it by vegetation; a climate warm and humid, in which the plant luxuriates, and which gives to the fibre that length, strength and those superior spinning qualities for which American cotton is so famous; a long season of vegetation giving the plant time to attain its utmost development, to bud and ripen again and again until checked by frost, and, above all, the experiences of a century to guide and direct, may we not, with such natural and acquired advantages defy competition in the future, as in the past, if but some means could be suggested to supply the loss of that skilled labor hitherto at our command, but now daily becoming more scarce and less reliable.

To the advantages already enumerated, may be added those which are to be found in a perfect system of railroad enterprises penetrating every section, and affording, in connection with our noble rivers, extraordinary facilities for conveyance to the seaports of the gulf and the Atlantic, and thence to the markets of the world.

It was this rare combination of favorable elements which gave to the cultivation of cotton such an extraordinary impetus that the crop of 1859, as given in the United States Census of 1860, footed up 5,387,052 bales of 400 pounds each, or 2,154,820,800 pounds; considerably more than double the amount raised ten years before, when the previous census was taken. So enormous a product gave to us practically the monopoly of the staple, and but for the occurrences of the years since 1860, that monopoly would still be ours. As it is, we think our supremacy as producers is only suspended, not totally forfeited, for every advantage remains with us save one, the old system of labor, and some of our most intelligent planters are beginning to question the economy of that system. The loss of our full agricultural force will temporarily embarrass us, but its place can be supplied by the gradual introduction of a more intelligent and effective class of workers, and by the instant adoption of all those improvements in farming tools which have stood the test of experience in the North and West.

Previous to the late war, the efforts of the British spinners, through their "Cotton Supply Association" and other agencies, to escape their dependence upon America for needed supplies, had proved abortive, and though the cupidity of manufacturers, merchants and brokers had been inflamed to the uttermost, and their selfishness thoroughly aroused by the most gloomy pictures of the consequences of an interruption to trade with this country, and by extravagant estimates of the increased profits which would accrue from a national control over the sources of supply, yet the result of long years of costly experiment served only to show the futility of these enterprises, and they were abandoned.

It is true that in many other countries cotton could be, and was, raised to a considerable extent; but in none other was there so perfect a combination of favorable conditions for its cultivation. One or more of the advantages possessed by ourselves was always wanting elsewhere, and the consequences were either the production of an inferior article, or, if of good quality, then in insufficient quantity to be remunerative. Perhaps, as in India, a large yield was attained, but the distance from the places of consumption, the marked inferiority of the staple, the carelessness with which it was gathered, the wretched handling to which it was subjected, and the immense outlays for transportation before it reached a market, were insurmountable impediments to successful competition with us; and those most deeply interested in promoting the growth of cotton in the British possessions felt and ad-

mitted that India could furnish no effectual safeguard against such a
contingency as interrupted communications with America would bring
about.

The extent of the monopoly enjoyed by the Southern States in 1860
was most clearly demonstrated by the course of the market during the
years, when, owing to a limited production and a rigid blockade of the
southern ports, the manufacturers had to look about them for supplies.
The surplus stocks in Liverpool and elsewhere were soon exhausted.
The mills of Lancashire, to which a hemisphere looked for needed cotton fabrics, and which afforded employment to tens of thousands, and
supported whole populations, were of necessity compelled to shorten
time, and many of them stopped altogether. The price of the raw material reached an almost fabulous point, while the value of cotton fabrics became so much enhanced that the poor millions engaged even in
their manufacture could not purchase the commonest article of cotton
clothing. Other goods sympathised in the general appreciation of values, and wool and flax rose correspondingly. All this time, encouraged
and stimulated by the unprecedentedly high price of the staple, the
merchants and manufacturers of England were putting forth every
effort to supply the deficiency, and in every nook and corner of the
globe where cotton would grow, the plant was put under cultivation.
The price being so high no amount of ignorance or slovenliness, neither
inferiority of staple nor even poverty in yield, could prevent profitable
results. Then came a demand from all these remote corners for seed,
for information and for machinery, and nothing was left undone that
enterprise and energy could suggest to seize the opportunity, afforded
by our domestic troubles, to establish the raising of cotton in the British possessions upon an enduring basis.

The question was to England one of vital interest. She had long before felt that a trade, in which so vast an amount of fixed capital was
embarked, which distributed such immense sums, weekly, among a
population dependent upon them, and which influenced the well-being
of every consumer in the state, in proportion as it was prosperous or
depressed, should not be so absolutely dependent upon a single source
of supply; but hitherto neither government subsidies, the liberal outlays of the East India Company, nor well directed private effort, had
produced tangible results. Now the apprehended evil was upon her,
but not in its worst aspect, as she was not a party to the conflict that
caused the derangement of supplies, and could meet it with all the
power of her resources. The most gigantic efforts were put forth, to

encourage the cultivation of cotton not only in her own dependencies, but in countries beyond her rule; yet the supplies from these new enterprises and from increased production in older districts, although heavy, have but partially filled the void, and prices are still largely beyond the old standard. It is only proper to warn our planters, however, that so great has been the impetus given to the production of cotton in India that it has gained a position which will enable it to compete successfully with us at much lower prices than those now prevalent, and if the growing crop in this country should turn out as well as expected, prices will be lower next winter, and the struggle will be fairly inaugurated.

Are we prepared for the impending conflict, or do we design tamely and inertly to submit to the loss of our natural predominance in this important industry? With all the advantages already enumerated we are in danger of being distanced by other countries, unless we surpass them in skill and enterprise in the adaptation and use of improved inventions for the cultivation and the gathering of the staple, and for its better preparation for market. We must select for cultivation only the best varieties and pursue an enlightened economy in all departments of the business. Nature has endowed us liberally, but will do neither the work of our heads nor of our hands. We must seek out and obtain the best plows, and must learn the best method of treating the various conditions of our soil both in its manipulation and as regards the use of needed fertilizers. It will not do to say, "it has always been done thus and so;" but rather let us inquire, "is this or that the better way?" The theories of our grandfathers are doubtless respectable, but the necessities of the moment are novel and pressing, and require new and pungent remedies.

To recover our imperiled prestige we must economize in the labor of planting, of scraping, of chopping, of hoeing, of packing, of ginning and of pressing. There have been many planting machines, some useless, others perhaps good. Encourage the mechanical talent of the country to produce a good and reliable cotton-seed planter if none such now exists. Why should you not? No corn raiser of the North plants by hand; even the ungainly potato has been reconciled and is now quietly and regularly inserted in its bed by the unthinking machine. Why should it not pay as well to plant cotton in this way? If such a machine be demanded it will *surely* come forth.

Scraping and chopping out can be done with one and the same implement as fast as the team will travel. The machine has been invented to do this, and if not yet entirely perfected it must be, for it has been shown to be entirely practicable and reliable. We have examined such an implement at the works of the Albany Cotton Gin Manufacturing Company in Albany, New York. . . . The importance of this contrivance in a labor-saving point of view can scarcely be estimated. It scrapes both sides at once, and chops out the spaces with perfect regularity, doing what was the work of ten or twelve men in the old way. It cannot be doubted that some device will soon be invented for picking which will supersede the present laborious, tedious and expensive process. Encourage the machinist to think; something will come of it. . . .

IV

SOUTHERN SOCIETY AND CULTURE

In November, 1846, James De Bow published "The Moral Advance of New Orleans" in the hope of encouraging the citizens of that city to develop a taste "for those things that are high and ennobling in themselves." A great city, or a great region, must, he thought, be more than a commercial center or a productive garden: "*A society must be formed, social institutions promoted, literature encouraged and sustained, intelligence broadly disseminated, and a fixed and settled order of things secured.*" Just as De Bow urged New Orleanians to aim at something higher than "mere trade and commerce," so *De Bow's Review* tried to cultivate southern society and culture and to introduce its readers to the history, culture, and literature of the South and the world.

De Bow modeled his journal on *Hunt's Merchant's Magazine*, a New York commercial review, but he also tried to emulate the great English reviews, such as the *Edinburgh Review*, in the breadth of his coverage. He frequently published travel accounts, historical essays on subjects ranging from the history of Louisiana to dim antiquity, biographical sketches, and essays on law, politics, and literature. In addition, nearly every issue contained a list of recently published books, and De Bow usually reviewed briefly those books he had read. Many of these pieces make for tedious reading today, though they no doubt had greater appeal when they were published. Some of the pieces on southern society and culture, however, retain their interest, not only as representative of these broader concerns of the *Review*, but also as revealing windows on various aspects of mid-nineteenth-century society.

Not all of De Bow's authors took a specifically southern line in their essays, particularly in the early years of the journal. Though De Bow never had many northern subscribers—111 out of 4,656 in 1855—articles such as those by Dr. D. McCauley on humbugs and delusions in education could have found amused, and perhaps embarrassed, readers on either side of the Mason-Dixon line. Amusing articles like "Humbugiana" served not only to lighten the heavy burden of trade statistics and commercial information confronting the reader of the *Review*, but also to alert the reader to the myriad frauds of the mid-nineteenth century.

De Bow was particularly concerned with improving the health and condition of southern society and with broadening its culture. His advice to New Orleans on social improvement and moral advance could have easily served as his program for the entire South. He viewed the South as a society with great potential, but one just emerging from its frontier and commercial crudities. In this light, his emphasis on social institutions, literature, education, health, and "a fixed and settled order of things" is understandable. Similarly, De Bow desired to correct unwarranted attacks on southern achievements. On the question of the healthfulness of the southern climate, however, De Bow's optimism could not overcome the grim reality of places like New Orleans. As Josiah Nott's essay in Chapter Two aptly demonstrates, diseases like malaria, cholera, and yellow fever were real obstacles to the development of southern society.

Until the mid-1850s, De Bow frequently printed articles on southern society that bore little or no relation to the problems of slavery and race. But, as the decade wore on, the lighter touch of "Humbugiana" was overwhelmed by the stridency of defending the peculiar institution. This stridency is clearly evident in the essay on James Russell Lowell by an anonymous citizen of Alabama who contemptuously dismissed Lowell's poetry as the rantings of a libelous Yankee. More insidious than the frontal assaults of a Lowell were the indirect attacks that threatened to poison the southern mind against its own institutions. Southern dependence on the North for such basic items as schoolbooks was particularly galling to many southerners, who felt that it gave the scheming abolitionists ready access to southern youth and the opportunity to undermine the slave system. Increasingly, such thinkers measured any social institution or activity by the degree to which it supported slavery and the South in the divisive struggle with the North.

By 1860, then, *De Bow's Review* reflected the constrictions that slavery and the controversies of the 1850s had imposed on southern society and culture. Gone was a willingness to broaden southern culture, and gone, too, was an ability to be amused by the varieties of human experience. The moral advance of the South had been subordinated to the defense of the peculiar institution, a defense that men like De Bow willingly undertook. The costs of this defense were high. Southern cities and southern society were unable to achieve the greatness that De Bow had predicted in the mid-1840s, and ultimately, of course, the defense of slavery itself proved futile.

Dr. D. McCauley

HUMBUGIANA

*In this essay, Dr. McCauley points to a serious problem in mid-nine-
teenth-century America—how to distinguish quacks and humbugs
from real doctors or other professionals. As McCauley recognized, the
existence of quacks was only part of the problem; the willingness of
people to be taken in by unscrupulous humbugs made the job of the
quack even easier. McCauley's etymology of* humbug, *although amusing, is apparently more fanciful than accurate. According to the* Oxford English Dictionary, *the word appeared around 1750, but there is
no agreement on its origin.*

*Dr. McCauley's warnings about quacks in medicine were particu-
larly apt. At the time he wrote, medicine was still, at best, an inexact
science with considerable room for amateurs and outright frauds of all
varieties. There were few reputable medical schools, few state licens-
ing boards, and almost no professional or federal regulation. The lack
of effective training and regulation meant that it was often difficult to
tell the frauds from the legitimate doctors. As McCauley points out,
these quacks, and not infrequently trained doctors as well, often con-
cocted some potion that was supposed to cure all diseases. Such patent
medicines ranged from harmless colored and flavored water to potions
laced with opium or cocaine. McCauley's call for increased training
for doctors was frequently heard, and by the end of the century the
situation had been improved by better medical schools and more rigorous professional and governmental regulation. Still, his piece was a
timely warning about the dangers of credulity in dealing with disease
and doctors.*

Aristotle, one of the greatest intelligences that ever appeared in the
world, asserted that *incredulity* is the foundation of all wisdom. Had
the good old gentleman, whose philosophy maintained such an unlimited sway over the human mind for centuries, lived in the age in
which we live, there is little doubt but his opinion would undergo a

Vol. I (May, 1846), pp. 444–48.

change, and he might probably declare it to be more in accordance with the experience and temper of mankind to say, that *credulity* is the foundation of all folly. To investigate the gradual development of rational belief would be, to the philosophic mind, a useful and an interesting employment, and the investigation would disclose to us much of the duplicity, deception, fanaticism, and bigotry of our species. We would find error borrowing something of truth, in order to make her pass off more readily; we would discover the subtlety of grand deceivers, and impostors, grafting their greatest errors on some well-known palpable truth, and we might learn from the investigation, that all men entertain and are influenced by opinions to a much greater extent than persons unacquainted with self-examination are aware, and we might perceive the necessity of rigidly examining every opinion or sentiment, before it is adopted as a principle from which any conclusion is to be drawn.

We all know how prone the mind is to believe that for which it most anxiously wishes. As Prince Henry, believing his father dead, took the crown from his pillow, the king in reproach said to him:

"Thy *wish* was, Harry, father to that thought."

Our judgments are often perverted by our affections and passions. Of whatever nature the passion may be, it prevents us from seeing clearly the object by which it is excited. If we love, we cannot see the faults, and if we hate, we cannot see the beauties of the object contemplated. If we hope, or earnestly desire a thing, we easily believe that it will be enjoyed; but if we fear, we magnify difficulties that are real, and actively employ our imagination in conjuring up such as are chimerical. But it is not the object in this article to trace the causes which might be assigned for the constant disposition of mankind toward credulity. They are many and contradictory. The object is to turn the attention to the fact, that, in this enlightened age—this nineteenth century—men too readily believe without evidence or examination, and are almost as easily gulled as were our ancestors in the days of Joanna Southcott. If anything peculiarly marks the present age, it is the prevalence of imposture, and the very great readiness with which men and women, and sensible ones too, allow themselves to be beguiled by the assumptions of ignorance, and the tricks of quackery. There is scarcely a single province of human speculation or action which the disciple of charlatanism does not occupy, in which the meretricious is not put for that which is genuine, and in which falsehood does not ape the garb, the language, and the actions of truth. To point out and expose completely every deception that exists is almost impossible. It would be a task not easily executed. Number the leaves of the forest—count the grains of sand on the desert if you can; and then attempt to number the impositions that have been practised upon the credulous and the simple in every age.

In imitation of a good old-fashioned plan, before entering on the examination of the above-mentioned, we will inquire into the etymology of the word. The word *Humbug* is not found in our common dictionaries, and like the word hoax, and a few others that have crept into daily use, their meanings are well understood without the aid of a lexicographer.

The word in question comes from a celebrated professor of the healing art, a German, of the name of Hombog, who made a considerable figure some years ago in diffusing his manifestoes through the medium of the newspapers. In order to show the estimation in which Doctor Hombog was held, a few of the shortest of the certificates addressed to the illustrious perfecter of his system may be given. They are as follows, and the cures are really remarkable.

Dear Doctor,

I was stone blind for sixteen years, and tried every medicine in vain, until I purchased a bottle of your invaluable mixture, and by merely looking at it was restored to sight immediately.

Your grateful friend,
James Stow.

My dear Von Hombog,

Some ten years since I was so unfortunate as to catch the *mania à potu*, along with another dreadful disease. I was sent to the hospital, but received no benefit from the prescriptions of the doctors, and was sent home. My wife heard of your invaluable medicine, and by her shouting six times in my ears "*Von Hombog's Mixture*," I was cured.

Yours ever,
J. Dewberry.

Dear Doctor,

For twenty years I was deaf as a door-post. Nothing gave me relief. Bought a bottle of your medicine. Smelt the cork, and was as sound as a trout.

Frederick Stretcher.

Dearest Doctor,

I was blown up by the explosion of a powder mill, a short time ago; when, happening to remember that I had some of your mixture about the house, I took but one drink, and came down light as a feather.

James Airy.

These are but a few of the seven hundred and ninety-one thousand certificates which, in the month of March, 1837, had already been filed, yet they will give some faint idea of the universal usefulness of the mixture for all diseases which afflict the human family. We make no remarks upon the certificates; the style is good, and if true that the mixture did so much, there is no doubt but the sales would be large.

I. And, first, of our subject in relation to Medicine. Medicine is, or ought to be a science.

For the Medical profession we have the highest possible respect. No class of men are more important benefactors of mankind. Nowhere have been found more illustrious instances of knowledge, talent, devotedness, and philanthropy. Not the less, however, has that honorable profession been infested by quackery and humbug. Nor has this been confined to that despicable class of quacks, who, without knowledge or experience, or a single qualification for the healing art, foist their odious drugs upon a credulous public, and live by the miseries and gullibility of mankind. Such thin-skinned monsters of "the ooze and the mire" are impervious to every weapon, and insensible to all shame.

What, then, is a QUACK? A quack is one who sells a pretended nostrum, the preparation of which is kept secret, but the term may be applied to every practitioner who, by pompous pretences, mean insinuations, and indirect promises, endeavors to obtain that confidence which neither success nor experience entitles him to. There is no disease of dreaded name for which the quack cannot furnish a cure. Asthma and consumption are disarmed of their terrors; gout is now but a harmless bugbear; and if any suffer or die of cancer, it must be the fault of their own obstinacy or incredulity. The diseases of children, with such savans, need give little concern; there are anodynes which allay the pain of teething; there are worm lozenges which no reptile can resist, and there are cosmetics which infallibly cure and beautify the skin. Laborious investigation of the causes of disease is unnecessary; the quack doctor does not wait to see his patient, who has only to send a letter describing his case, with the *usual fee*, of course, and the remedy will find its way to the most distant corner in the Union. Even this trouble may often be dispensed with; a patient has merely to consider for himself whether his skin or his stomach is in fault, and pills, and cordials, and balsams of unerring efficacy are to be found in every village and town ready to his hand.

Of the truth of these statements there cannot be a doubt, as numberless cases are to be seen every day attested in our newspapers, by those who have tried them, and whose benevolence prompts them to publish, for the benefit of mankind, the advantages they have experienced in themselves or their families. Let us look into this for a moment. These attestations, though honestly given, are given generally in ignorance. A person is afflicted with a certain combination of symptoms to which medical men, or the unskilled, assign a particular name, as fever, dropsy, scurvy: he recovers his health after the use of some particular medicine, and is perfectly convinced the medicine cured him. He rejoices in his success, and confidently recommends the same drug to his friend, who is said to labor under the same disease. But there is here a double fallacy. The first patient cannot be sure that he had the disease he supposes, and he cannot be certain that the remedy cured him. As it is doubtful whether the second patient is afflicted in a similar way, the same medicine may not be applicable to him.

When we consider the endless variety of the human constitution, its delicate and almost evanescent changes in health and disease, it must be obvious that a remedy which will suit one person may be very unfit for another; and that a medicine which to-day is salutary may be attended with disastrous results if repeated to-morrow. In popular language, and even in the language of physicians, it may be said with truth, that ten persons have the same disease, as small-pox, fever, or a cold, but it will require correct and accurate observation to discriminate the differences of each, and to apply the remedies which are proper to them. But by the same patent medicine, and in the same dose, 80,000 cases are said to be cured in a year; and patients indiscriminately are invited to apply a composition in a case which they call a disease of some particular name, though a skilful physician would consider a totally opposite remedy as necessary.

Besides, there is something in the moral aspect of a secret remedy that ought to put mankind on their guard against it. The possession of health is to all so valuable, pain and suffering are so dreadful, that it is the duty of every one to communicate every assistance in his power to relieve it. With all the industry and accumulated knowledge of ages, there are too many diseases which baffle all the skill of the profession, and there must be something suspicious about those who, affirming themselves to be in possession of a remedy for cancer or consumption, conceal the knowledge of it to their own bosoms. It may be asserted then with perfect safety, that credulity with respect to quack medicines, is not free from danger. We know that there are some patent medicines which are harmless and insignificant, and their only effect is to amuse the patient with delusive hopes, and to trifle away the time during which the constitution could bear the employment of active remedies. To acquire a competent knowledge of the structure of the human frame, to become acquainted with the diseases to which it is liable, and the remedies for these diseases, require study and talent; and it is matter of regret that the course of education requisite to obtain a license to experiment on the bodies of our fellow-creatures, is so circumscribed. We hope the time has come when it will be decreed that the course of education necessary for the medical profession will be more liberal and enlarged; and since it is considered one of the learned professions, *let its professors therefore be learned.*

Dr. D. McCauley

POPULAR DELUSIONS IN EDUCATION

Dr. McCauley's attack on popular delusions in education was a response to several significant developments in American education. Under the influence of Enlightenment ideas that man was infinitely perfectible, that the environment was crucial to the making of the individual, that knowledge was power, and, consequently, that education was the foundation of a free republic, Americans after 1820 began to expect more and different things from their educational system. An educated man was now expected to be able to do more than read the Bible and newspapers, keep accounts, and write letters. Education began to mean having a broad knowledge of history, government, natural history and science, and mathematics. Furthermore, education was coming to be seen as a relatively pleasant process under which a child could develop naturally in a healthy environment with the aid of trained instructors. The spread of these ideas between 1820 and 1850 through the work of Horace Mann and others entailed new implications for American schools.

If Americans placed greater demands on their schools, they also placed greater demands on their teachers—at a time when teacher training, as McCauley aptly demonstrates, was woefully inadequate. The teacher of the mid-nineteenth century was expected to combine wide knowledge with patience, kindness, and a willingness to live in poverty. He or she was also expected to be Christian, moral, and patriotic. The new appreciation for the role of the teacher resulted in a push to improve the training of teachers through the establishment of normal schools, a movement McCauley would no doubt have supported.

If McCauley's alarm about charlatanism in education led him to support some progressive measures, it also drove him into opposition to others. Though he condemned cruelty and violence in corporal punishment, McCauley continued to believe that, so long as fear was one of the most powerful human emotions, "the rod of correction will . . . be a necessary instrument in the hand of the teacher of youth." The newer educational philosophies, as McCauley suggests, took a dimmer view of corporal punishment. If the child was not inherently evil,

Vol. I (June, 1846), pp. 528–33.

but rather basically good and perfectible, then kindness and reason, rather than the rod, should dominate a classroom. Here, the question of quackery was less clear-cut than with the issue of untrained teachers.

In both "Humbugiana" and in this piece, McCauley reflects the growing reliance of mid-nineteenth-century Americans on professionalism to eliminate incompetence and fraud. Professionalism promised greater training, more rigorous regulation, and greater assurance of quality in an increasingly complex world. As the century wore on, the ideals and values of professionalism came to dominate the lives of many middle-class Americans.

. . . Of the importance of a sound, substantial education, we need not speak. Its utility all proclaim. No nation, whether barbarous or polished, was ever known entirely to neglect education. Even savages, who have scarcely sufficient skill to erect themselves a hut, as a protection from the inclemency of the weather, soon discover the importance of communicating to their offspring a knowledge of those practices which necessity teaches them to adopt, and which experience convinces them are advantageous; and in every age, and in every country, men have evinced their sense of the importance of education, by bestowing upon it such attention as the circumstances in which they have been placed, and the degrees of civilization which they have attained, have enabled them to bestow. Education is in fact the grand engine on which, as it is well or ill conducted, the prosperity or ruin of states and nations ultimately depends. That it is badly conducted in many respects, there is not a doubt. With all our schools, and colleges, and universities, is it not remarkable how few good scholars are really made? Now, the cause must be either in the incompetency of those who profess to give instruction, or in the mode of teaching pursued. Let us look at each of these for a moment, and we will probably see that there is ample room for improvement in both cases.

In the first place, we maintain that to become an able, efficient teacher of youth, candidates for it should begin at an early period of life to qualify themselves for their future employment; and it is a strange anomaly that the aspirant to every handicraft should be compelled to serve an apprenticeship for several years, in order to make himself acquainted with its mysteries, while the teacher of youth is permitted to enter on his office without any previous training at all. There is no public provision for the professional education of school-masters. Some few years ago, while traveling on the Erie canal, we entered into the following conversation with a young man at the helm: Well, how do you like this business? Tolerable; not hard work. Are you well paid for your services? Twenty dollars a month and found. Is it not a cold, disagreeable employment in winter? Yes, but I give up before winter, always. And what then.do you do? *Keep school.* Where? In the country. And do you like that business? O yes, it is an easy kind of going business, and one needs not sweat. And what do you teach? Everything almost that's going, reading, writing, geography, *Bells Letters*, and astronomy. Pray, what is *Bells Letters*? O nothing but English *in high style*. Then, Mr. Bell writes good English, does he? I suppose so, said the scholastic pilot, swinging his long rudder to one end, to let another vessel pass, I know nothing of the gentleman, but that he has written a book. Such was a part of a conversation with one who professed to "teach the young idea how to shoot," in the winter season, when he could get nothing else to do, and there is no doubt he is not a solitary instance of teachers not trained to the profession in early life.

The canal boatman is only *one* of the thousand cases of individuals who engage in the difficult and responsible profession of training the tender mind, and inspiring it with a love of knowledge and virtue. It is, therefore, to be deeply regretted that so many instructors of youth are incompetent to the task, and that the young should suffer from their want of the proper qualifications. Passing down a street in an obscure part of a city, we were much amused in reading the following notice of one of the "school-masters who are abroad:"

> *Plane reeding* and spelling taught here for 25 cents per week.
> Reeding with explanations 30 cents.
> *Grammer* by the month, a dollar.

The following method of teaching mathematics, though correct in spelling, is also in point: "Those who attend the classes under my care, must bear in mind, that the proposition and demonstration must be fairly written on a wafer with ink, composed of a cephalic tincture. This must be swallowed by every student of mathematics, upon an empty stomach, and for three following days he must eat nothing but bread and drink nothing but water. As the wafer digests, the tincture mounts to the brain of the student, bearing the proposition and demonstration along with it. The above should be regarded as the royal road to geometry." This professional card was somewhere published, and we are inclined to regard it as a fine satire upon ignorance aspiring to teach knowledge; though the progress of quackery has been such that we should not at all wonder if it was intended to induce, and did in fact induce, the attendance of pupils.

But not only in the teacher, but in the methods of teaching, do we find the same gross perversions. We have good reason to be suspicious of new plans and discoveries, and locomotive speed in matters of education. The man that professes to teach reading in twenty lessons, geography in six, and writing in four, is a charlatan. What Archimedes said to Dionysius, there is no royal road to mathematics, is true of every branch of literature and science. The steps of learning can only be mastered by time, diligence, and toil, and we may rest assured, that whatever system states the contrary, is all deception. The greatest scholars, and the profoundest philosophers, were formed in schools where the good old ways of assiduous application, and strict mental discipline, were established and prized. Feeble sciolists and empty praters may be formed without study, but the scholar and the philosopher, never. The most eminent are generally the most laborious; and it is not to be doubted, that all whom we are now accustomed to admire, attained excellence by the gradual process of persevering industry. Away, then, with the idea of acquiring science and languages and geography *in a few lessons*. The fact is, ease and simplicity are too much in vogue now. Science comes in the changing form of Proteus; it must be stripped of its difficulties; it must be popular. Mathematics must be brought down from its lofty pedestal and made to prattle in the language of childhood. Abridgments, and explanations, and conversations without end, rise upon the labors of Euclid, Playfair and La Place. In this benevolent age, it is to be feared, the helps to learning are multiplying so fast, that the young will abandon all effort to help themselves.

Another popular error, in conducting the education of youth, is, lengthened confinement at school. Nothing is better calculated to make a dolt—nothing better fitted to stupefy and injure the intellectual powers—than long, continuous plodding over books in childhood, without a change of position. In the "statutes and regulations" of a school in our city, there is the following—"Day scholars must remain in the institution from seven o'clock till half past six, with the exception of the hour set apart for dinner and recreation." We are inclined to think, that five or six hours' mental employment per day is quite sufficient, because the improvement of the mind, and success in the acquisition of knowledge does, by no means, depend on the length of time professedly engaged, but in the intensity of mind put forth. We know that some parents fancy long hours at school are essential to improvement; and ill-trained children are so troublesome at home, that mothers feel a preference for the school that keeps them longest out of their sight, if they have, at the same time, the assurance that they are out of harm's way. Hence, a sort of competition among teachers, who shall give the *longest hours*, which, in many instances that have come under our own observation, are extended, particularly during the summer, from eight in the morning till six in the evening, with only one regular hour of intermission. Thus are the interests of the youth, both as to health of body and soundness of mind, too often sacrificed in a contest between the folly and selfishness of parents on the one hand, and the cupidity and imbecility of teachers on the other. It might be a good regulation to have the hour of meeting at school *fixed*, when that of leaving it should be a movable point, to be determined by the degree of successful exertion put forth. Tell a boy that he has a certain series of tasks to perform, with the assurance that when they are thoroughly well done, his time shall be at his own disposal, and it is astonishing with what alacrity he will address himself to the work put before him. Indeed, such will be the rapidity of his execution as, at first, to confound and embarrass his incredulous teacher, and make him half repent of the experiment. Nothing, then, we believe, has a more prejudicial influence on the juvenile intellect, than long hours, the half of which are generally spent in indolence, rather than in mental activity.

On the subject of corporeal punishment, there have been, and still are, conflicting opinions; and when writing on popular errors connected with education, it may not be improper to offer a few observations on discipline.

We believe it to be a fundamental principle, on which all good teaching may be said to rest, that corporeal punishment, if not banished altogether from school, should not be resorted to till every other method of correction has failed. Those who maintain that corporeal punishment should be abolished from schools, argue on the ground, that the lash is an unworthy mode of influencing the youthful mind; and that fear has a tendency to corrupt the young heart. We sincerely believe that suffering is not of itself a good thing for the young; that unhappiness at school is of no use for mental discipline or the formation of character, and that many teachers have erred in the way they have inflicted punishments on the young delinquents. We are opposed to the indulgence of all pique, prejudice, partiality, and, above all, of anger, and violence, and cruelty, in administering correction to youth; but till the commencement of that blessed era, "when He that made the earth and created man upon it, shall raise him up in righteousness and direct all his ways," we fear the rod of correction will, as it has been from the earliest of ages, be a necessary instrument in the hand of the teacher of youth.

Dr. Goldsmith, who at one time of his life was a teacher, says, that "whatever pains a master may take to make learning agreeable to his pupil, he may depend it will be at first extremely unpleasant. The rudiments of every language, therefore, must be given as a task, not as an amusement. Attempting to deceive children into instruction of this kind, is only deceiving ourselves; and I know," says he, "of no passion capable of conquering a child's natural laziness, but *fear*. It is very probable that parents are told of some masters that never use the rod, and, consequently, are thought the most proper instructors of their children; but though tenderness is a requisite quality in an instructor, yet there is often the truest tenderness in well-timed correction." Let us hear the opinion of that colossus of literature, Dr. Johnson. A gentleman having expressed to him his wonder that he should be possessed of such an immense stock of scholastic lore, particularly as he acknowledged his constitutional indolence: "My school-master beat me *most unmercifully*," said the doctor, "else I had done nothing;" and it is well known that Johnson dictated a speech to Boswell, in palliation of the conduct of a school-teacher who was prosecuted for criminal severity, in which he justifies corporeal punishment in cases of moral delinquency, and even with respect to the use of the rod, as an excitement to duty, though he seems rather to condemn the practice, yet in some particular cases, he admitted it might be necessary. Strict discipline in childhood and early youth, is essential to the formation of virtuous character; but all cruelty, and punishment unnecessarily severe, we condemn. No one can doubt, however, that fear is implanted in the human breast for the wisest and best of purposes; and it is not the least influential of the passions. We are rather inclined to believe, how little soever it may redound to the honor of our nature, that fear, in its various modifications, exerts a more powerful influence over the mind of man, in restraining him from vices and inducing rectitude of conduct, than the love of virtue, and the desire of acting in conformity with the external fitness of things, have the power to produce; and that upon the generality of youth at school, it has a more salutary effect in preserving order and enforcing attention than the "appetite for knowledge," though stimulated by the most effectual training.*

We have touched on a few of the popular errors in education, and, if what has been advanced are the words of "truth and soberness," they can be offensive only to charlatans. The antagonist of every system of error is truth. The love and cultivation of truth will go far to secure us from imposition of every description. Let us cherish it.

*We do not understand our contributor to advocate *corporeal punishment* at school, except as an extreme measure, justified only by the grossest delinquencies. Even in this case we ourselves *doubt*, and the question can by no means be considered settled. The present age is decidedly against all violent coercion at schools, and if it goes too far, the error is on the side we would far rather have it. Theorizing and speculating upon Education will never be at end until mental philosophy is perfect, and man's intellectual nature comprehended in all its delicate manifestations; a thing we regard as impossible.—Editor.

J. D. B. De Bow

THE MORAL ADVANCE OF NEW ORLEANS

When J. D. B. De Bow established his Review *in New Orleans in 1846, he adopted the city as his own. He hoped New Orleans would become the economic, commercial, and cultural center of the South. For that to happen, however, New Orleans would have to surmount several formidable obstacles. As a propagandist for the city, De Bow tried to counter New Orleans' well-deserved reputation as an unhealthy, culturally deprived port.*

Disease, De Bow notwithstanding, was the greatest obstacle to the growth of New Orleans. The city was periodically swept by the three great epidemic diseases of the nineteenth century, smallpox, cholera, and yellow fever. Smallpox and cholera devastated many American cities in the nineteenth century, but yellow fever was particularly identified with New Orleans. The city's reputation as a "charnel house" was well deserved, for the great cholera epidemic of 1832 had killed at least 6,000 residents, while the four yellow fever epidemics between 1837 and 1843 killed between 1,500 and 2,000 citizens each. De Bow, as he did so often, appealed to the facts, but in this instance they could not help him make his case.

Despite his commercial interests, De Bow believed that New Orleans must become more than simply a trading center if it was to become a great city. He encouraged the development of the public school system, which had been established in 1841, and his hopes for the establishment of a university in the city came to fruition in 1847 with the founding of the University of Louisiana. De Bow did more than simply support the establishment of such institutions. In 1848 he was appointed Professor of Commerce, Public Economy, and Statistics at the university. He was also active in the Louisiana Historical Society, helping to reorganize it in 1846 and then serving as its secretary for a number of years. Without these and similar institutions, De Bow feared that New Orleans could not become a "great and growing community."

Vol. II (November, 1846), pp. 348–51.

At the opening of a new commercial season, when our merchants, departed for a few short months on business or on pleasure, are returning among us—when the rich steamers of the Mississippi are crowding in with the immense resources of the valley country, scattering them at our feet—and a thousand ships of all nations and flags seek employment and gain it at our crowded levees, reviving the spectacle of Tyre and Venice—it is natural to indulge a few reflections upon the past history, the present condition, and future hopes of the city.

New Orleans, disguise the fact as we may, has had abroad the reputation of being a great charnel-house, in which disease and death usurp forever a horrid empire. We meet this *libel* with the facts. For six years there has not existed an epidemic of any kind in the city. The summer through which we have passed is no exception. A few sporadic cases only of fever have occurred, attracting far more attention abroad than at home. In no other part of the Union have we passed the same season more pleasantly and more healthfully than here. Excluding the chances of visitation from yellow fever, now reduced very low, there is not perhaps in America a city that will show in the past six years a less proportion of deaths to population!

But we have had a worse reputation still. Our city has been considered a great depot of merchandise, one vast warehouse in which every inhabitant is a mere transient adventurer, without any kind of local feeling or bond of union, constituting together a heterogeneous mass of material from all the world. This charge may have been true—*but that time has past.* Let any man mark the change within a year or two, a change even now in wondrous progress. The increase of private residences, and the neatness, elegance, and in many instances, splendor with which these are finished, evidence that something more than mere temporary abodes are intended. Our American citizens are becoming citizens indeed, and the portion of the city which they administer exhibits at this time a spectacle the most surprising and gratifying. This new state of things demands much at our hands. Something higher must be aimed at than mere trade and commerce, high as these may be. *A society must be formed, social institutions promoted, literature encouraged and sustained, intelligence broadly disseminated, and a fixed and settled order of things secured.* To this we are rapidly approaching, and may the day hasten on. From our position, advantages, and prospects, the world has much to expect, and must not be disappointed.

The winter on which we verge cannot fail of being one of great business activity among us. A wider European market must stimulate our exports, and a high degree of prosperity throughout the Union must enlarge and magnify our trade in even greater proportion than before. How shall New Orleans then meet her position?

Let a laudable public spirit take possession of us all. We have made the first step in establishing a system of common schools unsurpassed in the Union. The next step is evident. Education must not be begun only, but completed. The people demand institutions of a higher nature—academies and colleges. The new Constitution establishes a University. This we must have if *men* are to be reared. Every branch of information can be communicated by it—the useful, the elegant, and the practical. A professorship of the arts, of the sciences, of law, of literature, of *agriculture*, and of Commerce—shall we not have these? Have we not wealthy citizens and public benefactors to endow them if that be necessary, and a liberal State Legislature? or if another mode be resorted to which would perhaps be better, and the professorships be required to sustain themselves by the attractions which they could throw around the lecture-room, as in Germany and Paris, have we not able men, and a population evidencing a disposition to be improved and enlightened?

Last year we had a course of public lectures from many leading citizens on every variety of subject, and with all degrees of interest. These assemblages were of the best order, and the largest hall in the city, night after night, was crowded by them. Here the scenes of dissipation, alas! so commonly represented in our city, temporarily lost their seductions, and youth appeared at last to have found a resort more congenial. Do we ask why the revelry by night has been heard among us, and why so many victims have yielded to the dread delusions of vice? The answer is ever made—*"The sources of domestic and social enjoyment are so few in New Orleans. It is impossible for strangers to find any access into society!"* Let us aim, then, to elevate public taste and enjoyment, and to arrest the progress of the mischief we have deplored.

The People's Lyceum or some other must be opened again. Have there been arrangements made to accomplish this end?

Some of our citizens have established a Historical Society. Meetings have been held, and officers elected. This society will aim as high as those of other States. It should have a *library*—it should have a *hall* and *public lecturers* of eminence at home and from abroad. We believe that these things will not be neglected. The period is most propitious.

Is it not a little remarkable, that almost nothing, we might say nothing, has yet been done among us in relation to *books* and Public Libraries? In the first place books. If we examine the shelves of those in the trade, will we find them stocked with the standard literature of Europe and this country? We hear of a valuable work published at the North, we must send for it or wait a tedious time, until it drags itself hitherward. We hear of a work published in Europe, *but it never reaches here at all.* Our booksellers say there is no general demand for such books. They would be unproductive capital. Is this true? Be it so then—shall we not find the works, at least, in public libraries? They *must* be had somewhere. Alas, they are often to be had nowhere, as we too well know, who have so often desired to consult them! What libraries have we at all?

The State has made a collection of public documents and some valuable volumes of a historical nature in its hall on Canal street, but these are intended for our legislators, and not for public use.

The Second Municipality has, with praiseworthy zeal, and in a great degree through the enterprise of our fellow-citizen, S. J. Peters, Esq., collected near five thousand volumes, large and small. Half of these are for the use of children; but among the rest, we have been delighted to find works of the highest character and value, and have had occasion to refer to them to great advantage. But neither can this be called a public library.

At the Merchants' Exchange there have been, within a few months past, some three thousand volumes, belonging to Mr. French, open to the subscribers of that admirable reading-room. This collection we have once before alluded to. It consists in a great measure of the *old Commercial Library*, sold some time since to the present proprietor. Many of the works here are of the highest interest and value. But what is to become of them? Shall they continue private property—not even accessible to the reading-room, as we understand they will not be in a short time—or will not some individual or society purchase them for public use?

Lastly, we would advert to the library of the *Young Men's Society*, on Exchange place. This collection of books, though small, is on the increase. The Legislature has evidenced a disposition to encourage it. The members of the society are those connected with commerce. During last season they had a few public lectures, but somehow or other it struck us that but a small degree of interest was manifested. Cannot this society take a stand on the highest ground? Will not the merchants unite in its support? *Strange is it indeed, that in the great Commercial City of New Orleans we have no Mercantile Association*: a thing that exists in almost every other city in the Union! In New York, Boston, Philadelphia, Baltimore, St. Louis, Louisville, and Charleston, these associations are well organized, and give occasion, often, to the ablest reports, and to some of the best specimens of eloquence and ability in public addresses, which our country has known; and yet, with all of this, everybody thinks it a matter of course that there should be no such institution in New Orleans! Will not our liberal and enlightened *Chamber of Commerce* take this subject into serious consideration? The period is at hand when they should act.

Finally, let us in all things, then, in the year that is before us, encourage a taste among our citizens for those things that are high and ennobling in themselves, and those only that can elevate us to the position which, as a great and growing community, we should so heartily covet.

JAMES RUSSELL LOWELL AND HIS WRITINGS

Southerners, such as this unknown citizen of Alabama, were sensitive to attacks on slavery wherever they appeared. Though many southerners were predisposed to view any critique of slavery as "blind and reckless fanaticism," James Russell Lowell, the New England poet, came close to fitting the description of a fanatic from a southern perspective. During the 1840s, Lowell supported William Lloyd Garrison, perhaps the most radical and uncompromising of the abolitionists. Lowell, like Garrison, advocated in his poetry and other writings the immediate abolition of slavery and opposed federal protection of the institution.

Lowell's The Bigelow Papers, *which the Alabamian here attacks directly, were written in response to the Mexican War. Like many northerners of an antislavery persuasion, Lowell viewed the Mexican War as a ploy to extend slave territory and thus strengthen the institution. Written in a New England dialect and presented as the writings of a Yankee farmer named Hosea Bigelow, these satirical pieces attacked the war, the government and politicians, and slavery. The Bigelow Papers began to appear in 1846, and Lowell collected them into a volume in 1849. Ten years later, after Lowell's own enthusiasm for Garrisonian abolitionism had waned and the controversy about slavery had intensified, the New Englander's scornful critique of the peculiar institution goaded the southern writer into attacking "the miserable balderdash" that was "intended to insult, to misrepresent, and to humiliate the Southern people."*

Nearly thirty years ago, Mr. Thomas Carlyle, with a self-complacency quite characteristic of himself, and of his nation, announced, in the pages of an English Review, that Americans were not a poetical people. As he was then profoundly ignorant of the literature and literary men of the South, it is fair to presume that he intended only to embrace within the range of this sweeping conclusion, that portion of the

Vol. XXVIII (March, 1860), pp. 272–78.

people of this country who hybernate amid the snows of the North; a people, who, with all their affectation of superior intelligence, and of ability to direct public sentiment at home and abroad, have hearts as icy as the air they breathe, and as narrow as the strips of ground on which they farm and build and thrive and grow impertinent. Beyond cavil, New-England once had, and still has, among her mountains and valleys, many wise, sagacious, industrious and honest citizens—men who fear God and love the state; but if, since the landing of the May-Flower at Plymouth Rock, up to the remark of Mr. Carlyle, she has warmed into being, a single *poet*, his name and his fame have escaped our recollection. What in our judgment was true at that time, is equally and essentially true to the present hour. There were then, and there are now, rhymers and versifiers and scribblers in abundance: then, as now, there were critics to commend, newspapers to puff, and a gaping crowd eager to buy and to read; yet the genius, the sentiment, the passion, the imagination, the purity and breadth of heart and mind, which illumine every line of poetry in its high sense, are among the unattained and we fear unattainable realities of the future. This opinion is expressed deliberately and in defiance of those *hired* laudations which undertake to form the public judgment in this country, and of those few faint notes of praise which occasionally float from the other side of the Atlantic. We are willing to admit, that the names of some American poets, at long intervals, have been found on the catalogues of English booksellers; that they have been honored with cold notices now and then in some English Reviews; and that they have been gratified to learn that their ill-omened croakings against the institutions under which they were born, have been echoed back in triumph by those English propagandists who throng the precincts of Exeter Hall. But these incentives to inspiration and stimulants to a vanity already morbid, have been utterly ineffectual. The stubborn and lamentable fact remains, that New-England continues destitute both of a poet and of poetry. It is worthy of an inquiry into the causes, how, and why, so little has been achieved, when so much has been attempted. They may lie in that sterile soil and ungenial sky, so familiar to every son of that inhospitable clime: or in that pharisaical self-gratulation which chuckles at its own perfections and sees nothing to commend in others; or, in that inherited puritanism which turns up its pious eyes in horror at all secular learning and accomplishment: or in that hard grasping and selfish nature, which distinguishes the genuine Yankee from the rest of his species, as distinctly as if he were an *orang-ou-tang*, or a South Sea Islander; or in that licentiousness of taste and manners which degrades one portion of Northern society by its pretensions, and another by its pollutions; or what is more probable still, in the prevalence of a blind and reckless fanaticism, which when it once usurps a place in the human bosom, strangles every noble and generous impulse. Such fanaticism as theirs, is of no ordinary kind; cherished alone by ignorant zealots—kindled into excitement only upon rare occasions, and soon extinguished by the intensity of its own flames; it is of that deeper and more dangerous dye, which is appalled at no injustice, which ever accompanies despotism, which unfailingly tramples liberty in the dust, and which in all ages and in all countries, has been the parent of infidelity. Nothing is too low to minister to its designs, too exalted to awe its insolence, or too sacred to escape its assaults; and as if to exhibit its own hypocrisy upon the grandest scale, while one hand is raised to implore mercy upon the slaveholder, the other is eagerly clutching at his property. We should be false to our convictions were we to declare that this fanaticism is confined to a few. Recent demonstrations, if others were wanting, on the hallowed soil of Virginia, as well as the wailings and the threats which have followed the Harper's Ferry conspirators to the tomb, prove conclusively, that it is deeply seated; that it is widely spread, and glows as fiercely at the fireside and the altar, as it does on the hustings or the forum, or the field of blood.

While this dark fanaticism has been exercising its baneful influences upon the mind, the morality, the social position, and the political relations of the North, it has engendered a sickly energy and activity in the stupid brains of some men and women, who, taking advantage of the ambition, prejudices, and ignorance of sects and parties, have been enabled to emerge from the twilight into the open sunshine. Following literature as a pursuit, these "poor insects of a summer's day," have made it the study of their lives to malign the South; to denounce in every possible way its institutions, and to deride its material advancement, its intellectual wealth, its polity and its people. By appealing to the worst passions of the worst people, some of them have reached an unenviable notoriety; others have earned their daily bread; while another, and perhaps a larger class, have slunk away into an obscurity so deep, that no friendly sexton will find them when they die. These pedlars of false ideas—these panderers to the lowest instincts of erring nature—these harlequins who attune their notes to any song for a drink of their own ineffably mean *rum*—these Swiss soldiers of literature who will write upon any subject for pay—these literary mus-quetoes, whose buzzing is more dreadful than their stings—are not confined to the columns of partisan or sectarian newspapers; nor to journalism in its broader sense; nor are they the mean froth and scum of society which the rising wave has thrown upon the surface. They are to be found in all the walks of life and pervade every variety of composition. They belch forth their venom against the South from the pulpit—from the bench—on the hustings—in the halls of Congress—in the social circle, and in the wilderness. Even the worn artisan, half-fed as he is, and the wearied girl at the factory loom, ignorantly, heedlessly, hopelessly, join in the same cry, and swell the current of opposition to an institution and a people who support them, as well as their imperious task-masters.

Since the great epics have ceased to be among the achievements of the human intellect, poetry has assumed in the main, one of two forms—either the patriotic or the sentimental. Under these capacious heads it has been, or may be, made to illustrate events, to delineate characters, to portray passion, to arouse emotions, excite action, or awaken remembrance. It remained for unpoetical New-England to invent a poetry which is the antipodes of these, and which may be termed the *libelous*. It seems to have a single aim—to wound, to weaken, to vilify, to degrade and destroy the institutions and the prosperity and the national influence of the South. It revels in the theme of negro-slavery. Ballads and songs and satires, and even the drama, are redolent with their chants against a system of servitude, which is better than their own; which they have been actively instrumental in introducing, and which they only abandoned when it ceased to be profitable. The motives which prompt these libels are bad enough—the depraved appetite which gulps them down with such greed is still worse; but the climax of meanness may be easily found in the poetry itself: its utter destitution of truth, its pointless allusions, its vulgar assumptions, its mockery of sacred things, and its ribald style, which has neither the charm of novelty, the force of originality, the sincerity of honesty, nor the virtue of a sound morality. Such productions could only emanate from a race of starvelings, stipendiaries, and hucksters, and could only be applauded by readers who are more degraded than the authors.

Prominent among this class, is James Russell Lowell, who has filled, of late, a large space in the annals of Northern poetry. His poems have passed through several editions; and he has become, in his own estimation, one of the magnates of the land. Perhaps it were a charity to forgive his vanity, for he has been petted with the prettiest of phrases; he has been applauded by the smoothest of hands; he has been received by the blandest of critics; he has been encouraged by the sweetest of smiles; and, more acceptable still to him, he has been rewarded by a shower of dimes. This Mr. Lowell, who has been thus commended and caressed, is a citizen of the Old Bay State, and is of that pilgrim stock which enslaved alike the negro, the Indian, and the white man, and would do the same now, if their pockets could be filled. He is also a lawyer without a client; a politician without principles; a poet without a heart; a pedant whose attainments are ridiculous; a satirist who never saw a point, a humorist who has never attained to the dignity of a witticism. Living, as he does, under the shadow of Bunker Hill, with its noble monument meeting his daily vision—with its history full of patriotism—with its associations full of poetry—with the names of Warren and of Webster shining in undying beauty upon every tree and rock, and hill and stream around him—it is a marvel and a mystery, a shame and a scandal, that no elevated thought, no genial sentiment, ever lighted up his brain nor warmed his heart.

If any one, who is disposed to be candid, and who has leisure to spend a few hours unprofitably, should deem these strictures too harsh, let him turn to the miserable balderdash, which is to be found at random in these poems, but particularly to those portions which were intended to insult, to misrepresent, and to humiliate the Southern people. We have space only for a few specimens. The first is from what the author calls the Biglow Papers, and is written in the true Yankee lingo:

> "Aint it cute to see a Yankee,
>   Take such everlastin' pains,
> All to git the devil's thankee
>   Helpin' them to weld their chains?
> Why, it's jest ez clear ez figgers,
>   Clear ez one an' one make two,
> Chaps that make black slaves o' niggers
>   Want to make wite slaves o' you.
>
> "Taint by turnin' out the hack folks
>   You're agoin' to git your right.
> Nor by looking down on black folks,
>   Coz you're put upon by wite;
> Slavery aint o' nary color—
>   Taint the hide that makes it wus,

All it keers for in a feller
'S jest to make him fill its puss.

"Ef I'd *my* way I hed ruther
We should go to work an' part,
They take one way, we take t'other,
Guess it wouldn't break my heart;
Man hed ought'o put asunder
Them that God has noways jined—
An' I shouldn't greatly wonder
Ef there's thousands of my mind."

Our second extract purports to detail an interview between the ghost of Miles Standish and the author. The old Puritan is quite indignant at the degeneracy of the pilgrim race, and is particularly wrathy at the annexation of Texas. The modest Lowell interposes thus:

"Good sir," I said, "you seem much stirred,
The sacred compromises—"

(Miles interrupting)—"Now God confound the dastard word!
My gall thereat arises;
Northward it hath this sense alone,
That you your conscience blinding,
Shall bow your fool's nose to the stone
When slavery feels like grinding.

"'Tis shame to see such painted sticks
In Vane and Winthrop's places,
To see your spirit of Seventy-six
Drag humbly in the traces,
With slavery's lash upon her back,
And herds of office-holders
To shout applause, as with a crack
It peels her patient shoulders."

This bad temper of the ghost, however, is a mere passing zepher, compared to the tempest which rises in the heart of Mr. Lowell, "On the Capture of Certain Fugitive Slaves Near Washington." He thus gives vent to his outraged feelings:

"Are we pledged to craven silence? Oh, fling it to the wind!
The parchment wall that bears us from the least of human kind—
That makes us cringe and temporize and doubly stand at rest,
While Pity's burning flood of words is red-hot in the breast.

"Though we break our fathers' promise, we have nobler duties first,
The traitor to humanity is the traitor most accursed;
Man is more than constitutions; better rot beneath the sod,
Than be true to Church and State, while we are doubly false to God.

"We owe our allegiance to the State, but deeper, truer more
To the sympathies that God hath set within our spirit's core;
Our country claims our fealty; we grant it so, but then
Before man made us citizens great Nature made us men."

But enough. These passages will suffice to exhibit the tone of his mind and the objects he seeks to accomplish. If ever a bad heart and a poverty-stricken genius conspired to inflict injury on the unoffending, it has been attempted in these volumes. But his anathemas have fallen on the innocent objects of his malignity, as innocuously as frosts upon the snowclad lawns of his native "Elmswood." They have not even provoked a smile of merited scorn and contempt; nor would they deserve or receive a notice from us, had not his bold, bad sentiments found an echo in the bosoms of a powerful, an aggressive, and an increasing political party, which is of resolute purpose and of dangerous tendency—a party which has declared that an irrepressible conflict exists in this country, between what is termed, the free labor of the North, and the slave labor of the South. This ominous declaration, so inconsistent with the views of our ancestors, who formed the Federal Constitution, and so utterly subversive of the Union, as at present existing, makes it the imperative duty of Southern journalists and of patriots everywhere, to take a close observance of what is passing, both in literature and politics. At the North they are very intimately united; and have combined, with other powerful elements, to overthrow the institution of slavery. This important truth gains slowly upon the minds of the quiet citizens of the South; but when they are convinced, we doubt not, they will be prompt in resistance, determined in purpose, fruitful in resources, rich in examples, and glorious in action. "If coming events cast their shadows before," the end is not yet.

J. W. Morgan

OUR SCHOOL BOOKS

Although southerners repeatedly asserted the "rightfulness and justice" of slavery, they were, especially after 1830, increasingly sensitive to any attacks on the institution, no matter how indirect. They feared the contamination of southern society and institutions, whether from Yankee peddlers, circuses, or school books. Abolitionist tracts, newspapers, and agitators were deemed particularly dangerous because they might incite a slave revolt, but Yankee school books that attacked slavery were considered by many even more insidious, for they might undermine the younger generation's confidence in the peculiar institution. In the years before the Civil War, De Bow published several articles that deplored southern reliance on school books published in the North. These authors, like Morgan, urged southerners to boycott northern books in order to protect their children from antislavery ideas and to buy southern books, when they could be found, in order to encourage southern writers.

Writing in the midst of the heightening crisis, Morgan was more strident than authors writing ten years earlier. His piece, however, reflects the southern fear of alien ideas and the insecurity of southern society. This campaign against abolitionist and other radical thought in school books was only part of a larger crusade to keep the South free of dangerous ideas. The crusade, which began with efforts in the 1830s to censor the U.S. mails, was not entirely successful, as Morgan's complaints in 1860 reveal, but the lack of success had not resulted from a lack of effort.

While opinions may differ as to the beauty, we must all admit the truthfulness of the old couplet, which runs in this wise:—

> "'Tis education forms the youthful mind;
> Just as the twig is bent the tree's inclined."

Vol. XXVIII (April, 1860), pp. 434–40.

What can be more natural than that the habits and opinions of mankind should receive their bias and direction from their youthful training and instruction? It is then that the mind most readily receives and adopts its principles and views. The school-boy of a dozen summers, however precocious or brilliant he may be, blindly receives and believes ideas which, if never presented to the same boy until he was a man of twenty-five, would have been first carefully scrutinized, and then utterly rejected. It is with the mind of youth as with the paper upon which we write. At the first both lie, untinged and untouched, waiting till some hand shall inscribe its views upon them. Whoever shall first disturb the primal purity, whether his task be one of good or evil, shall thereon leave an influence which will not speedily be lost. Other and later inscriptions may make their impress, and, to the eye of the careless observer, they may seem to efface all traces of what has gone before. Believe it not, these early impressions may be somewhat weakened and obscured, especially to the outward gaze, but they never can be obliterated; there will always linger some traces of their former power. It will not do to say that we may at first write upon the virgin page or the untrained mind whatever fancy or eccentricity may dictate, and trust to a later date to remove all traces of that which we have inscribed. This is neither wise nor true. It may be that after-education can remove the more glaring features of error which original training has created, but some blot or blemish must needs remain. Moreover, even supposing that early error could be quite counteracted and corrected by after-teaching, wherein lies the wisdom of giving that error an original lodgment in the mind? It is both an easier and a more pleasant task to create impressions and views than to destroy them. I would much rather undertake the instruction of a youth who had never been taught, than to attempt to teach one who had been previously taught upon a plan essentially and fundamentally erroneous.

These preliminary remarks have been uttered with especial reference to a subject of the weightiest import to us of the South, and one upon which and every matter connected with it, we cannot be too keenly sensitive. I mean the institution of Negro Slavery.

When the public mind of our section was divided as to the justice and propriety of this institution, when probably a large majority of even our own people regarded the existence of slavery among us a blot on our fair name, and when sundry wild and impracticable schemes of general emancipation were devised, it was not then to be wondered at

that we should remain indifferent as to the views presented to our
youth, on this subject, and that we should carelessly allow them to
peruse, even in their tender years, works in which slavery was denounced as an unmitigated evil, and the universal race of Ham's descendants were blazoned forth as a set of dusky angels and martyrs.
Such a course may have been defensible at that period, but tell me,
what show of propriety is there in its continuance at the present day?
We have become awake to the rightfulness and justice of our stand; we
have come to know that we are "more sinned against than sinning,"
and we have witnessed the complete failure of the many quixotic attempts to transform negroes into prosperous and thriving freemen.
Why then should we wish that the rising generation, who are to frame
and control public opinion, after we have passed from being, should be,
on this question of vital importance, taught doctrines which are in direct conflict with what we now believe? Common sense, the dictates of
self-preservation, the interests of what we deem to be the truth and
the right, all equally forbid such a line of policy; and yet I make bold to
say that our present conduct in this regard, is worthy of utter and complete disapproval. We are very properly, extremely solicitous that no
books of doubtful or evil moral tendency shall come within the range of
juvenile reading. We refuse admittance to our firesides to the works of
Eugene Sue, Reynolds, Tom Paine, or any others which may, per-
chance, injure youthful morals or principles of belief; indeed, many are
so very careful on this point as to taboo many of the political and general newspapers of the day, lest their frequent recital of crimes and
enormities may prove prejudicial. And yet on the general question of
slavery, the question which, most of all, lies at the very foundation of
Southern Society, the question upon the answer to which depends our
acquittal or condemnation, upon this question are we criminally careless. Wherein consists the good sense of prohibiting, to a Southern
school-boy, the perusal of the works of George Sand or Paul de Kock,
while the same youth is allowed, at will, to devour the abominable
sophistries and jingling rhymes of Stowe and Whittier, is more than I
have ever been able to discover. I have, however, long since learned
that the custom is a very general, indeed, nearly a universal one. What
earthly improvement a girl, not yet "in her teens," or a boy not yet free
from the reign of the "round-about," can derive from reading works
wherein they are constantly informed that their fathers, and ancestors
generally, for the last two hundred years, have been a heartless, cruel,

bloody-minded set of robbers, kidnappers, and slave-whippers, I cannot imagine. The course of the Southern public, in this particular, is quite indefensible.

But, if our conduct in regard to works of fiction and the like, is improper, how much worse is it, when we come to consider the department of school books? I was led to write this article by the perusal of a school history of the United States, which I chanced to glance over, a few days ago. The work is evidently meant for the mere tyro in historical study, being essentially of an elementary character, and is doubtless the first of a series, in the more extended volumes of which the views advanced in the work now under notice, shall be given more at length. What is the language of this book? In a chapter which treats of the introduction of African slavery into America, we find this observation: "Las Casas, in his earnest desire to spare the Indian, little thought he was arousing a spirit of avarice which would inflict cruel wrong on the poor African."

And again, in the same chapter we read: "The negro thrives best in a warm climate; it is, therefore, in the South alone, that slavery, which originally existed in all the colonies, has taken such a hold, and continued so long, that the removal of the evil, though much to be desired, has become, year by year, a question of greater difficulty."

Now, who can fail to question the propriety of inserting such sentiments as the above, in an historical treatise which, so far from descending into the philosophy and relation of events, pretendedly deals with merely the dry bones, the *disjecta membra* of the science? Where a mere chronological narration and enumeration of events is proposed, what right has the author to step aside from his proper course, to drag in his own private views on vexed questions of great national import? He might quite as properly branch off into a disquisition of the exact sciences or the atomic theory. A work of this mere outline character, and which does not pretend to give matters in all their minutiæ and philosophical bearings, had best maintain an impartial stand on great mooted points. If such books are designed to open up or prosecute a crusade against slavery, methinks it would be more fair and honorable to come among us, in their true garb. Let them not sail under any friendly or neutral flag, but show in full view the black piratical ensign of Abolitionism.

Do not imagine, however, that the work from which I have above quoted, is of an uncommon character, or that the course it pursues is one unusually followed. Far from it, *ab uno disce omnes* [from this one, know them all—EDS.].

In every department of school-literature will you find numbers of such. Indeed, the one to which I have referred, is far less objectionable, in this respect, than many others I have seen. It would seem as though Northern cunning and ingenuity had exercised its utmost power in the furtherance of this system, regarding it, doubtless, as a most efficient mode of corrupting the minds of Southern youth, and introducing their dangerous heresies among us.

A very large proportion of the histories used in our schools are built upon this plan. They are filled with praise and glorification of the first settlers of the New-England and Northern States generally, as a set of incorruptible patriots, irreproachable moralists, and most exemplary models for future imitation. And their descendants are depicted as fully equaling the standard set for them by their distinguished ancestors, of unexceptionable demeanor. On the other hand, the individuals, who organized society in the Southern States, are pictured as a race of immoral reprobates, who have handed down all their vices and evil habits to their descendants of this day. While the institution of slavery, and its introduction into our country, are made the occasion of much violent invective, there is but a slight effort at rebuke, and a large amount of apology is offered, for the amusements of burning witches, hanging Quakers, and banishing Baptists, formerly so very popular in New-England. While we, who now support and defend the institution of slavery, are either denounced or pitied, the residents of the Northern States, who have always been the chief prosecutors of the slave-trade, are allowed to pass uncensured. Such is the state of the histories.

In many of the collections of speeches, works which are put into the possession of our boys, so soon as they become infected with the oratoric fever, will be found sundry poetical lamentations over the sad fate of the lamb-like, innocent, intellectual *darkey*, and *a heavy seasoning* of curses, deep and manifold, against the cupidity and hardheartedness of Southern people generally. Here and there, too, will you stumble upon some prose article, dwelling extensively in the pathetic, wherein the imagined sorrows and troubles of certain *dusky* specimens of "nature's noblemen" are fully considered.

In the reading books, even in the spelling books which the North furnishes us, with a few honorable exceptions, are found allusions, more or less covert, and observations, more or less disparaging, according to the policy of the author, upon our peculiar institutions.

Those of our scholars who may chance to pursue the study of moral science, will very probably have furnished them some lengthy and abstruse reflections upon the enormity of slaveholding, its sinfulness, and its violation of every precept of moral government. These bring their false logic and windy sophistries to bear upon us, and introduce long exploded dogmas to prove the immorality of slavery, and the heinous turpitude of slaveholders.

Thus it is in every branch alike. Wherever, by any possibility, a discussion and denunciation of slavery can be introduced, even by never so great a departure from the object legitimately under notice, that departure is made. The *animus* pervading many of these works would seem to indicate that they are the chosen agents for conducting a warm, vigorous crusade against us, the poor, benighted sinners of the South. They seem to regard Southern society as composed of a race so blind, morally and in a literary point of view alike, that they will gladly receive without questioning the books sent them, even though filled with foul calumnies against themselves.

Let us prove the falsity of this belief. Let us drive these incendiaries from among us. We forbid the abolitionist an abode in our midst, whenever he dares openly to declare and promulgate his opinions. Why should we be more considerate and forbearing toward his published or written sentiments than we are toward his spoken ones? We guard, by heavy penalties, against the possibility of his tampering with our slave population. We allow no interference with them on his part. Shall we be less careful when our youth, the growing, future rulers of our country, are concerned?

If it be deemed desirable that our school books should assume a positive, instead of a neutral stand, on the momentous subject of slavery, by every consideration of reason and common sense, by every dictate of self-preservation, let us have sentiments expressed in them which will accord with our own. Let us no longer pursue the foolish, suicidal policy of which I have spoken. It is full time that the Southern mind was aroused on this subject. Now, when we have awaked to the vital necessity of carefully guarding every avenue of approach, when we are so very careful on all other subjects, let us not be found wanting in vigilance upon this, so essential a point. Let us not be content to banish the wandering, incendiary Yankee schoolmaster, but let us also send his incendiary schoolbooks to keep him company. It can scarcely be needful that I should here enter a disclaimer as to any intended attack in the previous sentence, upon those gentlemen of Northern birth who now fill so worthily posts of honor in both our public and private institutions of learning. I know men, professors in our colleges and teachers in our schools, who, from long residence in our midst, have become thoroughly identified with our institutions, and whose views upon the question of slavery will call forth the admiration of even the most exacting of our Southern-born and Southern-bred citizens. My remark only had reference to those wanderers over the country, whose influence and presence are as great a curse as the locusts of ancient Egypt.

If some of the many men among us who are well-suited to the work, will but prepare a series of school books which Southern parents and teachers can with safety and a good conscience place before their children and scholars, I predict for them a success commensurate with what gratitude and self-preservation would demand. All that could be needed to insure them success, would be that the Southern people should be informed as to their merits, and their especial claims upon their confidence. Will not some one speedily undertake the good work?

COUNTRY LIFE

Even the South, which prided itself on its plantation and agrarian society, could not escape the increasing urbanization that the United States experienced in the nineteenth century. The move to the cities occurred more slowly in the South than in the North, but the number of residents living in urban areas in the South increased from 6.6 percent in 1840 to 9.5 percent in 1860. All of the major cities of the South— New Orleans, Mobile, Savannah, Charleston, Richmond, Washington, Baltimore, Louisville, and St. Louis—experienced substantial growth in the years before 1860. When the Civil War began, Baltimore, with 212,000 residents, and New Orleans, with 168,675 residents, ranked fourth and sixth in size of all American cities. Although the largest cities of the South lay on the perimeter of the region, the interior had some twenty places with more than 8,000 residents.

De Bow had, from the beginning of the Review, *been a champion of city growth, regularly publishing statistics, proposals for city improvement, and generally advocating cities as centers of commerce and industry. But even De Bow may have had some second thoughts about the virtues of city life, for in publishing this piece in 1860 he provided a platform for the anonymous author's nostalgia for the glories of plantation life. Although the writer clearly values agrarian society, he admits that the city has undeniable attractions. Interestingly, his solution is not to retard the growth of cities in general, but to encourage the growth of southern cities so that southerners could enjoy the benefits of city life without contributing to the prosperity and strength of the North.*

Within the last forty years country life has quietly and almost imperceptibly undergone great changes, and, under the influence of modern discoveries and inventions, will, ere long, be wholly revolutionized. The pursuits and amusements of our parents are not our pursuits and amusements, nor has anything new come in to supply the place of what

Vol. XXIX (November, 1860), pp. 613–17.

has passed away. The whole tenor and complexion of country life has changed, and that change consists in the country having become more and more dependent on the towns. Whether in pursuit of business, pleasure, or information, men leave the country and visit some neighboring city. Agriculture is the only rural avocation, and country is mere plantation life. The private social festive board is rarely spread; the barbecue, with its music and its dance, is obsolete and almost forgotten; the report of the fowling-piece disturbs not the slumber of the woods or the fields; the huntsman's horn is not heard, the cry of the hounds, and the clattering hoofs of the pursuing steeds enliven but rarely the dreary monotony of country life. The boys, like the men, look to visiting town for amusement, and neglect their traps and snares, their guns, and their boats, and their fishing tackle, their dogs and their riding horses. The anvil rings no longer under the sturdy strokes of the stalwart smith, the shoemaker has ceased to ply his awl, the seamstress neglects her needle, and the sounds of the shuttle and the spinning-wheel are forgotten. Our fields are clothed in living drapery of black negroes, black mules, black birds, and black crows, with here and there a forlorn looking master or overseer. Our bodies are in the country, our souls in town. There used to be far more variety, more leisure, more refinement, and more social enjoyment, in country than in town. Each farm was a little community, producing within itself most of the necessaries and luxuries of life, and each neighborhood a little world within itself, with its store, its post-office, its church, its school-house, its carpenters, blacksmiths, tanners, tailors, doctors, lawyers, and farmers. Men used to make fortunes in town and retire to the country to enjoy them. Hospitality was unbounded, and the guests always in attendance. Now the tables are sometimes spread, but the invited guests have gone to the city or the springs.

Men used to go to town to labor and to make money, and return to the country to enjoy it. How sadly is this changed. The country is the scene of mere monotonous agricultural labor—labor neither lightened by variety nor relieved by amusements. Men endure country life merely to make money, and go to town to spend it—to cease work and give themselves up to enjoyment.

Steam, and other modern inventions and improvements, but principally steam, has effected these great changes, and will bring about, ere long, much greater. Towns are become the foci of all art, industry, education, wealth, amusement, and civilization. They will rob the country at a distance of its wealth and its civilization, and only shed their en-

livening rays over little neighborhoods that encircle them. Countries
with many and large towns will become enlightened, powerful, and
wealthy; countries without them, dreary, poor, ignorant, weak, dependent, and tributary.

It has become cheaper to visit New-York or Saratoga than to keep an
equipage to visit our neighbors, and as every one goes now to cities and
watering-places, 'tis there we are most likely to meet with our friends,
neighbors, and acquaintances. Railroads and steamboats enable farmers to send daily to town for every article they need, and this breaks
up country stores, villages, and mechanic shops. Men are wholly seg-
regated in the country, and meet each other in the cities in pursuit of
business or pleasure. Our daughters mope and pine at home, and desire to visit town for amusement, or for religious, social, moral, and
intellectual association. Our little girls beg to be sent to school in town,
in order that they may see something of the world. Our boys long for
the holidays, and hoard every cent they can get, in order that they
may go to town and see the great world—the theatre, the legislature,
the ships, the printing establishments, the factories, and the great
stores. Our wives, too, wish to go to town because there is no society
in the country, because there is nothing going on to improve the minds
of their children, because there are no openings for business of any
sort in the country, in which a talented or industrious child can get a
living or attain reputation. The women all hate the country; and they
are right, for in the country woman is now a mere fixture, with few
occupations and no associations. The domestic manufacturing, the
sewing, knitting, weaving, cutting, and making the clothes for her
children and the negroes, which she formerly superintended and took
part in, gave some interest and variety to life. These occupations su-
perseded and done away with, and visiting all tending townward, has
left woman solitary and disconsolate. The negroes are the most social
of all human beings, and after having hired in town, refuse to live again
in the country.

No doubt the census will exhibit proofs of our theory. It will be found
that population increases much more rapidly in all well-located towns,
than in the country. This tendency to aggregate population in the cities, will be of great advantage to the South, which has all along suffered much from the opposite tendency. Mr. Jefferson has taught us
that cities were evils. So they are, great evils to distant country people
that trade with, but great blessings to their neighbors. They afford variety of occupation, increase wealth, and improve civilization in their

immediate vicinities, by robbing their distant customers. They hoard the wealth which their far-off customers make. The wealth of London, of New-York, and of Paris, is not made in those cities, but transferred to them by trade, from a tributary world. Agriculture as the sole or common pursuit, impoverishes a people; and the larger their crops, the greater the draft on their land, and the more rapid the process of impoverishment.

We must have cities, towns, and watering places, in the South, for country life is daily becoming more unpopular; and unless we have cities at home, our rich people will spend half their time and all their money abroad. We must not leave trade, commerce, fashion, manufactures, taste, education, and public amusements, to take care of themselves, and to pursue their natural courses and direction. The great centres of trade, fashion, taste, manufactures, literature, and education, are all without the South, and all exploitate, tax, and fleece, the South. If we let things alone, they will daily grow worse for us; and the great foreign centres will daily become more wealthy, enlightened, and attractive, while we daily become poorer, more ignorant, and dependent. We must make country life tolerable, nay, fashionable, by bringing the country nearer to the town. We must have many small towns, and in each State, at least one city. We must have attractive centres at home, or become daily more and more the tributaries and dependants of centres abroad.

Disunion alone will not cure the evil—non-intercourse must be superadded to disunion. Indeed, if disunion restore friendly relations between the sections, we shall become more than ever the mere slave colonies of the North. We want actual, not technical and nominal disunion. Our quarrel with the North is rapidly building up Southern trade, manufactures, literature, fashions, thought, &c., and establishing actual independence. Make up that quarrel, whether within or without the Union, and we are ruined.

Town life and country life are both required, in order for the full development of human character. He who has lived always in the country, is a mere rustic or clown; but he who has spent his whole life in town, is a far more awkward, uncouth, and artificial character. His notions are narrower than the rustic's, because there is more of the world in the country than in the city. A Londoner is proverbial for his narrow notions, his bad English, his vulgar conceit, and his uncouth deportment. But cockneys are not peculiar to London. Every town rears them; and the smaller the town the more intense the cockney. To mistake London for the world, makes a man ridiculous; to take a small town for the world, makes him absurd.

Country youths should spend some years of their lives in business, or at school, in town. It not only varies and enlarges their experience, but it teaches them orderly, systematic, and industrious habits. Every pursuit in life is carried on more systematically in town than in country; and men are more industrious, because they gain their daily bread by their own daily work, while in the country, people, rich or poor, can idle away half their time, and yet get along tolerably well. Two years as clerk in a store in a city, is the proper education for a farmer. He learns to keep accounts, and becomes habituated to calculating and balances, expenses and profits, outgoings and incomings. Merchants always make the best farmers.

V

THE SOUTH, THE NORTH, AND THE UNION

From its first issue, *De Bow's Review* had been a southern journal, but De Bow took up the cause of the South with special fervor in the 1850s. Responding to the growing sectional tension over slavery and its extension into the territories, De Bow began to shift the focus of his magazine. He always retained his interest in the agricultural, commercial, and industrial development of the region that had spurred him to journalism, but more and more the cause of the South came to be identified with a defense of slavery. The economic development of the South could no longer be seen as a goal in itself, but rather as an essential element in strengthening the South for the coming contest with the North over the peculiar institution.

De Bow, like many Americans North and South, hoped that the Compromise of 1850 would resolve the sectional tension, though he was skeptical that any political agreement could long protect the South against the growing antislavery crusade. In the midst of the Congressional debate on the compromise, De Bow voiced his fear that the South would concede too much in her effort to preserve the Union. He admitted that "the Union is the source of our greatness and strength," but he admonished his readers to remember that "there must be an end, somewhere, of concessions." Political agreements and concessions might preserve the Union, but they could not ultimately be relied upon to defend slavery. In "The Cause of the South," De Bow challenged southerners to take up "the vigorous prosecution of their industry, resources, and enterprise" in order to break the northern stranglehold on the southern economy. Only thus might the South successfully resist the "reckless fanaticism or ignorant zeal" of the northern abolitionists and secure the safety of the peculiar institution.

Southerners who put their faith in the Compromise of 1850 were quickly disillusioned. Whatever hopes De Bow had in July, 1850, were dashed by November of that year as many northerners openly opposed the Fugitive Slave Act. That opposition seemed to confirm the belief that the South had conceded too much in the compromise. Southerners would not acquiesce in the destruction of their institutions, and De Bow reiterated his conviction that "the rights of the south, and the full and unlimited rights of the south under the Constitution, without compromise of any sort, *must be preserved*, or the Union will become a snare rather than a blessing."

Throughout the 1850s, De Bow devoted increasing space in his *Review* to discussion and examination of the differences between the North and the South. Some pieces, like his essay "Fugitive Slaves" and the appeal of the Law and Order party in Kansas, were polemical and written to arouse southern fears. Others, though they may have had the same effect, were astute analyses of the southern position, of its strengths and weaknesses, and of the background to the conflict. Edmund Ruffin, in "Consequences of Abolition Agitation," provided the readers of *De Bow's Review* with a penetrating and frightening analysis of the election of 1856. Rather than take comfort in the election of James Buchanan with his southern sympathies, Ruffin pointed out the dangerous power of the newly formed Republican party in its first presidential contest. Ruffin realized that the numerical superiority of the North and the existence of more free than slave states would soon allow the "abolition party" to control the presidency and both houses of Congress and, ultimately, to amend the Constitution. Ruffin fully expected that such power would be used to abolish slavery. He predicted that if the abolition party gained such power the South would have no choice but to secede to protect her interests and rights. He also concluded that the North would accept southern secession and would not resort to force to maintain the Union. He was, of course, more accurate in forecasting the actions of the South than of the North.

On the eve of secession and civil war, *De Bow's Review* mirrored the hopes and fears of southerners in the face of Harper's Ferry and the election of Abraham Lincoln. Authors like Joseph A. Turner in "What Are We To Do?" attempted to chart a course to safety but, ironically, only revealed southern weaknesses. More than a decade after De Bow had issued his first calls to develop and strengthen southern industry, Turner was still bemoaning the lack of development and urging southerners, once again, to "patronize home industry." That Turner found it necessary to repeat such urgings suggests the lack of response over the previous fifteen years. In 1860 the call to patronize home industry was pitifully inadequate.

If Turner's support of home industry was an inadequate solution to the problem facing the South, he, like the anonymous author of "Our Country—Its Hopes and Fears," considered secession essential to the protection of southern interests, particularly if the Republicans captured the presidency in 1860. The Mississippi essayist advanced the argument that only in the South could one find any survival of the American revolutionary tradition. The North had madly succumbed to abolitionism, "freeloveism," and other equally outrageous fanaticisms and had destroyed the heritage of freedom left by the founding fathers. The South, by resisting such madness, had preserved the legacy of liberty for the white race. Slavery, he argued, was not a crime, but necessary to the maintenance of white freedom. That being the case, southerners were fully justified in seceding to protect slavery, white liberties, and the great legacy of the American Revolution.

Throughout the decade of the 1850s, then, De Bow and his contributors tended to subordinate economic and political considerations to a defense of slavery and the South. A good example of De Bow's political analysis from the point of view of a committed southern advocate is his discussion of the potential presidential candidates of 1860. Almost the sole criterion was the candidate's position regarding slavery and its protection and expansion. De Bow condemned all Republicans, though he did make some distinctions between Abraham Lincoln, "a low and vulgar partisan of John Brown," and William H. Seward, whom he described as "the ablest man" in the Senate. De Bow's animosity toward the Republicans, and toward Lincoln in particular, suggests why Lincoln's election, carrying not a single slave state in a frightening vindication of Ruffin's prediction, convinced many southerners that the time had come to secede. The cause of the South could no longer be achieved in union with the North.

J. D. B. De Bow

THE CAUSE OF THE SOUTH

De Bow took up the cause of the South in this editorial during the Congressional debates on the territorial question and slavery precipitated by the acquisition of the Mexican Cession. By 1850, the sectional balance in the Union was disappearing. The South was already outvoted in the House of Representatives, and the admission of additional free states would tip the precarious balance in the Senate. As the decade opened, many southerners believed that they had only two choices: they must achieve some solid guarantees for their institutions within the Union, or they must secede before the North could abolish those institutions. Many at the time believed that only a comprehensive compromise could preserve the Union. As he had in 1820, Henry Clay began to work toward such a compromise. Clay's first effort to create an omnibus bill that embodied all the points of compromise was long debated in the first half of 1850. His proposals probably conceded more to the North than the South, including the admission of California as a free state, the organization of the Mexican Cession as neither slave nor free, and the abolition of the slave trade in the District of Columbia. The South obtained the recognition of slavery in the District of Columbia, promise of a stronger fugitive slave law, and rejection of the concept of the Wilmot Proviso. Southerners hoped that these provisions would safeguard slavery and contribute to the cessation of the slavery controversy. When De Bow wrote the following essay as an editorial for the Review, *it was clear that Clay's omnibus bill was in trouble, which may account for some of his concern.*

De Bow, however, doubted that the provisions of the proposed compromise could achieve their dual objective of protecting the South and molifying the North. He clearly recognized the growing power of the North and questioned whether any purely political solution was possible. Part of his fear was grounded in the apparent unwillingness of the South to take the steps necessary to defend its society and institutions. Specifically, he cited the failure of southerners to support his Review *and the southern convention that was meeting in Nashville, Tennessee. The convention, which began on June 3, was the work of more rad-*

Vol. IX (July, 1850), pp. 120–22.

ical southerners who had been trying for a number of years to call such a meeting as a means to southern unity. But unity could not be manufactured where none existed. Five states sent official delegations, four sent unofficial groups, and six states, including De Bow's Louisiana, were unrepresented. Southerners of many persuasions were determined to maintain their rights, but the vast majority were also determined to avoid even the appearance of disunion.

The delegates to the Nashville convention, like the rest of the nation, waited on events in Washington, and in the months after De Bow's editorial the Compromise of 1850 was achieved. Following the defeat of Clay's omnibus bill in July, Stephen Douglas took over the direction of the compromise efforts. By September, he had achieved separate passage of the various parts of the compromise, and the crisis was averted. Although De Bow agreed with southern extremists on slavery and the territorial question, he acquiesced in the Compromise of 1850. He was unhappy with some of the provisions, as his piece on the fugitive slaves demonstrated, and, as a result, he saw no reason to slacken in his campaign to maintain southern rights and to convince his fellow southerners of the need to strengthen the South in every way possible.

We have long ago thought that the duty of the people consisted more in the vigorous prosecution of their industry, resources and enterprise, than in bandying constitutional arguments with their opponents, or in rhetorical flourishes about the sanctity of the federal compact. This is the course of action, which, though it may not convince, will at least prepare, us for this crisis which it needs no seer's eye to see will, in the event, be precipitated upon us by the reckless fanaticism or ignorant zeal of the "cordon of free States" surrounding us on every hand. "Light up the torches of industry," was the advice of Dr. Franklin to his countrymen, on discovering that all hope from the British cabinet had fled forever. Light up the torches, say we, on every hill-top, by the side of every stream, from the shores of the Delaware to the furthest extremes of the Rio Grande—from the Ohio to the capes of Florida. Before heaven! we have work before us now. Who conducts our commerce, builds for us ships, and navigates them on the high seas? *The North!* Who spins and weaves, for our domestic use (and grows rich in doing it), the fabric which overruns our fields and not seldom fails to remunerate the labor that is bestowed upon it here? *The North*. Who supplies the material and the engineers for our railroads where we have any, gives to us books and periodicals, newspapers and authors, without any limit or end? *The North*. Who educates for our children, and affably receives the annual millions we have to expend in travel and in luxury? *The North*. Is there a bale of cotton to leave our ports for Liverpool, shall not a northern ship transport it? Is there a package of broadcloths, or a chest of tea, to be landed at our warehouses? There is a tribute, first, to Boston, or New York! We look on and admire the growth of this tremendous power there, scarcely admitting any excellence in ourselves or willing to make an effort to secure such excellence. Yet we expect to be respected in our rights, and deferentially bowed to by the rulers of the North! Vain hope, if history be credited. Let the scepter depart from Judah, and his brethren will not long desire the pretext to trample upon his inheritance.

It is not too late for hope. Perhaps it is not. No man, with his eyes about him, can have failed to mark the change which is coming over us imperceptibly, and working out a higher and better destiny for the South. To promote this change, we entered the vanguard in the early hours of the day, and have devoted ourselves, with energy, zeal and conscientious devotion, for many years, to the work. We proclaimed to the South, *action!* ACTION!! ACTION!!!—not in the rhetoric of Congress, but in the busy hum of mechanism, and in the thrifty operations of the hammer and the anvil. We have preached this doctrine on the hill-tops, from the day of our first editorial until now—through every defeat, every pecuniary loss and embarrassment, amidst every discouragement, oftentimes with the faintest possible applause. The mead of praise came to us oftener from the North itself in our labors. "*Stop the Review*" was a familiar word that was heard often, often, often, from all quarters, from the highest to the lowest; "I have not time to read;" "I take too many other works;" "You are now getting on too well to need my subscription;" "Perhaps next year I will subscribe;" "I admit it *is* a valuable work and should be encouraged," is denied in none of these letters. More frequently the word is "*refused*," as the number comes back, saddled with postage; and, on reference to the books, it is discovered one, two or three years' subscription remains *unpaid*! These have been our trials, struggles, bitter discouragements and defeats. Verily perseverance, in such a cause, is a virtue higher than that of Hannibal in climbing the Alps, or of Kepler in calculating the laws of planetary motion.

Was the fault, in all of this, ours? We have much to atone for, and admit, with sorrow, many short-comings, and less of merit than the cause, so dearly at heart, demanded. Yet, the early dawn and the midnight lamp have witnessed our labors; and meat and sleep and pleasure, have been sacrificed, cheerfully, to them, without one desponding thought. Why, then, the discouragements and the defeats? The unsolicited tribute of hundreds and thousands in every part of the South—indeed, of the Union—has given assurance, that, wherever the fault may be, it is not altogether ours. We say not this with immodesty, but rather in justification. If wrong, will it not be a friendly part to convince us of it, and point where the mischief lies, that we may apply the remedy. Let the "invisible nightmare," that is "crushing out the life" of us, take a shape, that we may see and fasten on it. "Come, behemoth, chaos or the Hyrcan tiger," anything than mystery and doubt!

We crave the reader's pardon for this personal episode, and resume our subject. It is customary to hear southern men declare the institution of slavery is in danger, and express the fear it cannot be maintained—hedged in, as it were, by the opposition of so many civilized nations, and attacked by the powers of the North. The more timid are reluctant to invest in the property; some, in the spirit of the tories of the revolution, have sold it all out, and, perhaps, from tender consciences, removed away. It has been quite common to emigrate northward, with the results of *unrighteously taxed* slavery, converted into cash, to be added to northern opulence, and enable it the better to make its crusade against our altars and our homes. The sons of these *slave-made* capitalists soon learn the endless cant of abolitionism and "free soil," if the fathers themselves do not set the example. Denouncing the "price of blood," they are the last to contribute a mill from their unrighteous hoards in the purchase of a "potter's field."

Two thousand millions of property (for it will reach this much) we are told is in peril—but what of this? The abolition of slavery at the South is an impossibility, without a servile war, continued struggles of the races of whites and blacks, desolation of fields, hearths and homes, abandonment of half a score of great States entirely to Ethiopian manners, industry and civilization! No southern man will dispute these propositions, since it is demonstrable that the negro cannot be removed away by all the resources and power of the nation. No southern man will argue these propositions. The time for argument has passed.

What then? can there be any hesitation about our true policy? If abolition involves our irretrievable destruction, and if resistance seems equally threatened with desolation and death, even the coward will not falter when death *certainly* impends upon flight or fight!

The cry, after all, upon the walls, is not war, but peace. "Concession" is the word upon every lip—"concession and compromise," for *peace.* What would you? Is it time to set the world upon fire about abstractions? Would you return to the days of the school-men and embroil nations and men in your hair-setting polemics? Away with your southern fanatics as your northern fanatics. Wilmot proviso, indeed! . . .

Various propositions have been brought forward, in the view of preserving the South from the common dangers of the times; but, whatever their individual merit, the result has proved how difficult, how almost impossible, it is to unite the people upon any measure whatever of security or defense. Distraction presides over our councils; and, in the jealousies of sections of parties or of men, a front is exposed, broken at every point, and inviting the assaults, if not the very contempt, of the assailants. Our protests are regarded but gasconade; our earnestness, hypocrisy; our solemn declarations of rights, the silly declamation of men, without concert, whom the first federal thunders will coerce into submission—unwilling and boisterous and fretful, to be sure, but still *submissive.* In sober truth, it is hard to conceive the South has any fixed plan at all, or cares to show more than *congressional valor*, in this struggle.

Great, indeed, superlatively great, to every one of its parts, is the value of this federal Union. Glorious is it, too, in all the associations of history, the defenses of liberty, the struggles of patriotism, and the advances of industry and enterprise. We hail the peaceful triumphs of its flag over all the world, and, in the name of American citizen, recognize a title of pride and power from the rising to the setting sun. We were less than men not to have the stars and stripes of a confederacy, which is now, and ever has been, without a parallel. By these stars and stripes we would breast every danger, and count death immortal when thus encountered. There is not a southern man that does not feel and acknowledge this; and in the sanctity of the relation, easy is it to recognize the cause of all the sacrifices they have made, and are making, and those, in all probability, they will continue to make, in the future. Far be it from us to characterize, as reprehensible, any such loyalty and devotion. The Union is the source of our greatness and strength—its dismemberment will probably be of our impotency and ruin; whilst all the world will look on, with amazement, upon the dissolution of a fabric so beautiful and fair in its proportions.

Thus, we should feel and think. Yet there must be an end, somewhere, of concessions. If not a *voluntary* end, a *necessary* one, when everything to be conceded is gone. It becomes the South to determine how far its safety will admit of concession. The stand should be made there. None can mistake the *anti-slavery* growth—it has no resting place. The cry is onward! When was there ever a "step backward" in its history? It will sweep over Mr. Webster as the whirlwind sweeps over the reed. Every concession made to it will induce a more imperious tone—every success will embolden and pave the way for a new and higher triumph. "Will you interpose the constitution?" There is a voice higher than the constitution! Will you make a compromise and hold up its sacred assurances? Majorities rule—numbers have assumed the sway—the edict of Congress goes out upon the land, backed by its fleets and its armies, potent as the nod of the autocrat of Russia and unalterable as the laws of the Medes and the Persians. The path is clear, the end undisputed. The protection of the national flag will be withheld from the slave, in his passage from one port to another in the Union. His arrest in a free State impossible. Slavery will go by the board in the District of Columbia—in the forts and navy-yards. The trade between the States will be prohibited. The final act is not yet, but soon. There is a precedent in the British parliament and the West Indies. *They will use the precedent.* We know the rest.

Where are we? There was an address of the southern members of Congress, admonishing the nation of the perils that encompassed it, and calling upon the South to indulge no ideal dreams of security. Perhaps this address was objectionable in its terms, in its time, and in its tendencies. We enter into no argument. It is a fact, that the "address" was *not* sustained by the *unanimous* southern voice!

There was a call, to meet in convention, at Nashville, to "consider the common danger and provide some measure of security." In our pages, no discussions, in regard to this convention, have been had. We have forborne an opinion. Perhaps such an assembly would add to the general flame, and precipitate the end it was intended to avert. Scylla and Charybdis illustrated. Perhaps violent men would have swayed its councils and plotted anarchy and treason. The example of "Hartford" was paraded in hideous colors. We heard, at last, the President, himself, would put it down. This is improbable, but he has been saved the trouble. The South, itself, has put the convention down. Legislature after legislature gave the cold shoulder. The people avoided the ballot-box, and let the elections go by default. Nashville feared the associations of "Hartford." A few men will meet, perhaps—have met; but to call that a "southern convention," or to say that the South had any active participation in it—preposterous!

The address and the convention are alike *failures*.

A new star arises in the darkness of the hour. Night after night, men gather in Washington, in some out of the way chamber, and venture grave discourse. They will give shape and system to their cause. They will change the issue from Congress to the people. No more speeches, but "articles" and "editorials." Money is collected—prospectuses are issued—editors are appointed, and a newspaper, a *"southern paper"*— a paper without party and without politics—is to emanate from Washington and be scattered over the land, attacking abolitionists in their lair, and confirming doubting and vascilating slaveholders in their fields. The excitement is fine, and money pours into the treasury. Good—but are all agreed now? Were the southern members of Congress *unanimous*? Are the southern people resolved the step is a prudent and wise one? Bye and bye subscriptions will slacken, editors will resign, and new ones, without public confidence, be appointed. The paper grows tamer—ambles—squints at politics—offends the whigs— offends the democrats—changes hands. 1852, advocates a southerner for the presidency. 1856, bought out by the free-soilers, and proclaims John Van Buren as the people's choice! . . .

J. D. B. De Bow

FUGITIVE SLAVES

De Bow's fears for the future of the South were not allayed by the Compromise of 1850. Writing four months after publishing "The Cause of the South," he reasserted the need for southerners to be vigilant and to preserve their rights "without compromise of any sort." What provoked his alarm in this instance was the new fugitive slave law and the hostile reception it received in the North. Part of the Compromise of 1850, the Fugitive Slave Act was designed to ensure that southerners could recover their escaped property wherever found. There was, of course, no problem with enforcement in the South; the act was to ensure the return of slaves who had escaped to the North. The very idea of returning slaves who had successfully escaped was repugnant to many northerners, but several provisions of the law increased northern opposition. Escaped slaves were not guaranteed a jury trial and their case could be decided outside the normal judicial system, thus removing certain safeguards. Furthermore, the commissioner who decided such cases was to be paid ten dollars when the slave was returned and five dollars when he was set free. Finally, federal marshals in enforcing the act could require the assistance of ordinary citizens. These provisions and the capture and return of several slaves provoked considerable opposition in parts of the North, opposition that extended in several cases to rescuing accused fugitives from jail.

It was these acts of opposition to federal law that De Bow found particularly obnoxious. He felt betrayed, for the South had made certain concessions to achieve a compromise, and yet within four months parts of the North rose in opposition to one of the key points of the compromise. If such defiance of the law continued, slave property would be no more secure than it had been before 1850 and the southern concessions would have been for naught. De Bow clearly did not believe that the fugitive slave law would be enforced and, as a result, he began to doubt more seriously than before that the North would long countenance the maintenance of slavery in the South.

Vol. IX (November, 1850), pp. 567–68.

Several of the southern states are about convening in solemn form to deliberate upon the proper course to be pursued by them in reference to the late action of Congress on the various phases of the slave question. We have no doubt that these assemblies will be guided by a high and lofty devotion to the principles which have sustained us in every period of peril; and that their wisdom will not be of that kind which looks only to the day or the hour, but will have reference to the remotest times to come after us. The rights of the south, and the full and unlimited rights of the south under the Constitution, without compromise of any sort, *must be preserved*, or the Union will become a snare rather than a blessing. We are not children to be frightened by "painted devils," nor madmen, to provoke or invite a danger, which may with honor be avoided; but we are men cognizant of our rights and duties, and brave enough to defend the one and just enough to observe the other. In our fellow-citizens we have an abiding trust, that they will, instigated by no passion nor excitement, take a full and impartial view of the whole subject of our slave relations, which are to us country, life, death—everything; and if there be found safety under the late adjustments, safety present and future to the south, they will accede to these adjustments, and rejoice over them. But if, on the contrary, danger still lowers in the horizon, and the "cry of peace, peace," be heard, "where there is no peace," we believe that our countrymen will act as patriots ever should act, doing and daring, and leaving the consequences to God. We await the judgment of the people on issues so momentous, and when that is given, are prepared to stand by it at every hazard.

God grant that the verdict be *peace*, and that some measure shall be devised for the preservation of this glorious Union, in a manner that may cause no section of it to blush. The south has done too much for the Union not to regard it fondly, as the artist who has just elaborated some stupendous piece of mechanism. Yet no son of hers, however moderate in his views, conciliatory and meek beyond all other men upon the face of the earth, can hesitate a moment, that the progress of free-soilism—agrarianism and abolitionism, are creating fearful breakers for us and our institutions ahead, if we have not our eyes wide about us; and that if we sleep for a single moment, the hand of the madman, ever brandishing his torch, will spring the magazine which shall destroy not us only, but whelm friends and foes alike in one wide ruin. It is no time yet, watchman, to cry *"all's well"* upon the wall.

The late fugitive slave law—one of the measures of adjustment— and which the south had to purchase at much expense, though it should never have been necessary at all, contradicts, as is evident enough now, the whole public sentiment of the north. Though one arrest that we know of has been made under it, no one is blind to the fact that *that* arrest was made without much publicity. From circumstances since transpired, there is reason to believe, had the affair been generally known, there would have been resistance, and without doubt *rescue*. If the intelligent people of the north be willing to carry out the law in good faith, there are ignorant or bad men enough to defeat its action, if they will. Already have meetings been held, not of fugitive slaves and free negroes only, but of white men, in many parts, who have solemnly pledged themselves *the runaway shall be protected at every hazard*. It will be found practically impossible for the southerner, we apprehend, even with this law, to reclaim his fugitive slave, as public sentiment will compel the commissioner, it is said, to resign, if rowdyism does not peril the master's life in the attempt. *There is no other country under Heaven where a man can only regain his property when out of his possession, by braving dangers, far beyond those that exist in a state of nature, when each man, with his sword or his rifle, is a law unto himself*! We have no faith in this fugitive slave bill, though we shall be rejoiced, if time prove us in error. . . .

Committee of the Law and Order Party

THE VOICE OF KANSAS—
LET THE SOUTH RESPOND

This appeal for southern aid by the leaders of the proslavery forces in the Kansas territory clearly shows why the latter became known as "Bleeding Kansas." A superb piece of proslavery propaganda and anti-free-soiler atrocity-mongering, the authors' self-styled designation as "the Law and Order Party" was more than a little ironic. The leader of the committee, David R. Atchison, senator from Missouri and later chief of the Atchison, Topeka & Santa Fe Railroad, was also the leader of the "Border Ruffians," bands of proslavery gunmen from neighboring Missouri—called "Pukes" by their free-soil enemies. Atchison, here so righteous in his denunciation of free-soiler violence and so fervent in his support of the rule of law, was well known in Kansas for having expressed his burning desire "to kill every God-damned abolitionist in the district."

Notwithstanding the self-serving nature of this document, some of the accusations leveled in it against the armed bands of free-soilers and their primary financial backers, the Emigrant Aid Societies of New England and New York, were well founded. The account of the "Ossawattamie murder," infamous thereafter as the "Pottawattamie Massacre," is fairly accurate and complete, lacking in only one significant detail: the identity of the leader of the abolitionist band that committed the atrocities with broadswords in the night. He was John Brown, who would, in 1859, seize the federal arsenal at Harper's Ferry.

[One of the Committee (Col. Buford) places the manuscript in our hands, and we commend it to the serious attention of the readers of the Review. The cause is one to which, without loss of a single day, every Southern man should contribute. Alabama, South Carolina, and Georgia, have been lavish in their aid. The loss of Kansas will give to the enemies of Southern institutions a victory more signal and more important than has yet been won over us. To avert the

Vol. XXI (August, 1856), pp. 187–94.

mischief, prompt and concerted action at the South is only needed. Those familiar with the state of affairs in Kansas *know* that it can only be abolitionized by the supineness of the people of this section, whose all is at stake in these contests.]

The undersigned, at a recent meeting of the party, were constituted a committee, charged, among other things, with the publication of this address.

That a state of insurrection and civil war exists among us is abundantly evident: the "law and order party" on the one side, opposed on the other by the abolitionists, sent out and sustained by the Emigrant Aid Societies of the North. A brief review of the points at issue, and their controlling circumstances, may be useful to justify this our appeal for aid.

In territorial politics, the question of free or slave State has swallowed up every other. The abolitionists on the one hand, in accordance with their early teaching, regard slavery as the greatest possible evil; they deem it a monstrous national crime, which their false theories of government impute equally to every portion of the confederacy, and thus believing themselves individually responsible for its existence, they feel bound each to struggle for its overthrow; to such extremes have wicked demagogues stimulated their fanaticism, that their perverted consciences justify any mode of warfare against slaveholders, however much in violation of law, however destructive of property or human life, and however atrociously wicked it may seem to others; nay, many of them already go so far as to oppose all law, religion, property, order, and subordination among men, as subversive of what they are pleased to call man's natural and inherent equality. And with them it is no mere local question of whether slavery shall exist in Kansas or not, but one of far wider significance, a question of whether it shall exist any where in the Union. Kansas they justly regard as the mere outpost in the war now being waged between the antagonistic civilizations of the North and the South; and winning this great outpost and standpoint, they rightly think their march will be open to an easy conquest of the whole field. Hence the extraordinary means the abolition party has adopted to flood Kansas with the most fanatical and lawless portion of northern society; and hence the large sums of money they have expended to surround their brother Missourians with obnoxious and dangerous neighbors.

On the other hand, the pro-slavery element of the "law and order party" in Kansas, looking to the Bible, find slavery ordained of God; they find there, as by our law, slavery made "an inheritance to them and their children forever." Looking to our national census, and to all statistics connected with the African race, and considering, too, their physical, intellectual, and moral natures, we see that slavery is the African's normal and proper state; since, in that state, that race multiplies faster, has more physical comfort, less vice, and more moral and intellectual progress than in any other.

We believe slavery the only school in which the debased son of Ham, by attrition with a higher race, can be refined and elevated; we believe it a trust and guardianship given us of God for the good of both races. Without sugar, cotton, and cheap clothing, can civilization maintain its progress? Can these be supplied without slavery? Nay, in the absence of slave institutions, must not social distinctions supervene among the free to the detriment of republican equality? This is no mere property question, but a great social and political question of races; it is not a question of whether A. or B. shall be owner, but of whether the slave, still having a master, shall still be a working bee, and not an idle drone in the hive; a question of whether the South shall still be a land flowing with milk and honey, or a land of mendicants and vagabonds; a great question of races; a question of whether we shall sink to the level of the freed African, and take him to the embrace of social and political equality, and fraternity; for such is the natural end of abolition progress. Fanaticism must defend its beneficiaries—first, by sending the federal army to protect them, and ultimately by giving them the right to bear arms, vote, testify, make and administer laws—in short, the right to eat out our substance, to pull us down to their level, to taint our blood, and bring us to a degradation from which no time can redeem us. Thus radical and marked the difference in theory between the two parties, and not less so their difference in practice; while we, in good faith, sustain and uphold the laws, the abolitionists on the other hand, in effect, repudiate and set them at defiance; with open disloyalty they assert the invalidity of the territorial laws, while they render our national insignia only the mockery of a hollow respect; indeed, more than once, they have openly resisted the marshal in the service of progress, and, in some places, their organized armed resistance to the territorial laws is so overwhelming that ministers of the law there never attempt the discharge of their official duties; they have repudiated payment of taxes, and have held and published the proceedings of large public meetings in which they resolved to resist, even to blood, the territorial laws, and especially the laws for the collection of the public revenue.

According to testimony under oath lately given before the Congressional Committee, they have secret military organizations for resisting the laws and for carrying out their abolition designs upon Kansas— organizations in which the members are bound by the most solemn oaths to obey their leaders, in all cases, not excepting even murder and treason. It is abundantly proved by eyewitnesses of unquestioned veracity, that at the present time, they have at different points in the territories banded together in actual encampment large numbers of armed men, subsisted and kept together by their aid societies for no other object than to make forays upon the country and drive our friends from their homes. By such banditti the murders near Ossawattamie, on Pottawattamie creek, were committed; declarations by the perpetrators contemporaneous with their foul deeds indubitably show the parentage of these crimes; six victims, whose bodies have been found, fell in that massacre, beside four others missing from the neighborhood, and not yet heard from. Of the six, one was Allen Wilkinson, Esq., a member of the territorial Legislature and postmaster at Shermanville; sick with the measles, for no other offence save that of being a law and order man, he was dragged at midnight from his bed, and from the side of a sick and imploring wife, by a band of abolition assassins, acting as they said in the name of the great northern army; within hearing of the terror stricken wife, with fiendish barbarity, he was flayed alive, his nose and ears were cut off, his scalp torn from his head, and then he was stabbed through the heart. Such is the sworn evidence of his widow lately tendered in Westport before the Congressional Investigating Committee. It revealed on the part of their friends such a picture of savage ferocity that that Committee for once blushed, and even stultified themselves, rather than receive the testimony as competent. They had already received and recorded the evidence of Pardee Butler, testifying that since their appointment as Commissioners he had been tarred and feathered for negro stealing; but this decision they unblushingly reversed, and erased the evidence rather than be forced to put against their friends this horrible tale of the Ossawattamie murder upon the record. Besides Wilkinson, Wm. Sherman and brother, and Mr. Doyle and two sons, were proved to have been murdered at their respective homes on the same night and by the same band; one of the Doyles' also had his fingers and arms cut off before he was finally dispatched. Incredible as these things may seem, they unquestionably happened in Kansas Territory in the latter part of last month; yet what is more incredible, but not less true, is the undeniable fact that these outrages are not, as some pretend, the mere extravagances of a few irresponsible individuals, but on the contrary are justly chargeable to the abolition party, as the legitimate fruit of their party measures and party discipline, and as naturally resulting from the public teachings, advice, and counsel of their chief men and most distinguished leaders.

The outrages above specified were preceded, and up to the present time, have been followed by others of a like character and dictated by a like settled policy on the part of our enemies to harrass and frighten, by their deeds of horror, our friends from their homes in the territory. Undoubtedly this policy (a well settled party system) has dictated the notices lately given in all the disturbed districts by armed marauding bands of abolitionists, to the law and order men of their respective neighborhoods, immediately to leave the country on peril of death. Under such notices our friends about Hickory Point, and on Pottawattamie and Rock creeks have all been driven out of the territory, their stores have been robbed, their cattle driven off, their houses burned, their horses stolen, and in some cases they have been assassinated for daring to return; some too of these outrages have been perpetrated under the very nose of the United States troops, who all the while assert that all is peace and quietness, and that they will afford ample protection, without the necessity of our banding together in armed bodies for mutual defence. Among many others of our friends thus driven away, we might specify the case of Messrs. Hargous, Jones, and Owens, of Hickory Point, whom two hundred United States troops stationed within two miles of their homes have been unable to inspire with a sense of security. Morton Bourn, a most exemplary, quiet and unoffending, man of our party, living within eight miles of Lecompton, the capital of the territory, where quite a number of troops are stationed, was lately driven from his home by a band of twenty-five armed men, who robbed him of all his guns, five saddles, three horses, the blankets from his beds, and over fifty dollars in money. The thieves gave him twenty-four hours to leave with his family, and threatened to kill him if he ever returned, saying, they intended to serve all the pro-slavery men in the neighborhood in the same way. Mr. Bourn is still out of the territory, and though anxious about his property and desirous to return, yet he dares not do so; although as often as he applies, the troops and the Governor assure him that all is quiet, and that he shall have ample protection; but he knows that unless they remain constantly about his house they cannot keep marauders and murderers away. This case is specified not for its peculiar enormity or hardships, but because it is a fair type of a large class of such cases, and because the undersigned have all the details from Mr. Bourn himself, and know them to be strictly true, indeed one of us assisted his family in their flight the day after the robbery.

It is but too evident the troops cannot enable our friends to maintain their ground in any part of the territory where the abolition element is in the ascendant; notwithstanding, we assure our friends that, after the most diligent inquiry and attention to that point, we firmly believe that our party has a well established, decided, and increasing majority of actual settlers in the territory. This majority, however, we do not believe can be maintained unless something be done to give confidence to our friends, where they are few and weak in number. This can only be done by colonizing large settlements together, under one common head with absolute control; let, say from one to three hundred agriculturalists, mechanics, and laborers so settle together in some suitable point, to be indicated by the undersigned, or some other committee charged with the general interests of the party. This can be lawfully, safely, and efficiently done, and by this means law and order can be maintained in the territory, and we say this, too, notwithstanding we are in possession of very convincing evidence to the fact, that the abolitionists of the North intend during the coming month to introduce large numbers of their hired bands to put their treasonable pretended government into operation by force. These measures of mutual defence and future progress, however, require means, and demand aid from our friends abroad. The colonists should be subsisted a reasonable time, and each individual furnished with adequate agricultural or mechanical outfit, so there can be no want of settlers coming and remaining at the points where they are most needed. Funds are required, and for these we call upon our Southern friends—upon all having a common interest—nay, we call on all loving justice and wishing equal rights to each State and section of the Union—we call on the honest free State man, who, sick of the agitation and strife brewed by the abolitionists, desires the restoration of peace and quiet to the country. These can be restored only by restoring to the weaker and attacked section the means of future defence, in restoring the sectional equilibrium disturbed by the measures of 1850. Fanatical aggression cannot be quieted by *giving*, but it may be by *taking away* the power to effect its ends. All fair minds who have looked this question full in the face, know and admit that it is not merely a question of whether Kansas shall be a slave State or not, but a question of whether the entire South shall not become the victim of misguided philanthropy. That man or State is deceived that fondly trusts these fanatics may stop at Kansas. To use that territory as the mere "key to the future"—the mere means of ulterior operations against the whole South—is unquestionably the settled policy of the ultra abolitionists, the head and soul of the aggression, and *whose opinions in the end must leaven and control the whole body*—the whole mass that acts with them.

The most convincing proof (if proofs were needed) of this was recently given before the Congressional Investigating Committee. Judge Mathew Walker, a Wyandott, an unimpeachable witness, and most reliable man, testified before the committee, that before the abolitionists selected Lawrence as their centre of operations, their leader, Gov. Robinson, attempted to get a foothold for them in the Wyandott reserve, near the junction of the Kansas and Missouri rivers; that in his negotiations for that purpose, Robinson finding it necessary to communicate their plans and objects, divulged to Walker (whom he then supposed a sympathiser) that the abolitionists were determined on winning Kansas at any cost; that then having Missouri surrounded on three sides, they would begin their assaults on her; and as fast as one State gave way, attack another, till the whole South was abolitionised. That this revelation was actually made the undersigned have not the slightest doubt; and we are equally confident that in that matter the abolition party was truly represented by Robinson, who has always been their chief man and acknowledged leader in Kansas.

It is widely reported, and generally believed, that the northern abolitionists are now raising large bodies of armed men, under military organization and discipline, to be surreptitiously introduced into the territory for the objects of driving out the peaceable inhabitants, setting the laws at defiance, and overwhelming the law and order party at the decisive election for a Territorial Legislature to come off on the first Monday in October next. It is not impossible they may partially succeed in their aims; their labors to inflame the northern mind are so incessant, their faculty of misrepresentation is so extraordinary—so fatally bent on mischief. Their papers, for instance, show up the Ossawattamie massacre as an outrage of our own; according to their account, "five pro-slavery men were hanging an abolitionist, when his five friends providentially came up and shot them in the act."

All have heard, through the papers, of the killing of Stewart by Cosgrove. The facts were these: Stewart being in Lawrence, when news reached there of an abolitionist having been just killed at Blanton's bridge, in the vicinity, started off with four others toward the California road, all swearing they would kill the first pro-slavery man they met. Lieutenant Cosgrove and Dr. Bratton, two quiet and worthy men of our party, happened to be passing just as Stewart and his men reached the road. The five halted the two at the distance of only five or six paces, and to the astonishment and horror of the weaker party, immediately after halting them began snapping and firing at them. Cosgrove seeing Bratton shot through the arm, fired and killed Stewart, and then with his wounded companion escaped under a shower of bullets. The next day a Lawrence man being taken as a spy and searched, a letter was found on his person to a friend in the North, detailing Stewart's death, in which he says, Stewart was met alone, unarmed, and without cause or excuse shot down by five border ruffians.

Indeed, it was proved before the Investigating Committee that the abolition party had travelling agents in the territory *whose duty it was to gather up, exaggerate, and report for publication,* rumors to the prejudice of the law and order party, and with the view to excite abolitionists to come to the territory; and the witness, Parrot, admitted in his examination that he, as agent, had prepared such a report, and placed it in the hands of Sherman, one of the committee, since his arrival in Kansas. Sherman was then on the committee, and did not deny it.

How can there be other than the most exasperated state of feeling between the two sections? How can civil war be avoided, when honorable committee men countenance such reckless mischief? Look the future in the face like men: if standing up to our rights, to our responsibilities, and to our trust, brings peace and security, so much the better; no other course can effect it. Send us men and means. We must have your help. Appoint agents, responsible, trusty, reliable men for every State, district, and neighborhood, whose sole business shall be to canvass for aid. Did we know suitable persons who would act, we would not hesitate to appoint them all over the country. Let our friends send their names, with details as to character and qualification, and we will duly accredit them. One gentleman, an Alabamian, Alpheus Baker, jr., Esq., of Eufaula, Alabama, whom we all know, who has been here, and has distinguished himself by the zeal, success, and signal ability with which for a while he canvassed the border counties in Missouri for aid, we take the liberty of nominating, without assurance that he will accept. We trust that he may. Friends of the cause must contribute according to their several gifts—we must not meanly abandon our birthright, and, without a struggle, yield to grasping monopoly this fairest Eden of our common domain—this land of flowing brook and fertile plain. Kansas is indeed the garden spot of America, and in every way adapted to Southern institutions; in no other part of the Union is slave labor more productive; and, in the present imperilled state of our civilization, if we do not maintain this outpost, we cannot long defend the citadel. Then rally to the rescue.

Any communications our friends in the South may be pleased to favor the undersigned with, will reach us most safely and certainly, if directed to us, at Westport, Missouri. Funds contributed may be sent to our treasurer, A. G. Boone, Esq., directed to him at the same place.

> David R. Atchison,
> Wm. H. Russell,
> Jos. C. Anderson,
> A. G. Boone,
> B. F. Stringfellow,

June 21st, 1856.   J. Buford.

Edmund Ruffin

CONSEQUENCES OF ABOLITION AGITATION

*Edmund Ruffin (1794–1865) was one of the foremost agricultural re-
formers and secessionists of the antebellum South. A life-long Virginian, Ruffin became a planter after attending William and Mary
College and serving in the army during the War of 1812. During the
1820s and 1830s, he performed experiments on his farms and pushed
for agricultural reform in the Upper South, particularly through his
editorship of the* Farmer's Register. *Like De Bow, he advocated the organization of agricultural societies, opposed protective tariffs, and
supported direct southern trade with Europe. In addition, Ruffin became, particularly in the 1850s, a fervent advocate of southern nationalism and independence. He rejoiced at the formation of the Confederacy in 1861 and later claimed to have fired the first shot on Fort
Sumter. The defeat of the Confederacy in 1865 so demoralized Ruffin
that he committed suicide rather than face life under the Union.*

*Ruffin's essay is an astute analysis of the presidential election of
1856 and the growing power of the newly formed Republican party.
The major contest was between James Buchanan, a Democrat from
Pennsylvania, and John C. Frémont, the explorer and Republican,
with Millard Fillmore running on the American party ticket. In winning 174 electoral votes, Buchanan carried 5 northern states and 14
slave states, while Frémont carried 11 northern states for 114 electoral
votes and Fillmore took Maryland for 8. As Ruffin realized, the North
had the power, if it voted together, to elect a president without a single
southern vote. Ruffin's fears were realized in 1860 when Abraham Lincoln won election without carrying a single slave state. Ruffin's predictions regarding the possibilities of peaceful secession were less accurate than his political forecasts. Like many southerners, he believed
that the North would not fight, though he was, of course, confident of a
southern victory if war came.*

*This article was only the first in a three-part series that Ruffin pre-
pared for* De Bow's Review. *In the subsequent articles, he attacked
northern fanaticism and defended the right of the South to control*

Vol. XXII (June, 1857), pp. 583–93.

traffic on the Mississippi River and, hence, access to the Gulf of Mexico via that waterway.

[The author of the present paper, which will be followed by two or three others on the same subject, is Edmund Ruffin, of Virginia, the distinguished agricultural writer and practical farmer of that State, who is believed to have achieved as much for the development of the South as any citizen within its limits, and who enjoys a reputation for elevation of character, and purity of sentiment, that might well be emulated in any quarter.

With no lack of faith in the ability and disposition of the men at present in control of our National Administration to carry on the Government in strict accordance with the Constitution, and for the protection of the rights of every section, we still see clouds enough in the Northern horizon to evidence that danger is not yet passed, and reasons enough for the South to keep vigilant sentinels at every outpost.

It was this fear of disunion, and the consequent losses of every kind it would bring to the North, that arrested the madness of its fanaticism in almost the very arms of victory; and among those who depicted these dangers, and urged these losses, were the leading statesmen from every section of the Republic— the Hunters, the Wises, Choates, Browns, Cobbs, Floyds, Slidells, Fillmores, Walkers, etc. The danger was averted, but it will not be amiss to burnish up the weapons with which it was won, and to keep them ever ready at our hands in case of emergency. In this spirit, and for these uses, we insert Mr. Ruffin's papers. They are adapted to Northern as well as to Southern minds.]

In the late presidential election a victory has been achieved for the constitutional rights of the Southern States. The Northern abolitionists and their auxiliaries have been repulsed, and their strongest assault has been foiled and defeated for the present time. But though defeated, our enemies are neither weakened nor discouraged. They have seen that with even their present numbers, if more adroitly marshaled and directed, they might have been victorious. And with their growing and certain gains, from the hordes of future ignorant immigrants from Europe, (most of whom will be ready tools for the service), the abolition party will be relatively stronger for the next contest, in the next presidential election.

And what is this victory that the South has gained, and its value? And by what means was it secured?

Even if Maryland had not been an exception to the otherwise unanimous vote of the slaveholding States, their unanimous vote would

have been overpowered by an united vote of the States under abolition
influence, and all of which will be ready hereafter, under different circumstances, to follow the lead of abolition to put down slavery, and to
crush the rights and the vital interests, and the very existence of the
slaveholding States. If the President had been a Southern man, and
even had equal or superior abilities and claims, he could not have been
elected, because he would have failed to obtain the necessary additional aid of Northern votes, adverse in feeling and interest to the
South. Therefore, however much we may rejoice for our victory, it affords but slight ground for triumph, and still less for assurance of
safety, or even of a like temporary defence hereafter, against the renewed and better concerted attack of our enemy. It has been truly said
that this victory has given to the South, not peace, but only a truce
from active hostilities. Let us of the South use this time of truce to
thoroughly examine, understand, and strengthen our position, and so
be prepared to meet and repel every future attack on our constitutional rights and our rightful interests.

It is often asserted, and is admitted by many among ourselves, that
so long as the Northern people and States use only their constitutional
power to assail our interest, the sufferers have no just right to com-
plain, and still less cause to resort for defence to extra-constitutional
remedies. No position is more false or dangerous. The forms or letter
of the Constitution may be so used as to destroy its spirit and substance, and the very benefits that the Constitution was enacted to secure. When one, and the much more powerful section of a country and
people is entirely opposed to and arrayed against the other section, in
interest or principle, or in fanatical sentiment, the constitutional forms
and literal restrictions of the government may be respected, and yet
the weaker section and party may be subjected to the utmost extent of
injustice, wrong, and oppression. The right of representation granted
for Ireland in the British Parliament, even if entirely fair and equal
in proportion to the respective populations of Ireland and England,
would have done nothing to guard the weaker from the oppression of
the stronger country. If the plan had been adopted of allowing to the
former American colonies of England representatives in the English
Parliament, as a measure of defence it would have been futile and contemptible. Our ancestors would have scorned to accept, as protection
for their assailed and threatened rights, a representation in Parliament, even if then greater in proportion to population than that of the
far more populous mother country. And, as the people and the States
of this Confederacy are now divided, by sectional lines, in sentiment,

opinion, and supposed interests, and are standing adversely, and in still growing opposition and hostility, the representatives in Congress of the Southern and weaker section, being a fixed minority in both houses, are no more a safeguard to the section they represent, than would exist if it were deprived by the Constitution of all right of representation. In the lower house of Congress, that result is already seen fully exhibited. In the Senate, the majority of members from the non-slaveholding States is smaller, and, owing to the longer term of service, and slower changes of members in that body, the cause of right and justice has not yet been trodden under foot by the brute force of a fixed and sure majority of voters. But the same end must be reached there also in good time. The Senators of the sixteen non-slaveholding States must hereafter truly represent the opinions of their constituents, as now do their fellow representatives in the lower house, and then both legislative bodies will concur in controlling the fixed minority of the fifteen slaveholding States. And, even without this certain, though slow change of voice of the Senate, and long in advance of its completion, there will be admitted other Senators from four or five new non-slaveholding States, which increase will make the abolition party as irresistible in the Senate, as it is already in the other branch of Congress. When this party is thus supreme, it will, of course, elect a President of the United States of like sentiments. And then, without the need of infringing the letter of a single article of the Constitution, the Southern States, their institutions, property, and all that is dear to them and necessary for their very existence, will be at the mercy of their fanatical and determined enemies. Under these circumstances it would be very easy to destroy, by legislation, all the value and security of the institution of slavery, and so lead to its necessary abolition, and the consequent inevitable ruin of the Southern States and people. But these would not be the only means to reach this end. If more power were needed for more complete victory and success, and the Constitution (even as construed at the North) stood in the way, that instrument, in accordance with its own provisions for amendment, may be altered, and put in any required shape. Owing to the actual much faster settlement and filling up of the non-slaveholding territories, (mainly by foreign immigrants,) and their greater extent, and even if no unjust furtherance were given by Congress, it will not be long before the non-slaveholding States will be so increased as to make three-fourths of the whole number of the members of the Confederacy. Then, the Federal Constitution may be legally altered in any manner by the votes of the Northern States only. Negro slavery may be thus abolished, either directly or indirectly, gradually or immediately. Can any man doubt that the full power and constitutional right, then possessed, will not be exercised as directed by the already existing fanaticism and hostility of the Northern people? The man who can entertain a hope of the contrary course may be, (indeed must be,) too virtuous to know or believe in the violence of fanaticism, or the baseness of party spirit. But he will be a poor judge of human nature, a novice in political history, and altogether unfit to be trusted to guard and protect our rights and liberty.

The present contest between the Northern and Southern States, in regard to negro slavery, has been growing in violence for a long time. It was begun with the iniquitous aggression of attempting to exclude Missouri from the Union as a slaveholding State, and in the successful exaction of the Missouri compromise, in relation to which, both the general enforcement and exceptional violation of its principle by the North, have been exercised and varied, the more to wrong and injure the Southern States. But it has been only since the (falsely so-called) compromise enactments of 1850, that abolition has been hastening towards its object with gigantic strides—and also the South has been partially roused from its sleep of fancied security. Unfortunate it has been, that this sleep had not been effectually shaken off thirty years sooner, and every means then used for defence that was abundantly possessed by the South at that time. If, when the Missouri compromise was submitted to, the proposed restrictions had been resisted by the South at all hazards, there would have been no further trouble about slavery. And if the fanaticism (or, more truly, the unholy grasping for political power) of the North, had then been so unyielding as to permit a separation of the United States, the southern portion would now have double of their present wealth and power—and the Northern States would not have attained half of their present greatness and wealth, which have been built upon the tribute exacted from the South by legislative policy. But no separation would have been produced. If, at the time of the Missouri compromise, the northern members and States had been firmly resisted, they would have drawn back, and the spirit of political abolition would have been crushed in the bud. The sincere abolitionists, who are actuated by what they deem moral and religious considerations, are but the simple and deluded tools of the hypocrites and knaves who are using them to further their own objects of personal ambition and political power.

Without looking even as far as twenty years into the future of the effects of the northern crusade against southern slavery, let us see what might have been the speedy consequences, if the contingency had occurred, which was so near occurring, of an abolitionist being elected President—he being the candidate of the Northern States only, and on the abolition question and principle. It is true that a more conciliatory policy would probably have been adopted at first, because the victorious party would not have risked the driving their conquered opponents to desperate and revolutionary measures of resistance. But it is fair to suppose that a party so fanatical, greedy, and unscrupulous, would have used every means to reach its object, that could be used safely and successfully. Let us, then, see what means, and all claimed as constitutional by the North, could be used by an abolitionist administration of the Government of the United States. If elected, it would have been supported by a majority of the people of the States, and of the House of Representatives. It would not have required much time, or management, (by corruption or other influences,) for the President to have also at his command a majority of the Senate—representing States that were already his supporters. Then, the President, with a majority of both Houses of Congress, might adopt any or all of the following measures, to weaken and destroy the institution of slavery:

The first and greatest measure, is already openly avowed by the abolitionists, and the majority of every Northern State, as their designed policy and plan of action hereafter. This is to admit into the Union no new territories as slaveholding States. This alone, even if nothing else is done, will soon increase the non-slaveholding States to three-fourths of the whole, so that the Constitution can be changed, and slavery abolished. But, in advance of the consummation of this great and effectual measure, various other auxiliary means might be used to hasten the end, as thus:

Each of the largest non-slaveholding States might be divided by act of Congress, so as to make two States of each, and so have four abolition Senators in place of two.

Every office and emolument in the gift of the Federal Government might be bestowed on abolitionists only, and in all the Southern States on Northern abolitionists, until corruption and fear, or despair, should induce conversions, or professions and acts of abolitionism in southerners, as offering the only road to office or gain.

The zealous and active exertions of all these many thousands of Government officials and employees, down to the lowest laborers on any Government work, would be counted on and secured, to operate against the institution of slavery and the interests of slaveholders.

This open, unassailable, and powerful influence, would be added to, and serve to increase a hundred-fold, the existing secret influence and concealed operations of the many abolition agents, male and female, lay and clerical, who, in various ostensible business employments, have long been operating on our slaves, often under the hospitable shelter of our own roofs, and as our pretended friends.

Every military and naval officer hereafter to be appointed, might be an abolitionist, and all now commissioned, and not abolitionists, might be dismissed from service on other pretexts, or otherwise not entrusted with any command.

The various lands held by the Federal Government, for forts, dock-yards, arsenals, light-houses, &c., in the South, and every national ship in Southern waters, would be made places of secure refuge for fugitive and even rebellious slaves, and secure positions for any other incendiary action.

The District of Columbia would be made non-slaveholding by law, and soon in sentiment. It would be openly and entirely what it is already partially, (by Northern and Government influence,) ground, within the Southern and slaveholding territory, where the enemies of the South have the greatest facilities for their most effectual and dangerous action. Already under the protecting shield of the Federal Government and its administration, at a former time, the agents of the abolitionists have been able there to effect more injury to slaveholders, and with more of impunity, than any where even in the abolition States.

The removal of slaves by sales from States where they were in excessive numbers, to other States or new territories where they were most deficient, would (as long threatened) be forbidden by an early law under the complete supremacy of a Northern administration. This alone would prevent the making of any new slaveholding States in the small extent of the remaining territory in which climate does not forbid slavery; while the increase of slaves in the old States, from which they would have no sufficient outlet, would render them an unprofitable burden and a dangerous nuisance to the whites. The condition of the slaves would thereby be made much worse, in regard to their own business, and the institution of slavery would be hastened toward its doomed extinction.

Some of these measures might require that liberal mode of construing the Federal Constitution which is general at the North, and especially on this subject. But even the strict construction of that in-

strument might be conformed to, literally, and yet an abolition administration, in a little more time, can as effectually extinguish the institution of slavery, and the prosperity and existence of the Southern
States as independent communities.

Such might have been, and, to great extent, such would have been
the earlier or later effects and operation of an abolitionists' election to
Presidential office. Such, and with more sure and extended operation,
will be the effects of the future election, by a much stronger constitu-
ency, of a Seward, or some other Northern abolitionist, or of another
Southern renegade and traitor, of more ability than the one who was
lately raised so nearly to the height of his ambition, only to be let fall
and sink in an abyss of contempt.

Will the Southern States wait for the completion of these surely
coming results, or will they take the warning so plainly to be read in
their enemies' acts and avowals, and save themselves from the impending ruin? The fast growing strength of the abolition party, and the
signal success of that party in the next Presidential election, may
cause every Southerner to regret that its candidate was not elected in
the recent contest, when the South was relatively stronger for defence
than it will ever be hereafter.

In such a contingency as we have just now barely escaped, the election of a President by abolition and sectional votes, there will remain
no chance for the slaveholding States to preserve their property and
their political rights, unless by another declaration of independence of,
and separation from, a despotic party, whose wrongful and oppressive
acts have already far exceeded, and threaten to exceed much more in
future, all the acts of actual and prospective oppression of our mother
country, against which our free and patriotic fathers revolted—prefer-
ring a struggle for freedom, with all the certain disasters and incalcula-
ble dangers of a war with a nation of ten-fold their power, to submission to unjust oppression.

We, the sons of those fathers, eulogize and glorify their act of separation from the previous glorious and happy union of these Colonies
with their mother country. Their act of separation and disunion we
deem a noble and patriotic devotion to freedom, worthy of all praise.
We, the children of those fathers, in maudlin love of, and devotion to a
union with those who were formerly deemed our brethren, but now
are our most malignant and dangerous enemies, have submitted to oppression and wrong incalculably greater than ever England inflicted,
or thought of inflicting on her Colonies. And still many of the South

continue to recommend patience, and endurance, and submission, to every wrong and evil, rather than the evil of disunion!

If Fremont had been elected, the consequences would have been so manifestly and highly dangerous to the rights and the safety of the slaveholding States, that they would scarcely have waited to be completely shackled, and powerless for defence, before they would have seceded or separated from the victorious and hostile States of the present Confederacy. It is proposed here to inquire what would have been the results of such separation, and especially to consider the question of the danger of war, which it is so generally believed would necessarily ensue between the separated communities, and the results of any war.

If the necessity was manifest to the people of the South, there would be no obstacle to their deliberate action, and no probability of opposition by the Northern States, nor by the then remaining fragment or shadow of the Federal Government of the previous Confederacy. The legislatures of the offended States would call conventions, and these conventions would declare their separation and independence, and, by subsequent acts, make a new confederation. If all the fifteen slaveholding States united in this action, they would be far stronger, at home and for repelling invasion, than would be the Northern States as invaders. Even if but five or six adjacent Southern States alone seceded, no remaining power of the Federal Government, or of all the Northern States, could conquer or coerce the seceders.

But, contrary as is the opinion to that which generally prevails, I maintain that such act of secession would offer no inducement or occasion for war; and that there would be no war, as the immediate or direct result of secession or separation.

The malignant hostility of feeling that is even now entertained by the abolition party, and perhaps by a majority of the Northern people, towards those of the South, is not here overlooked or underrated. If they could, by merely willing it, they would ruin us, even while united with them under one government—and still more readily if we were separated. If the mere wish of abolitionists could effect the destruction of our system of negro slavery, even by the destruction of the entire white population of the South, I would fear that consummation would not be a remote event. But *to will* and *to do* are very different things. And even Northern fanaticism, (to say nothing of Northern self-interest and avarice,) would be glad to forego these gratifications, if they were to be purchased only at the cost, to the North, of hundreds of millions of dollars, and hundreds of thousands of lives. Even if admitting, what is so arrogantly and falsely claimed by the North, that it could conquer and desolate the South, any such victory would be scarcely less ruinous to the conquerors than the conquered.

But there would be no such war, and no movement towards it—because war could not subserve or advance any interest of the North. It is unnecessary to maintain the like proposition in regard to the South, inasmuch as it is universally admitted. No one, of either side, has ever asserted, or supposed, that the South would assail, or make war upon the North, in consequence of their separation. Whether this peaceful disposition is ascribed to a greater sense of justice, or to the weakness, or the timidity of the Southern people, all concur in the belief that the South would desire peace, and would avoid war, unless necessary for defence. Then, passing by this contingency, deemed impossible by all parties, we have only to examine the supposed inducements for offensive war and attack by the North on the South.

"But," it is urged by many among ourselves, "even if the North refrained from making war, still it would retain the direction of the Federal Government, and exercise its rights and remaining power—and also hold possession of the Seat of Government, the army and navy, the fortifications, and the public lands. How could the public property be divided peaceably? And, without resorting to war to enforce our right to a fair share, would not all be necessarily lost to the South? I answer that, even if admitting all these premises, still there would be no need, and no advantage, for the South to seek justice through war—and no benefit to the North would be gained by withholding our just dues, either by war, or in peace. Nations, in modern days, do not often go to war, and never in advance of negotiation, to recover debts, or to settle pecuniary accounts and obligations. There are other means, in many cases, to induce, and even constrain nations to render justice; and, luckily, in our case, the means available for the South would be of the most cogent influence. These will presently be discussed. But first, I will say, that even if the result of separation to the South was, indeed, the loss of every value named above, (except the few spots of Southern ground, heretofore ceded to the Federal Government, and which would necessarily go finally to the States in which they were situated,) the South would still gain, by separation, much more than it would lose by this great spoliation. As to the army, it would, probably, like the present Federal Government, cease to exist, as soon as the Union was dissolved. The public buildings, fortifications, and navy, and all other material values held by the Government of the Union, and the annual revenue, have been mainly (at least two-thirds of the whole) acquired from the contributions of the Southern States—while the larger proportion of all disbursements of Government, and pecuniary bounties and benefits of all kinds, have as regularly gone to enrich the Northern people. If, then, this regular and very unequal apportionment of the burdens and bounties of Government were stopped, as it would be by separation, the South would gain more in retaining, for the future, its own resources for its own benefit, than the actual pecuniary value to the South, in the Union, of its share of all the present national property. And these retained resources, within a few years, would amount to a fund sufficient to more than replace the forfeited values of army, navy, and all the public edifices. As to the public lands, vast as is their extent, and enormous their value, the South has already been virtually deprived of them. No Southerner can safely remove with his slaves to any new territory. They were thus unjustly and illegally shut out from the rich fields and richer mines of California, by the action of the North and the Federal Government. The conquest of Mexico was achieved by men and money supplied (as of all other contributions) in much the larger proportion by the Southern States. By their much larger expenditure of both blood and treasure, California and New Mexico were acquired. Yet the people of the South, as slaveholders, were excluded from the territory; and Southern men have had no access to or benefit from the rich mines and lands of California, that were not as open to, and equally enjoyed by, the semi-barbarians of China and the Sandwich Islands, the former convicts of Australia, and the needy and desperate outcasts, invited by these benefits, from every foreign land. A like virtual exclusion of slaveholders will be effected hereafter as to every other new territory. And even from the sales of public lands, and through the Federal treasury, it can scarcely be expected that any considerable benefit will hereafter accrue to the South, or serve to lessen its greater share of the burden of taxation. For nearly all the resources from the public lands have, in latter years, been squandered by Congress, and mainly to benefit Northern men and Northern interests. So little revenue from the public lands will hereafter reach the treasury, that the amount will probably not more than defray the great expenses of the land surveys and sales, and the much greater expenses incurred in governing and protecting the new territories. If the gigantic and much urged and favorite scheme of either one or three railroads to the Pacific ocean should be adopted by Congress, (as seems probable,) all the net proceeds of future sales of public lands, and that amount doubled by additional grants from other funds of the Government, will not suffice to construct and to keep in use this work of unexampled magnitude and unheard of national folly or extravagance.

According to these views, the entire loss to the South, and at once, of all the public property, would be no greater damage than the former and present and prospective unjust apportionment of contributions and disbursements. Still, this is no reason why, in the event of separation, the South should submit to lose its just rights in the common public property. And in this respect, the independent South would be more able to obtain redress for spoliation, or to save something out of the general wreck of the present public property, than will be possible if remaining united to and governed by the stronger Northern States. As a separate power, wronged by spoliation, the South would negotiate for redress, calmly and peaceably. And, if necessary, until redress was obtained and an acceptable composition made, a prohibition should be enacted against the introduction or sale of all Northern commodities, and the employment of any Northern vessels in the Southern States. These peaceful means would soon produce satisfactory redress or, otherwise, ample retaliation for any amount of previous injury. These measures would be far more potent than war, and yet entirely peaceful, and such as could not be opposed or countervailed, or even complained of by the Northern States.

Joseph A. Turner

WHAT ARE WE TO DO?

Joseph Addison Turner (1826–68) was a planter, writer, and publisher in Putnam County, Georgia. The son of a Georgia planter and legislator, Turner received a college education, read law, and was admitted to the bar. He began writing in his teens, and his first publishing venture was Turner's Magazine, *launched when he was twenty-one. His own journal did not survive its third issue, but Turner's literary inclinations found expression in his contributions to* De Bow's Review, *the* Southern Literary Messenger, *and other antebellum periodicals. Turner in the prewar years also practiced law and ran his plantation. In 1860 he began another new journal,* The Plantation, *devoted to a defense of slavery, but like his previous venture, its life was brief. Turner is today best known for publishing* The Countryman, *a weekly newspaper published from March, 1862, to June, 1865, that has the distinction of having been the only paper published on a plantation. He is also given credit for having been the mentor of Joel Chandler Harris.*

Turner's essay reflects the fears and suspicions of southerners following Harper's Ferry. Not only had John Brown and his motley band invaded the South, captured federal property, however briefly, and attempted, though unsuccessfully, to incite a slave revolt, Brown had also left plans and maps that seemed to indicate that a vast and violent conspiracy was underway to attack slavery in the South. Southerners took little comfort from the obvious absurdity of Brown's schemes and the failure of his invasion and, for months afterward, saw every fire, every murder, and every disobedient slave as the harbinger of slave revolt. Though Turner obviously shared the southern paranoia, he could think of no more effective remedy than urging his countrymen to "patronize home industry."

Turner's call to support southern industry and commerce would have been familiar to readers of De Bow's Review *where it was a favorite theme of the editor. Turner recited the usual complaints that southerners were more inclined to buy from the North and even to vacation in the North than to spend their money in the South. Turner pleaded with his fellow southerners to boycott the North completely and to*

Vol. XXIX (July, 1860), pp. 70–77.

build southern industry as the best ways to force the North to abandon abolitionism. Had the South strengthened her industrial capability beginning in the 1840s, Turner's arguments might have had more force. But the mere fact of their repetition in 1860 indicates that the South had not heeded the earlier warnings and that Turner's hopes were in vain. In addition, by the summer of 1860, secessionist sentiment had reached such a pitch in many quarters that these measures seemed wholly inadequate to the crisis. Only after secession and the start of war would the South be thrown completely on its own resources, and only then would it discover how inadequately its "home industry" was prepared.

In view of the Harper's Ferry affair, and the developments which have followed it, a question of very grave import presents itself to the Southern people. What steps are we to take to effectually resist the spirit and the attacks—the actual invasions, of Northern abolitionism? It is our intention to discuss this question calmly and dispassionately, with all the reason, all the judgment, which nature has allowed us.

Probably, in presenting our views, we shall wound the feelings of some Northern men who may chance to read this article. Possibly, even some of our Southern brethren may become offended at the reflections in which we shall indulge. If we offend a true friend of the South, from whatever section he may come, it will always be to us a source of regret, and we tender apologies in advance.

But, to those who are our determined and uncompromising enemies, who are ready to apply the torch of the incendiary to every house in the sunny South, who are all the time compassing heaven and earth to obtain the means by which to kindle a servile war, and to raise the assassin's knife against every Southern breast—to such we have no word of explanation, farther than to say, that in meting out justice even to you, we would let reason and not passion direct.

In order to protect ourselves and our families, we must first find out who are they that threaten us. What we are called on to guard against now—this very day, this very hour—is the host of abolition emissaries who are scattered abroad throughout the length and breadth of our land, who permeate the whole of Southern society, who occupy our places of trust and emolument. To alter a little the language used by the Abbé Dubois to Morton Devereaux—"The plagues of Egypt are come again—only, instead of Egyptian frogs in our chambers, we have the still more troublesome guests—Yankee adventurers."

Let us examine, for a moment, the plans of these people. Take the following extracts from Thatcher's letter to John Brown: "While at Brownsville, Texas, I addressed a letter to the schoolteacher, Mr. H. He says there is no avocation in which a man can do so much good for our cause as that of school-teaching. . . . He says that we must send our more well-qualified men to the South as school teachers, and work them in everywhere. . . . I sometimes register one name, and then another, to suit the circumstances, as I travel about. Sometimes I pass for a travelling preacher, and at others for a New-Orleans merchant, looking at the crops and talking of speculations in cotton, etc. *Southern people are easily gulled.*"

What a text for comment is afforded by the above passages! They help to prove that many of the Yankees who come among us as teachers, preachers, merchants, drummers, pedlers, etc., are base, bitter, malignant abolitionists, bearing in their hearts a determined and implacable hatred toward us and our institutions; always seeking every opportunity to instil the poison of their opinions into the minds of our slaves; working silently, slowly, insidiously, but constantly, till, as they imagine, they shall be able to kindle a fire of servile insurrection, which shall wrap in flames and involve in ruin the whole broad expanse of our now happy and prosperous Southern country. It is folly—it is wilful blindness—any longer to shut our eyes to the fact. The danger is in our very midst, and we must meet it now. Whence come all the fires of which we read? Is it at all probable that so many, in so short a time, are the result of accident? Some time during the past winter, four towns in Georgia—Atlanta, Griffin, Newnan, and Warrenton—were on fire at the same hour, and while these were burning, the flames were sweeping over the capital of our sister State, Alabama. On our plantations, we hear of the burning of smoke-houses and gin-houses. It has almost come to the pass described by John Randolph, when he said: "The night-bell never tolls for fire in Richmond, that the mother does not hug her infant more closely to her bosom." So, now, the planter's wife never sees the flames shooting up from her husband's burning out-houses, that she does not involuntarily shudder at the thought of impending calamities.

On the maps found in John Brown's possession, were certain marks, designating certain localities all over the Southern country—in Georgia as well as other States. What mean these marks? Nothing? They at least indicate that abolition emissaries have been on these spots, and have cast an evil eye—an eye of blighting—upon these portions of our beloved soil. These our homesteads have been polluted by the tread of vile murderers, who have, doubtless, partaken of our hospitality, while they were taking counsel how they might assassinate us.

No one, we think, who reads the journals of the day, and considers the matter carefully, can doubt that our enemies have been, and are, among us, scouring the whole country and scheming our destruction, and that these enemies are, in many instances, teachers, preachers, drummers, pedlers, etc. What are we to do in the premises? That all Northern men who come here are abolitionists, or unworthy of confidence, we do not pretend to assert; but that many of them are, we do believe and affirm. Which of them are wolves in sheep's clothing, which of them are worthy of hanging as traitors, we cannot often determine. At the same time, could we *know* who of them are friends worthy of confidence and countenance, nothing would delight us more than to take such *gentlemen* by the hand, and welcome them to our houses with all the warmth of hospitality for which Southerners are celebrated.

But it is impossible for us to make the distinction, and we must, in some way, reach the guilty, if we would maintain our position, if we would retain our property, if we would preserve our homes from desolation.

It may be right and proper to call conventions, to consider the propriety of dissolving the Union. It may be right and proper for our State legislatures to take such action as may seem best—to pass such laws as are calculated to protect us. But it is well known, by those who have been observant on this point, that legislative enactments accomplish nothing, unless they are in accordance with public sentiment. In public opinion, and in the action, the every-day practice of the Southern people, lies the evil; and a change in these respects must prove the remedy, if we ever find one. *We must do something, independently of conventions and legislatures.* There is a course to be pursued, which alone, whether the Union shall be severed or not, will insure our safety.

We must patronize home industry. At the risk of doing injustice to a great many Northern men who come among us, merely with the view of improving their private fortunes, and who attend strictly to their own business, leaving us to manage ours, we must set our faces against immigration into our borders from the North. Especially must we frown upon all *itinerants* and *stragglers* from beyond Mason and Dixon's line. Let us, in no instance, trade with a fresh Yankee merchant, employ a raw Yankee teacher, or mechanic, or *in any manner tolerate* a Yankee pedler. Let them all be placed under a ban. Let them all be watched, and let them know that they are objects of suspicion.

Of course, there are those among us who have been here so long, who have become so identified with us in feelings, whose lot, for weal or woe, is so completely cast with us, that we feel confident they entertain our sentiments, and would join us in action. Especially is this the case with those who are holding negro property. We would not, for our right arm, be guilty of the gross injustice of expatriating such men. Every one must acknowledge, however, that the class described is not a very large one, and that some even of those who have long resided in our midst, and have long enjoyed our confidence and esteem, are hostile to us and our institutions, and would, if an opportunity should present itself, strike us a mortal blow.

Southerners should also content themselves within their own limits. Let those who have money to spend distribute it, in future, among their own friends and neighbors. For those who have the means and the leisure to make a tour every summer, and to whom this annual excursion has become a sort of necessity, there are numberless places of interest in our own borders. It is useless to enumerate them, for it is hardly to be believed that any intelligent Southerner is ignorant concerning them.

Every one who wishes to become travelled, must, of course, go North. It seems hard to say that a tourist must avoid any particular part of the world. It does appear, though, that at this time Southerners should not go North. Admit, however, that under ordinary circumstances, an occasional visit to the land of black-republicanism is admissible; still, what are we to think of those who, after the late developments, will continue to go every summer to expend their means among those who treat them with apparent respect, merely for the sake of their money? Under the present aspect of affairs, it would be best, even for those of us who have never made a Northern tour, to defer it, until we have taught the people who are striving to injure us a lesson.

At one time, during the summer of last year, it was estimated that there were two hundred thousand strangers in the city of New-York, one half of whom were probably Southerners. Say, then, there were one hundred thousand of these. A Northern guide-book sets down the ordinary expenses of a traveller at five dollars per day, and we hardly believe that, in such matter, a Yankee would over-calculate. People who have seen tourists from the Southern States, scattering their money among newsboys, posters, cabmen, and the whole host of street blood-suckers who can scent a Southern man from afar, and who recognize immediately one who will bear bleeding—to say nothing of gambling shops and *other* shops—those who have witnessed all this, will readily believe that most of the class of travellers spoken of spend twice five dollars per day. Including everything, I am confident that they do spend, on an average, ten dollars per day, while at the North. But we will not speculate. Multiply the number in New-York—one hundred thousand—by five, and we have the snug little sum of a half million dollars, expended by Southerners, in that city alone, each day during their stay in it.

But New-York contained certainly not more than one third of the travellers from the South who were at that time flaunting their purses and displaying their folly at the North. Three half millions make a million and a half, and all this in one day. Suppose each one of the tourists spoken of goes on at this rate for thirty days—and this is a very low estimate—then the fact stands that Southern travellers, as such, leave in the Northern states, in the course of one summer, forty-five millions of dollars. If, as we think, every one who has had an opportunity of observing believes, these travellers spend ten dollars a day instead of five, they leave ninety millions in the North in the course of one tour.

In another place we may enlarge on the idea that we support a large class of Northern people—that they subsist upon the contributions we make to them. At present we will simply remark, that the above is merely a calculation of what Southern people, in their capacity as travellers, spend when they go North; and that the millions and millions expended by us besides in the purchase of Northern goods and manufactures, in attending Northern schools and colleges, & c., are not taken into the account. How many of us are compelled to cry *peccavi*, either in the matter of throwing away our money in Northern towns, or supporting straggling Yankees here at the South, instead of helping our own people! How many of us are guilty of the gross inconsistency of *professing to be ultra Southern Rights' men,* and still *invariably employing Northern teachers and mechanics, in preference to Southerners!*

On the other hand, it cannot be denied that many of our Southern teachers and mechanics are so idle and worthless that they allow these shrewd, hard-working Yankees, to slip in before them and bear off the palm on all occasions. It is the great fault of Southern people that they are *too proud to work*! and very often they perform the work that they do in such a manner as to show that they are half ashamed of it. They forget that whatever is worth doing at all, is worth doing well. But we do not wish to censure one class more than another, and have not done so. The truth is, all of us—employers and employees, capitalists and laborers, rich and poor, producers and consumers—all have acted wrong, and it remains for us to reform.

It is now pretty generally conceded at the South, that strict non-intercourse is the only thing which will bring the Northern people to their senses. We cannot convince them that it is right for us to hold slaves, but we can cease to furnish them with the means of making war upon us and our institutions. We can touch their pocket-nerves, and send a thrill—like an electric shock—through the whole of their money-loving systems. It has always been in our power to do this, and their well-informed men have long known it; but they have never, till lately, believed there was any danger that we would exercise the power we possessed. At this time they *do* believe that we are ready to seal the fountains which supply to them their very life-blood, and great is the consternation exhibited among the sensible, thinking, far-seeing portion of the community. Witness the Union meetings held in their large cities, which are proper enough, and the speeches made at which are sensible and patriotic enough; but what a pity all these things were not done before. Why have not the conservative men at the North frowned down the infamous black-republican party, when they knew so well how disastrous to the country would be the effect of the increase of this party in numbers and power? Why have they allowed theories which they knew to be subversive of the Constitution, to be promulgated till they have acquired such potency for the accomplishment of evil? They have permitted a party built upon treasonable principles to originate, grow, and flourish in their midst, and have forborne to crush it, till now it overrides almost everything at the North. True, some of the men who hold these meetings and make these speeches are convinced that we are at last thoroughly aroused, and they are sincere in their efforts to turn the tide of opinion which prevails with their fellow-citizens. But these are comparatively few in number. We are credibly informed that many avowed and open black-republicans signed the calls for these Union meetings. The body of the Northern people still believe, that all the writings, talking, resolutions, and proceedings of all kinds, following upon the Harper's Ferry affair, are so much "sound and fury," so much gas and vaporing, which will soon subside; and that we will always continue to pay them tribute. No amount of argument will convince them. Nothing but action will open their eyes, and we ought to think of nothing else. Further appeals to them, in the way of argument, will stamp us as spiritless cravens.

Let us stop the supplies we have been so long furnishing them, and watch the result. Let them fail to get the millions which we have been pouring into their coffers every year. Let us refuse to purchase goods from them for one twelve months, and see their ships idle, their manufactories stopped, their mercantile houses closed. Hotel servants, cabmen, sailors, mechanics, drummers, will be thrown out of employment. The mob of vile abolitionists who throng round the ballot-box at their elections, and vote down or drive away by brute force the conservative men who approach the polls, will be parading the streets and raising riots for bread; and there will ensue at the North ruin and desolation, which will bear some faint resemblance to that which they have been so long endeavoring to prepare for us.

There has been, during the present spring, a falling off of orders from the South for Northern goods. The purchasers from our section have been fewer than formerly. An intelligent merchant remarked, in my hearing, that it was thought in New-York the falling off from Georgia, Alabama, Mississippi, and perhaps one or two other States, was about forty per cent. It has been greatest in Alabama. All honor to her for it! In the purchases of the slaveholding States at large, from the North at large, the decrease cannot be estimated at more than twenty-five per cent. Yet, see what an effect can be produced by even this slight cause. See the strikes in the shoe-manufacturing towns of New-England. The contest which the Republicans declare is constantly going on between capital and labor, has broken out at their own doors, in spite of their cunning efforts to keep it away from them, by opening it at the South. And this is not the first time this has been the case. These strikes and riots are not new to the Northern people. Twenty-five per cent falling off in the amount of Southern orders for Northern goods has opened the eyes of the fanatical Natick and Lynn shoemakers and other mechanics—the class which has been studiously kept in ignorance of the true relations between North and South, by abolition teachers. A mechanic among them has had the good sense and manhood to make a speech in which he told the black-republican leaders, that they had abundance of sympathy for the black man, but would contribute nothing for the relief of a suffering white mechanic.

What a glorious effort, then, would be produced by complete non-intercourse for one year!

But, if we expect to live independently of the North, we must go to work and supply ourselves with those things for which we now look almost exclusively to her. It is true, that even now, we are supplied with *all* the necessaries of life, and many of its luxuries; but by taking the proper steps we could command everything. There are manufacto-ries to be built; foundries and machine-shops to be put in operation; importing houses established; ships launched. Our wearing apparel, our agricultural implements, our engines, both of peace and war, must be made at home. True, there are some manufactories among us; some foundries and machine shops. The Central Railroad, for instance, turns out some beautiful locomotives, said to be equal to any in the world; and this example is worthy of imitation by all companies that possess capital. (Per parenthesis, what a *great* pity that the surplus funds of the Central Railroad and Banking Company, which were de-voted to the purchase of steamers to ply between Savannah and New-York, were not applied to the establishment of a line between Savan-nah and Liverpool, or better still, between Savannah and Marseilles!) But the articles we purchase from Southern manufactories are as a drop in the sea compared with those we obtain from the North.

A bill was up before the last Georgia legislature, having for its ob-ject the establishment of a foundry for the manufacture of firearms within our own borders. Our legislators passed a bill authorizing the appointment of commissioners to *inquire* about the matter, and, also, Georgia passed a bill appropriating seventy-five thousand dollars for the *purchase* of firearms. And from whom will they be purchased? From the North—thus continuing the old process of furnishing our en-emies with money—sinews of war. Will Southerners—will Georgians—never grow wise? Will their eyes forever remain sealed?

No people on earth—none that ever lived—are, or were, so well supplied by nature with all the resources from which may be derived wealth, power, and prosperity, as those of the slaveholding section of the United States. Georgia alone has, within herself, every element of a great and powerful empire. We possess, or may possess, not merely the necessaries of life, but most of the luxuries demanded by the high-est grade of civilization. All we lack is the determination to make our-selves independent of the world. We of the cotton-growing States of

America alone, with insignificant exceptions, produce the staple which has become a necessity to the *genus homo*, while other countries produce nothing essential to our comfort and convenience, with which we cannot supply ourselves, by properly-directed skill and labor, within our own borders.

If we take the proper steps, we can, in a very short time, place ourselves in a condition to declare non-intercourse, without experiencing any inconvenience from it. Direct trade with Europe, *now*, would afford us facilities for disposing of our cotton, and obtaining the luxuries to which we have become accustomed. If we should cease, now, to trade with the North, there would probably result pecuniary embarrassment, but it would be temporary and slight. We need not curtail our cotton crop. Suppose we had not a single ship, how long would it be before whole fleets, with agents for European manufacturers on board, would be riding at anchor in all our Southern harbors, freighting themselves with cotton, to be carried across the broad Atlantic, wrought into countless fabrics, and shipped back to the Yankees, even, who would be compelled to have them?

The price of cotton might go down, but it is not at all probable that it would remain so long enough to produce any serious results. The Northern manufactories might be idle, but would we not, by selling direct to Europeans, save the commissions at present taken out of our profits by Northern exporters? Because Northern manufactories were stopped, would Northern people cease to be purchasers of manufactured cotton goods? Would the number of consumers in the world be reduced? Besides, it must be borne in mind, that Southern manufactories would, all this while, be springing up, and becoming bidders for cotton almost at our gin-houses.

Grant, however, for the sake of argument, that we would be subjected to inconvenience, pecuniary embarrassments, want of luxuries, or even great hardships, by cutting loose from the North—has all patriotism, all devotion to the country, passed away from our land? Are the sons of our fathers so degenerate that they can sacrifice nothing to the cause of independence? Are they willing, for the sake of present ease and luxury, to remain in a state of virtual vassalage? Is the spirit of the Habershams, the McIntoshes, the Tatnalls, the Troups, and all that gallant host, whose name is legion, extinct? It is not dead, but sleepeth; and the day will come when the North, with all her radicalism, her agrarianism, her infidelity, and all the wild theories and speculations which render her people insecure, restless, and unhappy, will be left to her own devices, while the South, the favorite of nature and of fortune, cleared of the clogs which now impede her progress, will proudly take her position as peer among the most powerful of earth's nations.

A Mississippian

OUR COUNTRY—ITS HOPES AND FEARS

In writing this paean to the possibilities of a southern nation, this anonymous resident of Mississippi employed several ideas common in antebellum America. Americans from all sections tended to see the United States as the hope of the world. They believed that the new government under the Constitution had inaugurated a new era for mankind. By 1860, as this writer suggested, southerners had come to see the North as the betrayer of the revolutionary traditions that the South still upheld. They believed that America could still become a nation "in which every element of moral and political success may be found," but now that nation could only be an independent South, rather than the United States.

To support the idea of an independent South, this author also relied on the argument that Negro slavery made possible white liberties. This idea received some support in the antebellum South and has recently been revived by historians such as Edmund Morgan, in American Slavery, American Freedom: The Ordeal of Colonial Virginia *(1975). Though historians like Morgan have tried to explain the paradox of slaveholding advocates of liberty like Thomas Jefferson and the other Virginia revolutionists, this Mississippi writer clearly saw nothing to explain. For him it was simply a given that liberty belonged only to the superior class and thus to whites. He shared the view of many aristocratic southerners that menial work was degrading and fit only for slaves and that true liberty could safely be enjoyed only by the upper classes. To extend full liberties, and especially the vote, beyond a small circle, as was happening in the mid-nineteenth century, courted disaster. If slavery was necessary to maintain white freedom, as this author clearly believed, then that was simply another good reason to retain the peculiar institution. This idea did not die with slavery. White supremicists continued to argue that white freedom could only be maintained by denying it to other supposedly inferior groups.*

Vol. XXIX (July, 1860), pp. 83–86.

A crisis impends the North. Her vagaries in moral and political philosophy are hastening her to anarchy, and if the present pernicious tendency of her passions is not checked, tumultuous chaos, or despotic rule, will close her career as a republic; and the weeping and wailing which she now wastes for the misfortunes of others, will be wanted to soothe the anguish of her own bleeding heart. How truly may it be said of that people: that "those whom the gods would destroy they first make mad." While these stars in the North furnish this reading to the view of the horoscope, let us turn to the constellation in the South, and try to read our own fortune.

We assume that the signs of the times are portentous of change, which may lead to revolution and the establishment of a Southern confederacy. If this event awaits us, it is our right and duty to consider what may be its effects upon us.

Should an independent government be established by the Southern States, an era will be inaugurated, the like of which the world has not before seen. In its institutions will be blended a series of harmonious principles, the effect of which will be to create a nation, in which every element of moral and political success may be found. Other times have seen other nations struggling nobly for the attainment of political grandeur and prosperity; and, too, with no little success. Gallant and classic Greece, proud and imperious Rome, and the perished nations of the East, trod far and high the paths of glory; they led but to the grave. The fountains of their youth dried up, and a waste of magnificent and astonishing ruins alone attest the powers that have so utterly passed away. The conquerors and the conquered have alike perished. Why is it that such has been the history of the past? Is it a law of nature; or was it the effect of their imperfect systems? We trust the latter; and if it was, it becomes us well to ponder the cause, and if it may be, to guide our bark from the rock upon which they split.

The South would be peculiarly circumstanced, and advantages would be hers such as no nation has heretofore been favored with. Many causes will contribute to our happiness, prosperity, and perpetuity as a nation, but pre-eminently in view stand two peculiar features: the one a pure religion; the other a perfect labor system. In religious sentiment the South stands a unit. Its pure doctrines are linked inseparably, though not by legal constraint, with the laws of the land. Religious persecution and intolerance are unknown among us. No 'isms and schisms rankle in our hearts. Christ is acknowledged as the common bond of union. Mormonism, freeloveism, and higherlawism, with their teachings so sensual in morals and so dangerous in politics, disturb not our harmony. What human tongue can tell the effect of such moral unity! No other nation ever possessed it. Let us, then, cherish the uncommon boon and confess its blessings! With this view of things eternal, let us turn to matters temporal.

Labor is the basis of all temporal prosperity. We mean wisely applied, it is the source, the very substratum, of every individual or national necessary, comfort, and luxury; it is the source of all wealth; it creates the commerce whose ships float upon every sea; it feeds, and clothes, and arms, and pays, the hosts of war; and on its strong shoulders, and by its rough hands, do gentle art and science live. The South appreciates the gift; she understands her duties, and knows the blessings she enjoys from her labor system, and those who would trifle with this, her sacred right, will arouse a spirit at which, in pallid horror, they will recoil!

Our laborers engaged in the production of the most important articles of human use, with a constancy unaffected by any political commotions, pursuing steadily their respective vocations, furnish at all times, whether in peace or in war, the wants of man, and the necessities of government.

Our labor in its application is peculiar; unlike a large portion of the labor of all other countries, its time and energies are not wasted in the creation of luxuries, in the expensive and often useless projects of art, and perhaps more important in its effects than all other things combined; in filling the ranks of armies, where so much labor is lost, and a precise corresponding ratio of consumption increased. The freemen of the South will fight their country's battles; the slaves will till the fields, and feed, and clothe, and pay her armies.

Where slavery exists, liberty is implied to belong to a superior class. In the South that liberty is the sole heritage of the white race. Unlike society, as it is found anywhere else, the whites are morally and politically equal. Who ever saw a Southern born man in menial service? Many live and die poor, but none are so poor and humble whose pride would not revolt at the thought of rendering degrading service. Here the happy negro is the servant; at the North, and elsewhere, the free-born Caucasian, bowed by poverty, and humbled by inexorable necessity, gladly wears the gilded collar of his lordly master. Can such a man be depended on when his country claims him, as a voter, to declare for the right, and if need be with a soldier's pride and courage to maintain it? We think not! The voters and soldiers of every country, save of the South, number very largely of this class.

The institution of slavery rests upon so many strong and deep foundations that it seems useless on our part to defend it and madness in our enemies to assail it; but, silence and apathy with us may be deemed pusillanimity, and we should be as ready to prove our patriotism by expostulation and argument, as in the bloody crucible of battle; and while it seems that proclaiming our rights and proving the justice of our cause have little or no effect upon our adversaries, yet truth is enunciated, and the great Southern heart will be prepared to respond to its mandates. It is not, however, intended in this essay to encumber the valuable pages of the Review with argument upon argument, and fact upon fact, to sustain our cause. Patriotic and able writers and statesmen have done this. The curtains have been drawn and a flood of light dazzles us with the glorious future of the South, and the mask has been torn from the black demon of the North, and his hideous deformities exposed. But comparisons are said to be odious, and doubtless they are when our adversaries wither beneath their truthful force. We will only add, that if disunion must follow the present agitation, and we are forced to become a separate people, in beautiful equipoise, it seems a Southern republic may well resemble a self-adjusting machine; religion and art, pure democracy and the noble aristocracy of virtue and honor and chivalry, peace and war, freedom and slavery, each responsive to the rest, would vibrate in harmonious unity to the perpetuity of our beloved and favored land.

We hasten to a close. It really seems as if Providence does not intend, however much we may desire it, that the present union of States is to continue. We seem designed for a separate people. Climate, pursuits, tastes, and even our common language, all proclaim that the laws of nature will direct and control the will and laws [of] man. If we cannot control circumstances, however, we may modify their effects. How can this be done and the Union maintained? By the love of the patriot for his whole country we humbly believe there is but one chance for hope. That hope rests upon the Constitution, so amended as to enable the South to protect herself. The South should demand the power to protect herself; if it is granted, the Union is, perhaps, safe for ages to come; if our petition for justice is rejected, it ought not and will not survive the present generation. Demand what Mr. Calhoun asked: a dual presidency, each section electing a chief magistrate, either president clothed with the power to veto legislation affecting his own section; or give to the Senate from the two sections this power. The latter, an idea advanced by a late governor, we incline to, as it does not multiply the co-ordinate powers of government, makes no new officer necessary, is more simple, more economical, and will be more acceptable, as it does not, apparently, change the fundamental principles of our system.

None can deny the aphorism that, "Self-preservation is the first law of nature." We have the right to protect ourselves; we should demand the power. If the poor boon of justice is denied us, the craven only is content with less, and the South is thus to be vanquished; Southern chivalry is a vagary of the wildest romance; Southern manhood a dream; and the truth and justice of our cause will be our damning shame.

J. D. B. De Bow

PRESIDENTIAL CANDIDATES AND ASPIRANTS

De Bow's Review *was not a journal of political opinion, and De Bow seldom commented on political events unless they were directly concerned with commerce and industry or the interests of the South. By the late 1850s, the fate of the South seemed deeply entwined in national politics, and De Bow and his writers turned increasing attention to political matters. The criterion for publication, as this piece on presidential aspirants in 1860 makes clear, was the interests and rights of the South, particularly with regard to slavery. Drawing on the biographical sketches published by John Savage in* Our Living Representative Men, *De Bow analyzed the fitness of the various candidates to be president. The major qualification in his eyes was adherence to the true interests of the South. Thus, De Bow praised men like Jefferson Davis and Alexander H. Stephens and condemned Republicans like Abraham Lincoln and William H. Seward. De Bow's critical faculties, however, were not entirely blinded by his allegiance to the southern cause. Though he attacked Lincoln as a "low and vulgar partisan of John Brown," he conceded that Seward, however repugnant his ideas, was perhaps the "ablest man" in the Senate.*

The selections printed below include fourteen of the thirty-five potential candidates De Bow discussed. The sketches of the more obscure candidates, or those for whom De Bow merely printed biographical details without commentary, have been omitted.

A work has recently been published, entitled *"Our Living Representative Men,"* the aim of which is to furnish biographical sketches of all the persons who have been prominently named of late, in connection with the Presidency, and from whom it was supposed that choice would be made by the several nominating conventions.

It is stated, in the memoirs of Mr. Calhoun, that, while a student at Yale College, it was remarked of him, by the venerable Dr. Dwight, "he had talents enough to qualify him, eventually, for the office of Pres-

Vol. XXIX (July, 1860), pp. 92–103.

ident of the United States." This, however, it must be remembered, was in the older and better days of the republic, when talents and worth were supposed to have something to do with such aspirations, and, in general, did exercise a controlling influence in the nominating and electoral colleges.

The doctrine of availability, which is now the substitute for qualification, is so large and liberal in its application, that almost anybody can be added to the list of presidential aspirants, without the slightest shock to the public taste, should some accident of residence, or the want of positive antecedents, seem to be in his favor. The volume before us gives evidence of this fact, for here are, at least, thirty-four names presented, of whom it might be said, with truth, not more than one third are entitled, by virtue of any intrinsic merit, to be thought of, for one moment, in such connection.

Still, it is the part of the philosopher to take the age as he finds it, and having a few hours of leisure before us, we shall skim over this galaxy of representative men, and see what their biographer has felt at liberty to say of them. In doing this, we follow the alphabetical order of the book.

John Bell, of Tennessee, is a man of remarkably pure private character, and a high-toned and accomplished gentleman. He is, perhaps, the ablest man in his State, and there are few abler in the country. As the candidate of the Union party for the Presidency, he may get some support. Like Mr. Fillmore, in 1856, we trust that he will be able to draw off, at the North, sufficient Republican or doubtful votes to break the backbone, in some of the States, of the dominant organization. Mr. Bell's antecedents are not such as would make him the choice of any slaveholding State, considering the concessions he has been willing to make upon a subject of the most vital importance to them. He was born in 1797, graduated at the Nashville University, served in the State legislature and in Congress; took lead as a whig, opposed General Jackson, was Secretary of War under President Harrison, and has since served, until very recently, and with high honor, in the Senate of the United States.

John C. Breckinridge, of Kentucky, has been one of the most fortunate of American statesmen, being elevated to the highest posts at the earliest age, with the least effort, and almost without solicitation. We should not be at all surprised to find his lucky star still in the ascendant at the approaching Baltimore convention. He is a man of fine person and address, and varied accomplishments. When a member of the

House of Representatives, it was occasionally our fortune to meet him, and we were always charmed with the interview. He was elected to the Vice-Presidency at the age of thirty-five, after serving with honor in Congress, and being tendered the Spanish mission, which, on account of the health of his family, he declined. It cannot be questioned that Mr. Breckinridge has still a glorious future before him, and that he is eminently worthy of it. He was recently elected to the United States Senate for six years. . . .

John J. Crittenden, of Kentucky. We made the acquaintance of Mr. Crittenden in 1849, when on a visit to Frankfort, at which time he occupied the executive chair of the State. We found him a frank, unpretending, yet exceedingly agreeable gentleman, full of anecdote and humor, and a most excellent type of the Western politician. A breakfast with him, ex-Governor Ousley, and some others, at the house of Captain Russell, in the vicinity of Frankfort, afforded us rare enjoyment, and left its impress upon our mind in a manner not easily to be erased. Wit and anecdote abounded, and we have often sighed for just such another breakfast. Mr. Crittenden was born in 1786, and is at present the oldest Senator in Congress, having entered the other House more than forty years ago. He has done military service, is a most eminent lawyer, has been twice Attorney-General of the United States, and is thought one of the first orators of the country. On a recent occasion he said of himself in the Senate:

"If my education is defective, it is on account of some defect in me, and not in the school. The gentleman is a young man, and a young Senator. I hope and wish for him a long life of public usefulness. He may have learned much more than I have done; and, if so, it only shows the superiority of his capacity to learn, for I am sure he has not been in a better school. Sir, *this* is the school in which I was taught. I took lessons here when this was a very great body indeed. I will make no comparisons of what it is now, or was then, or at any other time; but I learned from your Clays and your Websters, your Calhouns and your Prestons, your Bentons and your Wrights, and such men. I am a scholar, I know, not likely to do much credit to the school in which I was taught; for it is of very little consequence to the world, or to the public, whether I have learned well or ill. It will soon be of no importance to this country or to anybody." . . .

Jefferson Davis, of Mississippi, is our warm personal friend, and therefore we are perhaps not the best qualified to speak of him. During his recent Secretaryship of War, our intercourse was frequent and pleasant. He was a most laborious and conscientious officer, and signalized his administration in every way. He was the very soul of President Pierce's cabinet, and found only in Marcy a rival, who had the advantage of him, however, in political experience and knowledge of party complications. Cushing had then his hands full amid the law-books, and Campbell was lost in the confusion of post-office routes and contracts; amiable and indefatigable Dobbin was immolating himself among his commodores and post-captains; Guthrie, like another Cerberus, was watching the money-bags, while McClelland, one of the best and truest men in the world, untiring and conscientious, was at work night and day bringing into shape the heterogeneous and discordant materials of the Home office. (We send him, to his retired shades of Michigan, this tribute of our affectionate remembrance, and the warmest desires of our heart for his prosperity and promotion.) Davis, during all this time, was felt everywhere, and well deserved the eminent trust reposed in him by the Executive. He was born in 1808, in Kentucky, but removed in childhood to the territory of Mississippi. In 1828 he graduated in the Military Academy at West Point, and did service for several years in the Indian wars of the West. Resigning from the army, he commenced his political career in 1844, as elector on the Polk and Dallas ticket, and was soon after sent to Congress. When the Mexican war broke out, the Mississippi regiment unanimously elected him colonel, and on many a well-contested field he won laurels which will never perish while history shall record the glorious events of that period. His repulse of the Mexican cavalry was effected under circumstances which are said to be without a parallel in history, except in one of the desperate conflicts of the Crimea. He was elected to the United States Senate in 1851, and again in 1857, where his career has been as distinguished as in the field or the cabinet, and where, by his bold, able, and unfaltering advocacy of the rights of the South, he has made himself eminently entitled to her plaudits and her honors wherever they can be bestowed. Though we regretted his language on some occasions when addressing the people of New-England, we make allowance for the *requirements of courtesy and the proper return of civilities*. Few of us can be proof against personal kindness!

Stephen A. Douglas, of Illinois, notwithstanding the large space he has filled in the public eye, and the distinguished honors accorded him, is still a young man, having been born in 1813, in the State of Vermont. He has risen by the force of native talent, having had a very defective early education, and a training in the workshop more than in schools.

His first appearance in the West was in 1833, where, having prepared himself for the bar, he soon won success and promotion, and was very nearly being elected to Congress just as he had reached the constitutional age. He was afterward elected judge, and served several years with distinguished honor in the lower house of Congress. For the last thirteen years he has been one of the most prominent members of the United States Senate—his recent election involving one of the most severe, protracted, and exhausting contests upon record, against the whole force of the Republican party, then having the popular majority in the State. The great theatres in which the extraordinary abilities of Mr. Douglas have been exhibited were the passage of the compromise measures of 1850, the Kansas-Nebraska bill of 1854, and the Lecompton constitution of 1858. In the last instance he appears in conflict with his party, having taken positions which are regarded by nearly the entire Southern portion of it as in conflict with his previous views, and at war with what we hold to be the sacred rights of the South in the territories, under the Constitution, as interpreted by the Supreme Court. This unfortunate position of Mr. Douglas has, up to the present time, interfered seriously with his prospects for the Presidency, and may yet cause his defeat in the nominating convention, or in an election before the people, or in the House. But a few years ago, there was no statesman who had more of the confidence of the South and none for whom she would have voted with more alacrity, as the proceedings of the Cincinnati convention evinced. It would have been well for the country, perhaps, had he been nominated at Cincinnati when sound, in place of the present incumbent, who is responsible for most of the difficulties that have subsequently occurred. Mr. Douglas, in the right of his first wife, is a slaveholder. He is a man of free and popular manners, an eloquent debater, and is possessed of herculean energies. His private fortune, which was recently large, is said to have sunk very low, and his health is much undermined.

Edward Everett, of Massachusetts, was recently nominated, by what is called the Union party, to the second place in the Republic. He was born in 1794, and after a very complete education, acquired in the best schools and colleges of our own country and Europe, became a student of theology, and then a Unitarian preacher and professor in Harvard College. For some time he edited the *North American Review,* and gave evidence of the highest literary attainments and scholarship. He served many years in the National House of Representatives, was Governor of Massachusetts, President of Harvard College,

Minister to England, Secretary of State under Mr. Fillmore, and United States Senator. Mr. Webster's celebrated letter to Hulseman is claimed to have been written by Everett, and his own despatch upon Cuba is a celebrated state paper. Of late, Mr. Everett's fine oratorial powers have been exercised in aid of the Mount Vernon Association, but his papers in the *New-York Ledger*, in the same connection, are utterly unworthy of his name. He signed the address complimenting Charles Sumner for his infamous speech, several years ago, and denouncing Brooks: which, to us, is a sin so dark, however explained, as to cover every supposed or admitted merit. . . .

John Charles Fremont, of California. We had hoped that the public career of Fremont was closed; but up he comes again, only, however, as a ghost in the play. A Southern man by birth, he was willing to sacrifice his section to the interests of an unscrupulous party, who rewarded him with the candidacy for the Presidency in 1856. Better for his fame had he been content with the world-wide interest which his explorations and adventures in the Western wilds had given him.

James H. Hammond, of South Carolina, was born in 1807. He has served in the State legislature, in Congress, and as governor, followed by a retirement of many years, relieved by contributions, occasionally, to agricultural journals, by addresses before literary and other associations, &c. His letter to Clarkson, in defence of the institution and policy of the South, exhausted the subject, and has never been surpassed or even equalled. It placed him in the highest rank, and was the means, more than anything else, of his being relieved from his unpopularity in the State; and eventually drawn forth to occupy the distinguished post of United States Senator. Here the public expectation has not been gratified; and it is claimed, we think justly, that in several of his speeches he did more to strengthen the hands of the North than those of his own section. We say this with regret, but at the same time add, that recently his position has been more satisfactory.

Sam Houston, of Texas. He was born in 1793, and, from swaying the destinies of the republic of Texas, came into the Senate of the United States, after annexation, and has ever since aspired to the seat of Jackson. At the present moment he is governor of Texas, but has announced himself as an independent candidate for the Presidency, upon the platform of the Constitution. In this we think he will be left high and dry upon the quicksands. Personally, we have enjoyed the society of Gen. Houston, and though we give him credit for many high and excellent qualities, he has been too recreant to the Southern interests, for us to wish him success, politically, in any arena.

Andrew Johnson, of Tennessee: born in 1809. Rising from the humble position of a tailor, taught the alphabet by his wife, this agrarian and socialist, as our friend Fitzhugh calls him, and we think justly, considering his whole career, has risen to Congressman, governor, and now United States Senator. His "free-farm" offerings fix him in the class of the demagogues, and his notions upon the rights of labor, slavery, &c., leaving him with few adherents at the South. He advocated the annexation of Texas, upon the ground that "it would prove to be the gateway out of which the sable sons of Africa are to pass from bondage to freedom."

Abraham Lincoln, of Illinois. It is creditable to the author of the work before us, that the claims of his personage were regarded to be too contemptible to entitle him to a place in the "Gallery." Still, by virtue of intrigue and perfidy in some quarters, he finds himself at the head of the Republican hosts, having distanced in the race all of his abler and more respectable competitors, including even the astute, profound, and, in some respect, virtuous Seward. Just Heaven, upon what times have we fallen, when the seat of Washington is in danger of being occupied by this low and vulgar partisan of John Brown! Should that day arrive, is there not virtue enough in our people to break the ignoble shackles, and proclaim themselves free? We believe it, and in that faith only find consolation. . . .

William H. Seward, of New-York. This author of the "higher law" and "irrepressible conflict," though, it seems, after all, he but borrowed the latter idea from Lincoln, was born in 1801, and after serving his State in various capacities, and winning high reputation as a lawyer, took his seat in the Senate in 1849, and is there to this day. He is one of the most dangerous, and is by far the ablest of the Republican, or what is much the same thing, abolition leaders. His policy is rule or ruin, and the aim and drift of his doctrines have been well shown on several occasions by our correspondent, "Python." Mr. Seward, though not technically an orator, has issued from the Senate chamber "speeches," which, for ability, polish, and effect, must be regarded masterly. We incline to think him the ablest man in that body. His remarks upon the death of our poor friend, Rusk, of Texas, which we heard, were regarded as one of the best specimens of "mortuary eloquence" ever listened to in the Senate.

John Slidell, of Louisiana, is stated in the book to have been born in 1793, but he must be several years older. As a politician he is practised and wily, and has long exercised controlling power in the State. His abilities are moderate, but his zeal and energies unflagging. Never having been of his political *family*, our judgment of him may be open to cavil. It puzzles us beyond measure to ascertain the grounds upon which he is named for the Presidency. He has the great merit of being true to his friends. He was born in New-York; was sent minister to Mexico, by Mr. Polk, and was beaten on one occasion for the Senate by the Hon. P. Soule. He was supposed at one time to exercise a controlling influence over Mr. Buchanan. It may be creditable to him if that influence has ceased. We shall be glad to ascertain the fact.

Alexander H. Stephens, of Georgia: born in 1812. He is in person frail and of most remarkable physique, but intellectually a giant. His first appearance in Congress was in 1843, from which time, until his retirement a year or two ago, he was, by all odds, the foremost man in the House of Representatives, and a leader in most of the great discussions that took place. John Mitchell said of him:

"At Crawfordville, a village on one of the piney ridges of Georgia, in an unpretending and somewhat desolate-looking house (desolate-looking it may well be, for no fair and kindly house-mother ever made it shine and smile), dwells one of the choicest and rarest spirits of our hemisphere. Youthful and almost boyish-looking, yet stricken by mortal malady—one who has made a 'covenant with death,' yet whose veins are full of the most genial life—with the cold hand clutching at his vitals, yet with a laugh clear and ringing as the marriage-bell; his thin face is of deathly hue, yet the dark eyes are blazing lamps. If you are his friend, he is gentle and affectionate as a girl; if his enemy, he will have great pleasure in standing opposite to you at any distance that may be arranged—in which case you had better look sharp, for he is cool as an oyster. A student and true philosopher, a laborious and conscientious legislator, a powerful lawyer, and a zealous cultivator of grapes (Catawba and Scuppernong), for he has faith in the virtues of wine—a generous friend and patron of humble merit, for the which many prayers and blessings arise every evening on his behalf—a noble imaginative orator, yet not of the Charles Phillips school of 'Irish oratory' by any means, his taste being too highly educated for that species of rigmarole—such is Alexander H. Stephens." . . .

VI

THE CIVIL WAR AND RECONSTRUCTION

Having beaten the drums for southern nationalism and secession for a decade or more, De Bow and his contributors welcomed the creation of the southern Confederacy in 1861 and did not flinch from the prospect of war with the North. De Bow simply shifted his emphasis from extolling the strengths and resources of the South and protecting her rights within the Union to celebrating the creation of a new southern nation and working to ensure its success. Like most southern enterprises between 1861 and 1865, *De Bow's Review* suffered during the decline of the Confederacy, but when he was able to publish, De Bow continued to compile information and statistics on the southern economy while adding significant new analyses of the Confederacy and the Civil War. Financial problems, shortages of supplies, and the advance of Union armies forced De Bow to suspend publication in August, 1862, except for one issue in August, 1864. In those first two years of the war, however, the *Review's* contributors reflected the initial optimism of the South in embarking on the creation of a new nation and a growing awareness that the challenges were greater than anyone had anticipated. By mid-1862, when De Bow suspended publication, his authors had begun to sense that the outcome might be a Union victory and, consequently, they redoubled their efforts to spur southerners to greater sacrifices on behalf of their cause.

The anonymous author of "What of the Confederacy," writing after the early Confederate victories of 1861, saw those events as the first act of "a great drama" sure to be enacted with "the most brilliant success." Confident that the southern armies were vastly superior to the "miserable hirelings of Lincoln" and that "independence is certain and secure," this essayist was so bold as to lay down southern conditions for peace. A Confederate peace would have left the South in full control of her economy, with access to the Pacific, protection of slavery, free contact with other nations, and the restriction of government to native southerners. In an argument familiar to readers of *De Bow's Review*, he asserted that the South was richly blessed with natural resources and that the Confederates had only to exploit those resources to achieve greatness as a nation. This early in the war, the predictions of the secessionists seemed likely to be fulfilled: independence would be achieved, and the Confederacy would join the ranks of the major nations of the world.

More sober advocates of the Confederacy, however, recognized the precariousness of the new nation's position, in spite of the initial victories. George Fitzhugh, better known for his defense of slavery, was also a careful analyst of the military position of the Confederacy. Although the South had considerable economic and industrial potential, the immediately available resources were considerably more limited. That suggested to Fitzhugh the virtues of a defensive strategy to wear down the northern armies and, with them, northern resolve. Fitzhugh found grounds for hope in the Trent Affair, which initially held the promise of British involvement, and in the discontent in northern areas that bordered on the Confederacy. Though counseling the wisdom of a defensive strategy, he urged southern leaders to take the offensive at the proper time and to strike North, where, in Fitzhugh's vision, many would welcome the Confederates as "deliverers from Yankee bondage, rather than as conquerers." It is doubtful that the Confederate invasions of the North in 1862 and 1863 were inspired by Fitzhugh, and, in any case, the defeats sustained by Robert E. Lee's troops, especially at Gettysburg, only weakened the southern cause.

If Fitzhugh placed his faith in the southern armies and their generally defensive strategy, other southerners thought that the Confederacy had an equally potent weapon in King Cotton. There had been much speculation in the South before the war that English and French reliance on southern cotton would ensure their support in any conflict with the North. Joseph Gribble, in "The Cotton Interest," reaffirmed his faith in the potency of the cotton weapon, but he also expressed his disappointment that cotton had not yet brought European aid. Gribble tried to explain the delay and to reassure his readers—and no doubt himself—that "'King Cotton' holds the balance of power, and will make his influence felt." But, to the surprise of the South, other factors—including new sources of supply, British trade with the North, and her reluctance to get entangled in a civil war—reduced the power of the Confederacy's main economic weapon, and Gribble's expectations would remain unfulfilled at the end of the war.

The war began to go badly for the South in 1862, though many Confederates remained confident that their armies could resist the northern onslaught and preserve southern independence. Still, the Union victories at Shiloh and New Orleans in April were worrisome, as were George McClellan's preparations to attack Richmond. James H. Thornwell wrote "Our Danger and Our Duty" to inspire the Confederate soldiers to greater sacrifices in their defense of their nation and their homes. When De Bow published it in his *Review*, he undoubtedly hoped it would have the same effect on his readers. Thornwell urged southerners to "look the danger in the face" and to resolve "that we will not be conquered." That resolve would help sustain the Confederacy for another three years, but it could not hide the growing strength of the North and the severe deficiencies of the South. The South's growing problems were reflected in *De Bow's Review*; Thornwell's piece appeared in the last issue before the suspension that lasted, with one brief exception, until 1866.

De Bow revived his *Review* in January, 1866, with the hope that it would contribute to the restoration of the southern economy and to the rebuilding of the Union. Reluctantly accepting the outcome of the war, he was determined to see that southern interests were protected in the reunited Union. As before the war, the revived *Review* emphasized trade, manufacturing, and agriculture, but two new concerns appeared: the reconstruction policy of the North, and the development of a new system of race relations to replace slavery and maintain white supremacy.

Southerners were well aware of their vulnerability in 1866, but they were determined to retain as much of their prewar world as possible. That goal could more easily be accomplished if the North instituted a lenient program of reconstruction. When De Bow took up the question of reconstruction policy in October, 1866, much of the South remained unreconstructed, Johnson's policies were under severe attack in Congress, and the Radical Republicans had begun to place reconstruction under Congressional control. Although De Bow assured all who would listen that the South was entirely subservient to the Union, the actions of his fellow southerners belied those claims. Continued harassment of the freed slaves, the enactment of the black codes, and the refusal of some southern states to repudiate secession fully spoke more forcefully than De Bow's soothing words and convinced Congress to institute a harsher program of reconstruction. De Bow's address to radical leaders reveals that, for him, the past was of less concern than the future, particularly a solution to the "negro question." Just as slavery had driven North and South to war, the status of the freed slave was the key issue separating the two sections during reconstruction.

The two selections by George Fitzhugh examine this problem of how to treat the freed slave. Fitzhugh had been one of the staunchest defenders of slavery and of white supremacy, and his two essays, written over a year's time, reveal how greatly things had changed in the postwar South and yet how greatly they had remained the same. Though he took a position with the much-hated Freedmen's Bureau, Fitzhugh had not changed his views on black inferiority. He saw the Freedmen's Bureau as only a temporary expedient to sustain the now-masterless blacks until the South regained full management of the Negroes. By 1867, Fitzhugh was appalled by the Radical proposals, particularly the enfranchisement of the former slaves. Such policies, he believed, would lead to the ruin of the South and of the Negro, who was totally incapable of playing an equal role in society. Their methods might differ but Fitzhugh's goal and that of most southerners remained the same—the reestablishment of white domination. Reconstruction forestalled that event for some years, but, as Fitzhugh predicted, the North eventually tired of protecting black rights and by the mid-1870s had largely acceded to the southern view of race relations.

Just as the problems of war had prevented *De Bow's Review* from serving as a window into the Confederacy after 1862, so De Bow's death in 1867 led to the rapid decline of the journal and deprived us of valuable views of the South under reconstruction. In the issues that were published in these troubled years, we can follow the changing fortunes of the South in war and reconstruction as De Bow's contributors found cause for both hope and despair. Throughout, they remained unreconstructed southerners, committed to the cause of the South and particularly to some system of racial subordination.

WHAT OF THE CONFEDERACY—THE PRESENT AND THE FUTURE?

This piece, written in late 1861, reflects the early optimism about the Confederate cause. Coming after the Confederate army under P. G. T. Beauregard had turned back the Union forces at Bull Run in July, and before the costly battles of 1862, the anonymous author had reason to be hopeful about the future. In the first flush of war, he could celebrate the "sublime spectacle" of a united South combining to resist the aggressor. Like many southerners, he believed that the martial spirit of the South had made possible an army superior to the "miserable hirelings" on whom Lincoln was forced to rely. Confident of the ultimate success of the South, the author went so far as to lay down the peace terms he could accept: payment for damages, half the Union navy, sole control of all commercial and diplomatic relations, and control of the lower Missouri and Mississippi rivers. Even had the first demands not posed nearly insurmountable obstacles to peace, Lincoln could not have accepted the last: free access to the Gulf of Mexico via the Mississippi had been one of the cardinal tenets of midwestern commerce and politics since the early nineteenth century.

This writer's policies for the Confederacy would have been familiar to readers of De Bow's Review. *The protection of slavery, the construction of a railroad to the Pacific, the encouragement of commerce (particularly with Europe), the sovereignty of the separate states, and the problems of the tariff for southern industry and commerce had been favorite themes of De Bow throughout the 1850s. So too, the potential greatness of southern material resources, agricultural production, and industrial development had long been celebrated in the pages of the* Review. *Given time, the Confederacy might well have turned those resources to good use, but what this author could not foresee was that the course of the war would deny the nascent nation the necessary time.*

Vol. XXXI (December, 1861), pp. 516–23.

["Beyond this eventful drama [the dissolution of the Union], should we be ruthlessly driven to its enactment, we would not now attempt to penetrate the view that closes from our vision the scenes behind it. But from the hope that is within us, and the faith which we have in things unseen, we may be permitted to predict that, when that curtain shall be raised, a fair, brighter future will present itself—opening to our view, in all its varied scenes, the progressive grandeur and brilliant destiny of the greatest power and happiest people on earth."—*Report on Federal Relations, Senate of La.,* 1858.]

The curtain has been raised, the great drama is being enacted with the most brilliant success, and the grand panoramic views are looming up in the distance, clothed in splendid and gorgeous drapery.

The first of the prominent pictures before us is that which exhibits the entire union, harmony and co-operation of the people of the Confederate States, in the great work of achieving their independence; and in this co-operation one of the most sublime spectacles the world has ever beheld presents itself. We allude to that which exhibits, at this moment, thousands and thousands of our noble women, throughout the Confederacy, of all ages and conditions, who are daily assembling together in cities, towns, villages, neighborhoods and cottages, busily plying the needle in preparing comfortable winter clothing, knitting woolen socks, and providing other necessaries and delicacies for the comfort of the brave men of our army—and all this without expense or burthen to the Government. Even as we write we can see, through the open windows of that splendid masonic temple in my own village, crowds of ladies earnestly and busily engaged in this holy work of patriotism and love.

Our soldiers are not like the miserable hirelings of Lincoln—the scum of infamy and degradation—hunted up from the dens, sewers, and filthy prisons of the North, with the low vandalism of foreign importations, picked up wherever they can be found. Yet such are the creatures our brave soldiers have to meet. Our armies are composed of men who have not volunteered for pay, nor for food and clothing; and it is even doubtful whether a solitary man can be found among them, now numbering over three hundred thousand strong, who would not be willing to serve the Government, cheerfully, if required, to the end of the war, being fed and clothed, without any pay. This is saying much; but if the test was necessary to be applied, there would surely be but few exceptions. Thus we find in our armies, even amidst all the privations incident thereto, the same spirit of union and devotion to the

Confederacy which actuates those whom they have left at home; indeed, with a large number of our people, there is being manifested a general feeling to give over the effort to make money or accumulate property during the continuance of this war. Such, then, is the state of the Confederacy; with a people so united, so determined, and so cooperating, there can be no such thing as fail, and the armies of such a people are unconquerable. Its independence is certain and secure.

What About the Peace?

There will be peace; will they offer to negotiate for it? We can propose no terms, but we must demand them. We desire nothing that is not right and just, and we will submit to nothing that is wrong. But no peace will be acceptable to the people that permits the Lincoln Government to hold its abolition orgies, and fulminate its vile edicts upon slave territory. Much valuable property of our citizens has been destroyed, or stolen and carried off by the invaders; this should be accounted for, and paid. The Yankees were shrewd enough to cheat us out of the navy, but we must have half of the war vessels and naval armaments in possession of the North at the commencement of this war. We should enter into no commercial alliances or complications with them, but assume the entire control of our commercial policy and regulations with them, to be modified at our own discretion and pleasure. They have closed against us all navigation and trade on the Mississippi, Missouri and other rivers; it is our right and duty hereafter so to regulate the navigation on these streams as may best conform to our own interests. It cannot be expected that we should permit the free navigation of the lower Mississippi to the West after they have closed it against us above, without the most stringent regulations. There is no palliation in the pretence that the blockade above was a war measure; they cannot so claim it unless we had been acknowledged as belligerents, and hence they have forfeited all right to free navigation as a peace measure. If, then, permission be given to the free States of the West to navigate the lower Mississippi, it should be under such restrictions as to afford a commensurate revenue to the Confederacy, and the strictest rules regulating the ingress and egress of passengers, officers and hands. The West is learning us how to do without her, and we thank her for it; we shall have but little need of her produce, as we shall soon have a plentiful supply among our own people. An absolute separation from all the North, with the sole and independent control of all regulations with its people, are our best and safest terms of peace.

Extent of the Confederacy

We have conquered an outlet to the Pacific which must be maintained, though we can desire no dominion on the Pacific coast but such as may be sufficient to secure the terminus to our great Pacific railroad through Texas and Arizona. Toward the north and east, the Maryland and Pennsylvania line, including Delaware, is our true landmark. Kansas, on the other side, must be conquered and confiscated to pay for the negroes stolen from us, abolitionism expelled from its borders, and transformed into a slave State of the Confederacy. Perhaps, after we have done with Lincoln, this arrangement may be very acceptable to a majority in Kansas, without force. We will have no desire to disturb Mexico so long as she conducts herself peaceably toward us, and, as a neighbor, maintains good faith in her dealings with us. Central America must remain as a future consideration; and, instead of the acquisition of Cuba, she has become our *friendly ally*, identified with us in interests and institutions, and, so long as she continues to hold slaves, connected with us by the closest ties.

Political Policy of the Confederacy

Throughout the bounds of the Confederacy, with its acquisitions wherever they may be, there must be established and protected the institution of domestic slavery. The world must be convinced of the great truth that slavery in the African race, as now held and regulated in the Confederacy, is in accordance with the model of divine government, and in fulfillment of the great purposes of God in his creative designs. That it is an unqualified blessing to the negro who is enslaved, and has unquestionably proven itself to be a general blessing to mankind by supplying with remunerative labor, bread and raiment, year after year, to millions and millions of laboring whites, more enslaved than our slaves, and actually saving them from nakedness and starvation.

With all nations and all Governments and people, the policy of the Confederacy should be Peace. We can have no interest or desire of interfering with the affairs of other Governments and people, or of entering into entangling alliances with them, while at the same time we ought not to permit, with impunity, any interference with the rights and concerns of our own. A free and friendly interchange of reciprocal commercial and national intercourse with all Governments and peoples, with such guards as may be absolutely necessary for our own welfare, safety and security, seem to cover the main ground desirable as to our foreign policy. The very name of peace brings order and harmony in its train.

> "Though source and soul of social life;
> Beneath whose calm, inspiring influence
> Science his view enlarges, Art refines,
> And swelling commerce opens all her ports."

We are decidedly in favor, and would earnestly urge a remodeling of the constitution after the Confederacy shall fully embrace the slave States, as it is but just that all these States should participate in the formation of their Government. The grand idea of their distinctive sovereignty must be preserved as the palladium of the people's liberties. There are very strong objections to some of the features of the present constitution, which it is needless now to refer to. It must be remembered that we have not to fix up a constitution for a day or a year, but we have devolving upon us the great and responsible duty of devising and instituting a form of government looking to a long future, or at least for securing the liberty and welfare of our posterity. How important, then, at the outset, to avoid all false steps that may tend to abridge popular government, or place the ruling power in the hands of a few.

There is no principle, we think, which should hold a more prominent and lasting position in the government of the Confederacy than that which is embraced in the idea that *Southerners should rule the South*. All resident citizens, whether of native or *foreign* birth, at the time of the adoption of this principle by the Government, to be held as *Southerners*, with all the political rights and privileges as if native-born. With the exception of these, and after that time, no more votes should be allowed, and no more offices be held except by native-born citizens of the Confederacy.

The naturalization law of the old Government has proved of little benefit to the Southern States. Whilst our Southern adopted citizens have proven themselves reliable, faithful and true to our institutions and the South, those of the North, who outnumber them twenty to one, have universally arrayed themselves foremost and in front of Lincoln's hordes in the work of rapine, murder and destruction against the

South. Hereafter, then, we can make no distinction between the Yankee and the foreigner, and both must necessarily be debarred of the privilege of citizenship in this Confederacy. We have viewed this question in all its bearings, and we can see no valid objections to it; indeed, with the lights before us, we look upon its adoption as eminently essential to the future stability and welfare of the Confederacy, and we believe that nine-tenths of the citizens of the Southern States, whether native or naturalized, will agree with us. There are cases in which it might be to the public interest to confer the rights of citizenship, and the power might be granted to Congress to pass special laws conferring citizenship on single individuals; further than that, the power should not be granted. We have spoken plainly upon this subject; we have the most sacred and vital responsibilities resting upon us as a people, and the highest duties to perform for the future welfare of our country; they should be discharged without fear or favor, looking alone to the glory of the Confederacy.

Among the most important questions which directly affect the interests of the people, that which relates to the ways and means of the Government has a most prominent position. Revenue for meeting the ordinary expenses of the Government and to discharge the public debt which will have been created by the war, will, of necessity, have to be raised. The times and the circumstances favor a change from the old revenue system of tariff or import duties—which was never an equal or honest system of taxation. It bore most heavily upon the masses, while the wealthy were almost exempt from its burthens; and those who possessed the greatest stake, under the protection and security of the Government, returned the least support to it. There are many reasons, indeed, not now necessary to refer to, which satisfy us that the old, corrupt tariff system of revenue will work heavily and oppressively upon the masses of the Confederacy. By abandoning this old system, we shall relieve the Government, to a great extent, of that venal curse, *official patronage*, which hung over and around the old Government like a black pall of corruption, infecting every avenue with its baneful influences, and which, most unfortunately, has already been transferred to our new Government, by quartering upon it the federal officials who have served under the most corrupt and infamous president that ever disgraced the old Union. The tariff, or import duties, under the old Union, has acted as the main cause in preventing direct Southern importations.

We feel confident that the people of the Confederacy are fully aware of and feel the necessity of unusual taxation, and that they are prepared to meet it willingly, cheerfully, and in the spirit of true patriots. Then let it be imposed in a manner and form that is not a deception and a cheat upon them, but which shall be plain and comprehensive to them and shall bear equally upon all classes and conditions. *We mean the abolition of all import duties, and the perfecting a system of direct taxation,* as economical in the expenses of its assessment and collection as can be made, *as a permanent policy* of the Confederacy. Such a system as this will act as a continual guarantee of a simple and economical administration of the Government, and a lasting blessing to the people.

The commerce of the Confederacy will soon grow rapidly in its extent and abundance—perhaps no power on earth will excel it—and the whole world will feel its invigorating influences. The rich resources and profuse abundance of the various products of the States of the Confederacy, with open ports, will attract the commercial world to our shores, and speedily build up a commercial marine of our own heretofore unequalled on this continent. With these bright prospects before us, and without a doubt of their realization, it becomes our Government to turn its attention to that arm of its power so essential to the protection of this vast interest, and hence a navy co-equal with and adequate to such protection and to keep pace with its growth, is indispensably necessary. Besides, our extended coasts, and the adjacent countries and islands southward of us, may involve large interests to the Confederacy, which it cannot be too soon prepared to overlook by the strong arm of an efficient navy.

In addition, an *inland navy*, of proper force and construction, has now also become indispensable for the protection of our river commerce, and the rights and interests of our Southern crafts or steamers, against the sneaking and unscrupulous aggressions of the Northwestern vandals and thieves. The branches of the Mississippi river penetrate into a large extent of territory under abolition rule, whose people abominate the South and her institutions, and whose characteristics give us no assurance against any kind of depredations upon us by them, even of midnight marauding and plundering. With such a people lining the navigable tributaries of the Mississippi, it becomes necessary, under the new condition of things, that a naval armament should be placed upon the waters of that great inter-commercial thoroughfare.

Resources and Productions of the Confederacy

There is no country upon the face of the globe that combines all the elements of greatness, power and wealth so bountifully as are embraced within the limits of the slave States. The resources of supplying all the wants of man, in peace or in war, and surrounding him with all the means of plenty, comfort, ease and happiness, are most profusely bestowed by a beneficent Creator upon this favored land; indeed, it seems that a gracious Providence, in scattering his blessings upon the earth, grasped a full hand and let them flow freely, when he swept it over the Southern States. Our mineral resources are already known to be most abundant, and yet we scarcely can see the beginning of them. In the upper States of the Confederacy the bowels of the earth are so richly stored with the leading mineral products most useful to mankind, that thousands of years to come will not exhaust the supply. But those rich and abundant productions of labor which are confined almost exclusively to the soil and climate of the Confederacy, challenge the world for a parallel. Never was there a people on earth so richly blessed of heaven, and never a people who should more fervently bow in thankfulness for the magnificent inheritance which is granted to them.

The soil and climate of the upper tier of States of the Confederacy, including Maryland, Virginia, North Carolina, and Northern Texas, embraces the finest grain and tobacco country upon the earth: wheat, corn, barley, rye, are most prolific, and mature to the fullest perfection; no portion of free soil can surpass it in the certainty and abundance of the yield of these products. We will take some interesting facts, as shown by the census as far back as 1850, exhibiting the comparative productions of the slave and free States in grain and stock. South Carolina produced six million bushels of corn *more* than the six New England States together, and more beef cattle than Pennsylvania by 1,740 head; more hogs than New York by 47,251 head, Virginia and North Carolina produced, jointly 13,363,000 bushels wheat—241,000 more than New York, and equal to the whole of the New England States, with New Jersey, Michigan, Iowa and Wisconsin added. Virginia, North Carolina and Tennessee produced 115,471,593 bushels of corn—exceeding by 300,000 bushels the quantity produced by New York, Pennsylvania, Ohio, New Jersey, Connecticut, Massachusetts, New Hampshire, Vermont and Maine, all put together. Taking all the free States together and all the slave States, and the aggregate quantity of corn produced by the latter exceeds the aggregate quantity produced by the former four million bushels. Nor are the Confederate States inferior to any region of the world for the production of cattle, hogs and sheep. Tennessee alone produced 3,104,800 hogs—being 16,306 more than the six New England States, New York, Pennsylvania, New Jersey, Iowa and Michigan together. Taking the State of Texas alone, and according to her assessment for 1860, her beef cattle numbers over 2,423,000 head and her sheep over 376,000 head; whilst her wheat region is much larger than Illinois, and produces the heaviest wheat grown in the limits of the old Union.

George Fitzhugh

CONDUCT OF THE WAR

George Fitzhugh (1806–1881) was, for most of his life, a lawyer in Port Royal, Virginia. Though a member of a large old Virginia family, Fitzhugh's upbringing was modest. After limited formal education and reading law with a local attorney, he established his own practice in Port Royal. Beginning in the 1850s, Fitzhugh joined other southerners in the growing chorus defending the peculiar institution. An effective propagandist rather than a rigorous scholar, Fitzhugh quickly became one of the best-known defenders of slavery in the South. He argued that slavery was the natural condition of man and that so-called free laborers were really "slaves without masters." Fitzhugh defended the patriarchical organization of society, such as existed in the South, as essential to the preservation of property, law, and government. He developed his views at length in Sociology for the South; or, The Failure of Free Society *(1854) and* Cannibals All! or, Slaves Without Masters *(1857). He also became one of the most frequent contributors to* De Bow's Review, *publishing over one hundred articles between 1855 and 1867. Though slavery was a frequent topic of these essays, he also wrote on technological progress, the glories of the Virginia countryside, English literature, and American and ancient history. A reluctant secessionist, Fitzhugh nonetheless supported the Confederacy. During the war he served in a minor post with the Confederate Department of the Treasury in Richmond. Afterward, somewhat to the consternation of his friends and colleagues, he accepted a position with the Freedman's Bureau in Richmond. He again took up his writing, first for* De Bow's Review *and then for* Lippincott's Magazine *of Philadephia. In the early 1870s, his health began to fail and he became increasingly inactive. He eventually moved to Texas to live with a daughter and died there in 1881.*

Fitzhugh's suggestions for the conduct of the war were similar to policies that underlay the actions of the Confederate government during at least the first half of the conflict. Though the Confederate government never fully articulated a strategic war policy, Jefferson Davis and his advisors placed great reliance on the idea of a defensive war.

Vol. XXXII (January/February, 1862), pp. 139–46.

The South could win simply by maintaining its independence, by successfully resisting northern efforts to bring it back into the Union. As Fitzhugh suggested, a defensive military strategy had certain advantages, especially for a nation of limited resources, but such a strategy also had other implications for the South. They could continue, for example, to portray themselves as the victims of aggression, thereby hoping to capitalize on northern opposition to the war and to attract European sympathy and recognition.

The problem with a defensive strategy was that it ran counter to accepted notions of warfare in the 1860s, which held that offensive action was necessary to achieve a decisive conclusion. By adopting an offensive-defensive strategy, as Jefferson Davis termed it, the Confederates hoped they could weaken the North through well-chosen battles on southern soil and then turn, invade, and defeat the enemy at the proper moment. Fitzhugh confidently believed that Maryland and perhaps the Northwest were simply waiting for the opportunity to release themselves from bondage to the Northeast.

Fitzhugh's prescriptions for the course of the war were born of overconfidence, as the later course of the war revealed. By July, 1863, Admiral David G. Farragut and General U. S. Grant had demonstrated that an army and navy could invade the valley of the Mississippi from the north or the south. A year later, General William T. Sherman, with his march through Georgia, would demonstrate that a Union army could operate successfully deep inside Confederate territory. Fitzhugh was more accurate in his assessment of the probable costs of a failed invasion of the North. Robert E. Lee tried twice. He was turned back at Antietam in September, 1862, and defeated decisively at Gettysburg in July, 1863. As Fitzhugh foresaw, such a defeat on northern soil was "a stunning and appalling blow."

Fitzhugh's second major concern in this piece was the Trent Affair, which took place in November and December, 1861. On November 8, Captain Charles Wilkes of the U.S. Navy stopped the British mail packet Trent *and seized James M. Mason and John Slidell, recently named as Confederate envoys to England and France. Wilkes took the men to Boston, where they were detained. Many Northerners viewed Wilkes as a hero, but his actions precipitated an international crisis. Wilkes's actions violated British neutrality and recalled the freedom-of-the-seas dispute between England and the United States in the early nineteenth century. Many southerners hoped the incident would result in British recognition of the Confederacy. The British were not pre-*

pared to go so far, but they did demand an apology and the release of Mason and Slidell. In late December, 1861, the Lincoln administration explained that Wilkes had acted "without orders," released the Confederate diplomats, and allowed them to finish their journey to Europe. Thus, the Lincoln administration avoided war with England over the incident.

The mob rules despotically among our enemies. Shall we instal it in supreme power at the South? So far, our President and all our officers have disregarded the senseless clamor of home-keeping people, who talk and write ignorantly, thoughtlessly and recklessly, about the conduct of the war, which they comprehend about as well as they do the Chaldaic language, or the Egyptian hieroglyphics. Out of danger's way themselves, they do not feel or care for the useless danger to which they would expose our troops. Our officers, whether volunteers or regulars, have exhibited remarkable prudence, caution, skill and sagacity. As conscientious men, they have endeavored to gain victory with little loss of life. In this they have succeeded, because they have fought the enemy at advantage, and never at disadvantage. An army acting on the defensive, in its own territory may, by retreating, choose its own position for battle. The invading army must either cease to advance, give up its project of conquest, or attack it at disadvantage, in the strong position which it has selected. Where such retreat is conducted in good order, the retreating army gathers strength daily from the surrounding country, and has little difficulty in procuring provisions, because it is always among friends whose resources have not been exhausted.

On the other hand, the invading army rapidly diminishes in numbers, from having daily to detail forces to keep open its line of communication with its base of operations. Besides, with it the difficulty of obtaining provisions increases with each advance. It must procure them from home, from which it is hourly receding; for if the retreating army have not entirely exhausted the supplies of the country through which it has passed, the people are unfriendly, and will not bring into the camp of their enemies the little that is left. If they send out foraging parties this still further weakens them, and exposes them to decimation in detail. Bonaparte set out for Moscow with half a million of men, and if we mistake not, had little over a hundred and fifty thousand when he arrived there. Russia, and the whole of Northern Europe, except Sweden, Norway and Lapland, is a dead level, interspersed with towns and villages. It has no natural strength, and hence, in past times conquest in Europe, with slight exceptions, has proceeded northwardly. The Confederate States present greater natural obstacles to an invading army than any equal area of country on the globe. Armies cannot march down our Atlantic coast, because of the great number of bays, inlets, creeks and rivers; nor down the interior, because of mountain ridges, impassable roads, sparse population, and scarcity of provisions.

The Mississippi is narrow, long, tedious, and easily defended, and its valley is subject to overflow. No invading army will attempt a serious invasion in that direction. It is our true policy to decoy the enemy into the interior, and then to cut them off as were Braddock, and Burgoyne, and Cornwallis, and Ross, and Packenham, and our own troops in the everglades of Florida. When we have defeated and captured their armies, exhausted their treasury, and cowed their spirits by defensive warfare, it will be time for us to begin to act on the offensive and to invade their territory. The northwest is as level a country as Northern Europe, teems with provisions, and abounds with towns and villages. Its population is a spiritless rabble, who have few arms and know little of their use, and who are endowed with no sense of personal or national honor. The northeast rules them with a rod of iron, and, by its protective tariff, robs them of half the proceeds of their labor. They should welcome us as deliverers from Yankee bondage, rather than as conquerors.

Cincinnati and Philadelphia are both weak and tempting points, and when we have well whipped the enemy within our own territory, it will be time to turn our attention to those cities.

We need not fear that we shall not have abundant opportunities, if we will be put prudent and cautious, to fight them at advantage. They have undertaken to conquer the South, and must advance. In Missouri, Kentucky, and northwestern Virginia, we may bide our time and opportunity, select our positions, and fight them only when it is policy to do so. They propose, too, to go to the relief of Eastern Tennessee. Let them try it; when they have marched through Kentucky it will be impossible for them to keep up communication with the North, and their invading army will fall an easy prey to our forces.

We must conquer Washington and Maryland on Virginia soil. McClellan is required by the whole North to advance. He must advance or resign. If he, or the general who succeeds him, advances, we will be sure to defeat them at Centreville, or Manassas, or at some point between Washington and Richmond. A half dozen defeats would not injure us. A single one would ruin them, and open the way to Washington and Maryland. We must break up their army before we advance into Maryland; and this they will afford us an early opportunity to effect, if we will be but patient.

Should they go into winter quarters in Washington, the North will see that the subjugation of the South is a hopeless project, and the nations of Europe will recognize our independence and break up the blockade. The press and the people of the North see this, and promise, as a dernier resort, a series of brilliant victories, to be achieved by land and by sea within the next few weeks. They must fight us within that time on our own soil and at positions selected by ourselves, and defeat us, too, or the illusion of subjugating the South will pass off from all Northern minds. Invasion alone can subjugate a country; and after nine months of threatening and preparation the North has not advanced ten miles into the well-affected portion of our territory, and has almost lost Missouri, Kentucky, northwestern Virginia and Maryland, which offered them no resistance when the war began. The grand result of their attempted conquest has been, so far, to add a third to the numbers and strength of their enemies.

Many who admit that it is both perilous and useless, so far as ultimate success is concerned, to attempt now to take Washington, who see that so soon as we cross the Potomac we divide our strength, and "have an impassable river behind us and an enemy in superior force before us," contend, nevertheless, that we are in honor bound to attempt the relief of Maryland.

Marching into her territory will be sure to transfer the seat of war from Virginia and carry it into her midst. She is now comparatively well treated by the federal forces, because they are trying to conciliate her favor, and retain her in the Union. When we attempt to relieve her by crossing the Potomac, we shall place her in the situation of Kentucky, Missouri, Western Virginia and Fairfax. The federalists will burn her farm-houses and villages and towns, and rob and lay waste her whole territory; and her own citizens, divided in their allegiance, will rise up and shed each other's blood. We can imagine no situation more deplorable than would be that of Maryland if we were now to march a part of our army into her territories. The time has not yet arrived when the federals would flee from her soil, panic stricken at our approach; and will not arrive until we have re-enacted on Virginia soil another Manassas. This we shall almost certainly have an opportunity to effect ere winter closes.

Should we be defeated in Maryland, our whole army, with their arms and ammunition, would be captured by the enemy. We might in a short time repair the loss of our men, but the loss of our munitions of war would inflict upon us a stunning and appalling blow. One defeat in Maryland would do us more harm than ten in Virginia. We have the selection of the battle-ground—Why choose Maryland?

We cannot conquer the North except by exhausting it, or by stirring up dissension between the northeast, East and northwest. Our victories but excite their indignation, increase their energies, stimulate them to enlist in the army, and keep down sectional and domestic broils among them. To avoid civil discord, by keeping the people engaged in foreign war, has been the common policy and practice of statesmen in all ages and in all countries. It is thus with the North. She fears the unemployed, destitute, agrarian mob of her large cities, and equally fears a rupture with the northwest. She has to choose between domestic war and war with us. She prefers the latter, and will carry on the war as long as her money or credit lasts. She will hardly be at a loss for men, as the wages she pays to her soldiers are better than those which she gives to her laborers. The prodigious expense which she is now incurring cannot be long continued, unless some rashness on our part enables her to recruit her failing strength from the spoils of the South. The cautious policy and strategy so far pursued by our armies, if persevered in, will insure us against any serious disasters, and gradually and slowly wear away and exhaust the strength and the means of our enemy.

Our soldiers and our officers have exhibited a noble specimen of the moral sublime, in the patience with which they have submitted to misconstruction, calumny and abuse. They prefer to pursue that course which is right, to that which only seems to be right. They will not sacrifice true honor to gain ephemeral reputation. They possess that lofty moral fortitude, that true courage, that can submit, even to the imputation of cowardice, rather than by failing in duty, to play the actual coward. With what truth and pathos did Scott exclaim (in effect), "I am a coward, because I have permitted popular clamor to swerve me from the line of duty."

It is easier, far easier, to face the cannon's mouth, or mount the deadly breach, than to prefer duty to reputation. Lucretia's virtue satisfies most men; for they are solicitous, not so much for self-approbation as for the applause of the crowd, and are satisfied to do what is wrong, provided they can win the plaudits of the mob. When the future historian records the story of our war, his pen will become most eloquent as he dilates upon that wise, cautious and prudent policy, that, despite of misconstruction, and sacrificing temporary reputation to ultimate success, often won victory by avoiding battle. He will place the men who have pursued this policy upon the highest pedestal in the Temple of Fame, along with Fabius and Washington, for the respect and admiration of endless ages. Horace has already written the appropriate eulogy for all such men, and the occasion is so appropriate that we cannot refrain from quoting a few of his well-known and eloquent lines:

> Justum et tenacem propositi virum,
> Non civiuim ardor prava jubentium,
> ....
> Mente quantit solida.*

We had written thus much more than a month ago. Since then, our ministers to England, Slidell and Mason, on their way from a neutral port to England, in an English national mail steamer, have been violently arrested by a federal naval officer, carried North and there detained in prison. This act met with the prompt and cordial approval of the people, the press and the Government of the North; and one of the federal cabinet, in his annual message, went so far as to more than intimate that Captain Wilkes erred in omitting to capture and make prize of the British steamer in which our ministers were found. When the news reached England, the whole nation, from the Queen to the peasant, was stirred up with indignation and anger. A messenger was forthwith despatched to Washington, bearing instructions to Lord Lyons to require a full and explicit apology from the Federal Government, and the release and return to England of our ambassadors.

Will the Government at Washington accede to the demands of England? We thought not; but, not because there is any depth of meanness or cowardice to which the weak, vulgar and perfidious regime at Washington would not descend. But it seems we were mistaken. The arrest of our ambassadors, even with their dispatches, could do no pos-

---

*The heat of fellow citizens clamoring for what is wrong,
  Cannot shake the just man and firm of purpose
  In his rocklike soul.—EDS.

sible good to the North and possible harm to the South. Our commissioners already in Europe were fully competent to treat and negotiate for the recognition of our independence; and the nations of Europe would not heed diplomacy, however cunning, but would only consult their own interests, and pay regard to our military exploits that proved our ability to sustain our independence, regardless of our professions of such ability, even were they as grandiloquent, as bullying and as boastful as the threats of our adversaries. But one result could possibly follow their discourteous and insulting action, and that was to alienate England more and more from the side of the North, and incline her further to that of the South, toward which her vital interest already most persuasively wooed her. Lincoln, Seward and Cameron, who were always peace men, reluctantly driven by the Northern mob into the war with us, have, from the beginning of their sway, been insulting foreign nations, especially England, legislating to injure them, and sending abroad coarse, crazy fanatics, like Cassius M. Clay, to do dirtier work in the line of insult and vituperation than even they could descend to.

They promised to conquer us ere this, and have not yet begun to invade us. By the admission of Northern men in congress, they have gained no victories and sustained very many defeats. They will be hurled from power, consigned to ignominious disgrace, and probably hung by the Northern mob for their want of success if they continue the war. They must make peace or conquer us.

All the States of our Confederacy have behaved nobly and gallantly throughout our struggle with the populous North. Each has done all that was required or expected of it—all that it had occasion or opportunity to do. We would make no invidious comparisons or distinctions, because there are no facts to justify such comparisons or distinctions. Yet, we are a Virginian in feeling, by birth, by remote descent, and by extensive connections and friendships. We feel peculiarly sensitive to what affects her interests or her honor. She, from her longer line of frontier, her many tide-water navigable rivers, and her vicinity to Washington, has been most exposed, and has had most to bear the brunt of the war. She has made the greatest sacrifices and exertions, simply because she was by her position required to make them. She was the first, and still is the great battle-ground. Soldiers have flocked from every State of the Confederacy to her assistance. She has received them with gratitude, entertained them generously, and fought side by side with them with a chivalry that added lustre to her ancient honor, and only emulated the chivalry of her allies because it was impossible to surpass them.

It is no small distinction to her that she was the first of the border States to secede; and this distinction we shall jealously cherish whilst readily admitting that the secessionists of the other border States were equally brave and patriotic, and only delayed in action by circumstances which they could not control. A few, a very few, cavillers have complained of the course of Virginia. It is true that, owing to her vicinity to the North, she has been flooded by treacherous Yankees, who, acting upon the fears and timidity of avaricious, selfish and cowardly natives, have neutralized, for a time, the patriotic action of some of our border countries. But only for a time! The people of Brooke county, in the midst of the Pan Handle, are as true to the South as the people of South Carolina. It is only the people of Wheeling, the lower order of tradespeople, whose Bible is the ledger, who are against us. That class of tradespeople who live for profit, the devotees of Mercury (the god of rogues and merchants), the worshippers of mammon, always go with that side that will pay best. Thank God! we have of this sort of people fewer in Virginia, than in any other country on earth. Most of our merchants, imbibing their sentiments, their principles and their morality from the country people, the farming people, are far too honest to succeed as tradespeople. In Virginia we have no trading class in sentiment and principle. The few who take to trade are often ruined by attempting to carry the morality of the country into the counting-room.

Virginia is now, and ever has been, an agricultural State. The farmers give tone and character to society. Her merchants are gentlemen, because they are the sons, friends, or connections of farmers. But there is an infamous class of low traders, who, like pickpockets and faro dealers, follow in the wake of armies and of governments. They have crowded to Richmond, and, by cheating everybody who deals with them, have given Richmond, a bad name. Her regular merchants, her native-born merchants, are as honorable a body of men as any in the Confederacy. Carry the capital where you will and it will be followed and flooded by pimps, panders, gamblers and cheats. A transient population begets a dishonest class who prey upon it.

The executive of Virginia, her army and her legislature have acted equally well. But for their zealous, able, efficient, and concerted action, the glorious results which have attended the campaigns on her soil could not have been attained. Those highest in position and purest in character are most exposed to the malignant shafts of every defamation and detraction: for defamation is a trade which pays best where its victims are noblest. Aristides, the Just, was ostracised,—banished from Athens because he was just.

> "He who ascends to mountain tops shall find
> The loftiest peaks most wrapt in clouds and snow;
> He who surpasses or subdues mankind,
> Must look down on the hate of those below.
> Though high above the sun of glory glow,
> And far *beneath* the earth and ocean spread;
> Round him are icy rocks, and loudly blow
> Contending tempests on his naked head,
> And thus reward the toils which to those summits lead."

The ultra abolitionists are already bitter and active enemies of the Lincoln administration; add to them all honest, brave, consistent and truthful men at the North, who clamorously applauded the act of Capt. Wilkes in taking possession of Mason and Slidell, and who will not now turn round, eat their own words, and basely kneel and knuckle to English threats, and an opposition party will be formed that will paralyze the action of the administration or expel it from power. Lady Macbeth but breathes the voice of natural indignation, when she denounces a like infirmity of purpose—

> Lady Macbeth.—"I have given suck, and know
> How tender 'tis to love the babe that milks me;
> I would, while it was smiling in my face,
> Have plucked my nipple from its boneless gums
> And dashed the brains out, had I so sworn as you
> Have done to this."

Joseph B. Gribble

THE COTTON INTEREST, AND ITS RELATION TO THE PRESENT CRISIS

The failure of Great Britain and France to come to the aid of the Confederacy was one of the greatest southern disappointments. Many considerations during the first year of the war had seemed to point toward eventual intervention on behalf of the South, and when such assistance was not forthcoming, more than one southerner wondered aloud as to the reasons for this European inaction. For Joseph B. Gribble, the cause of the delay in the inevitable movement by Britain and France to force open the Union blockade of southern ports and to recognize the Confederacy was intimately bound up with the demand for "King Cotton," the leading export of the South.

For decades, increasing quantities of southern cotton had moved northward to the textile mills of New England and eastward across the Atlantic to the great factory centers of Great Britain and France. This commercial connection, with its presumed European and Yankee dependence on the supply of southern cotton, was to Gribble's mind a powerful weapon in the Confederate arsenal. In fact, he greatly exaggerated the sensitivity of British foreign policy to the fortunes of the British textile industry. The excess supply of raw cotton in European warehouses that had accumulated during the depression of 1857–60 and alternative sources of fresh supplies of cotton were not the only influences at work to restrain the European, and particularly, British, interventionists.

By 1861, the net output of Great Britain's textile industry accounted for less than 5 percent of that nation's national income, compared, for example, with a 7.6 percent share for the iron industry. Although the Civil War years produced a "cotton famine" in Britain, sharply arresting the growth of the textile industry there, the British economy was sufficiently resilient and complex to withstand the drastic reductions in imports of American cotton—from 819,500,528 pounds in 1861 to 13,524,224 pounds in 1862 and 6,394,080 pounds in 1863—resulting from the blockade and the destruction of southern agriculture. A considerable part of the falling off of southern cotton exports to Great Britain in 1861 was due not to the northern blockade but to a quasi-

Vol. XXXII (March/April, 1862), pp. 279–86.

formal embargo imposed by the South in an attempt to bring Britain and France to heel. Jefferson Davis, president of the Confederacy, worried about the possibility of European nations recognizing this none-too-subtle attempt at extortion for what it was. Nevertheless, the "Cotton Supply Association" persisted in its efforts to constrict the supply of cotton leaving for Europe and, in 1862, several Confederate states passed laws to curtail the acreage planted in cotton. Gribble, apparently a free trade advocate—as were many southern writers for De Bow's Review *in the 1850s—counseled against any measures designed to coerce Britain and France to a pro-South policy. The proper course, he argued, lay in supplying Europe with cotton sufficient, but only just, to meet its needs, keeping the Continent on a taut leash that might at any moment be painfully tightened. As for the blockade, economic malaise in the North would probably induce the Union to lift the blockade before Great Britain and France smashed it. Gribble failed to recognize the intensity of northern resolve and of British aversion to war with the United States. Both considerations would frustrate his hopes. More importantly, Gribble and many of his fellow southerners did not realize that the realm of King Cotton lay mainly in the South.*

Having an abiding faith in the potent influence of "King Cotton," the writer is free to confess that he had anticipated an earlier movement on behalf of England and France, as the powers most largely interested, looking to the supplying of their manufactories, before the effect of a diminishing stock should have so materially enhanced the value, to say nothing of the political results likely to follow the curtailment of labor. Certainly, the "Cotton Supply Association" had never before so good an opportunity of pressing upon the government their claims to attention and support, and, viewing the subject from their standpoint, their efforts are commendable enough. But we cannot for a moment believe that the shrewd and far-seeing statesmen and merchants of England entertained any expectations of supplying the immediate demand for raw cotton outside of the Southern Confederacy. The combined power and wealth of Great Britain could not accomplish it, if silly enough to make the attempt.

Under the stimulus of a pressing necessity and high prices, and by diverting from the Chinese market part of its usual supply, about

988,000 bales have been drawn from India, equal in weight to about 750,000 bales of American, and greatly deficient in quality. We venture the prediction, that so much will not be received from the same source in 1862.

Notwithstanding these powerful influences, the supply received from Egypt and Brazil was ten per cent less in 1861 than the year before. The receipts at Liverpool from Africa were 1,600 bales in 1860, and only 1,300 in 1861. From the West Indies 5,500 bales in 1860, and 6,500 in 1861.

The time will undoubtedly come when, from various parts of the world, a larger supply of raw cotton will be derived; but, in the meantime, the demand will have increased in a larger ratio. Commerce is the hand-maiden of civilization; and the wild or ignorant tribes who may hereafter become the producers of cotton, will become consumers of the manufactured article.

We must look for other grounds on which to account for the long-delayed action of foreign governments. It seems very clear that, what with the old and deep-rooted prejudice against slavery, the double fact that the South was deprived of all postal and commercial intercourse with other nations, and that all that was known about us abroad was derived from the most false, malignant and debased press in the world, prompted by the most corrupt and venal government that ever disgraced a professedly civilized country, if we could get behind the scenes of the state departments on this and the other side of the Atlantic, we should probably find Jonathan pledging himself to John to do that which he knew to be impossible, and the latter believing him for want of better information. When, however, the British government and people awoke to a knowledge of the facts as they really existed, both interest and sympathy inclined them toward the South. Finding, however, that to do that which interest and sympathy, rather than inclination, prompted, it must come in conflict with an unprincipled government, and a reckless and infuriated mob to back it, the English government found it necessary to take some little time for preparation. We can already see the "beginning of the end;" but there seems little doubt that if our great Southern king had not interposed, and compelled them to respect his silvery locks, the governments of Europe would have left us alone to fight it out. Six months ago the South had no friends, and now the North has none. We have bought our new friends, let us hereafter compel them to respect us; we can hold them only by the ties of interest and of fear.

Much has been said and written about the policy of curtailing the growth of cotton, for the purpose of enhancing its value, or making other nations feel the want of that for which they *professed* to care so little.

Nothing could be more impolitic; and any legislative or conventional action looking to this end, is simply absurd. While we admit the fact, that years must elapse, before any very material addition can be made to the production of other countries, especially of quantities analogous to New Orleans cotton, still, there is no reason why we should force the wealth and enterprise of England and France, to test their utmost ability in this direction. It is clearly for our interest to supply the general demand, at a fair and remunerative price. So long as we do this, we defy competition and hold all Europe at our feet. It would be neither neighborly nor politic to flaunt defiance in the face of the world; though the cord that binds be never so strong, let it be so finely drawn as not to attract observation.

While every article of staple food should be raised at home, and coarse fabrics of cotton and wool, shoes, implements of husbandry, and the heavier work of cast and wrought iron should be manufactured in the Southern Confederacy; still, for all goods requiring cheap labor and careful manipulation, especially when the material is the product of other countries, we should go into the markets of the world, where the products of our soil would be gladly received in exchange. We are as essential an agricultural as Great Britain is a manufacturing and maritime nation. Commercial reciprocity is the surest basis of permanent peace and national prosperity.

Notwithstanding the antagonism of feeling, race and character, the North and South would yet be united, had not the former lost sight of this fundamental truth, and sought by coercion to obtain from us what they were not willing to grant in return.

We have frequently been inquired of by planters, "What would you recommend us to do as regards preparing to grow another crop?" The reply has uniformly been: make, first, all you can possibly for your own use, both of food and clothing; and in addition, *as much cotton as you conveniently can.*

Under the existing state of the country, and with the experience of the past four years pressing so severely upon the attention of planters, there is no probability that more cotton will be raised the coming year than will find a ready market. In all the northern portion of the cotton belt, grain will take very largely the place of cotton, for the present;

while over the whole country, more or less labor will be diverted into other channels. On the supposition that, of the past crop, 3,500,000 bales will be available so soon as the blockade is raised, and that 3,000,000 will be grown the coming season, we have, then, for two years use 6,500,000
add total stock in Europe, 1st January last 1,000,000
add product of other countries, two years 2,000,000
we have supply for two years, say 9,500,000
bales on a broad basis of calculation.

The actual amount taken for consumption during 1859 and 1860 was 9,525,000 bales; during which time the amount produced by other countries than the United States was but 1,705,000, or 300,000 less than the very liberal estimate made for this and next year.

The present offers an excellent opportunity for cotton planters to turn more attention to spinning and weaving, when they have the means. To repair fences, dwellings, gin-houses, negro quarters; clear out their ditches, etc. All such needful work has been more or less overlooked during the speculative excitement of the past few years. The great crop of 1859–60 was made too much at the expense of corn, etc., the scarcity of which has had so important a share in bringing about the large indebtedness of the planting community—the Providential influence of drought had not all to do with it. If the course indicated above be carried out, we shall then be in a position in 1863 to raise such a crop of cotton as the wants of the world may demand: the independence of the Southern Confederacy and unrestricted trade with Europe being considered a foregone conclusion. . . .

On the 1st of January, 1861, the continental manufacturers were said to hold 150,000 bales more than usual, yet the combined export to the continent during 1861, from this country and England, was fully as large as the year before; at the same time, we are given to understand that they are now no better supplied with stock relatively than in England. If this be true, there has been an increase rather than falling off in continental manufactures.

Neither the annual statements from Great Britain or the continent are yet at hand. The latest reliable accounts from Liverpool are to the 27th of December, and giving the business of that port only. The amount taken for consumption was 2,180,000 bales, against 2,526,000 the year before—a difference of only 346,000 notwithstanding the high prices—while spinners only held about 70,000 bales, against 183,000 a year ago. The stock on hand was of all sorts 558,700 packages, of which only 216,000 were American, with about 70,000 bales only known to be afloat from India, Brazil and Egypt. During the first seven months of the year, nearly 51,000 bales per week were taken for consumption and 13,000 bales for export, say in all 64,000. At present, about 32,000 are being bought for home use and 8,000 for the continent, say in all 40,000 bales. At this rate and allowing 150,000 for import, the entire supply will be exhausted by the first of May. Another important fact must not be overlooked, namely: that the proportion of American cotton used per month is 5-7ths, or 5,000 bales, against 2,000 of other sorts, so far as home consumption is concerned; of the exports, about 2-5ths are American. On the basis of calculation, it would seem that the supply of American cannot last beyond the first week of March, without allowing a bale for export; though, by a further curtailment of time, the final stoppage of machinery may be postponed to April. The holders of the debris of the dusty crops of 1858 and 1859, will be able to dispose of it at a handsome profit; such as could not be sold at three pence, will now realize perhaps eight.

On the supposition that the blockade were raised on the first of March even, cotton could not go forward fast enough even by steamers to meet immediately pressing wants; the London Economist of January 4th, estimates the amount from India, Brazil, etc., to be received by the end of June, at only 300,000 bales—it is always the case that the largest receipts from those sources come to hand during the fall months.

This is a state of things sufficiently embarrassing and critical, so far as other nations are concerned, and cannot possibly be of long continuance. In the absence of positive information, we may infer either that under the combined demand of England and France, backed by the presence of a fleet, for the fulfillment of treaty obligations, the government at Washington will raise the blockade, perhaps by the time this appears in print, or that the combined powers will do it by force at a very early day—the former seems most probable.

Though the value of cotton may be kept up to a high figure for some months to come on the other side of the water, still, so soon as the first shipments are at hand, there must be a gradual decline till middlings get down to about 9d., below which they are not likely to go so long as there is any disturbance of commercial relations, and consequent uncertainty as to the future supply.

On this side, many circumstances will combine against the value of cotton; though prices may be good they are not likely to be very high, because so soon as trade opens the supply will be continuous up to the summer of 1863; freights, insurance and exchange, will all be against us. If the ports were now open, the crop lately gathered could not be brought to market before the next would be forthcoming; the railroads would be fully occupied, but, so far as the Mississippi valley is concerned, there are not steamboats enough available, even if the interior rivers should keep up. On the waters of Alabama the war has not reduced the tonnage very materially, and a larger proportion would come to market before summer. As regards the crops of Texas, upper Red river, Arkansas, Washita and Yazoo, as well as the bayous of Louisiana, a large quantity will necessarily lie over till next winter. No accumulation of stock can occur at the ports, as the receipts will be taken off as fast as they come to hand.

The crop of 1861 will be good in staple, but a large portion low in quality in other respects, as the result of rainy weather during the earlier picking season, the extensive prevalence of rot, the injury done by worms in dusting the pods with excrement and fragments of leaf, less care than usual in gathering, and the injury resulting from housing so much in pens and sheds in the fields. Up to the middle of August, the prospects were favorable, but from that period to the first week in October, the rains were general and constant, causing too much growth of weed, and the loss by rotting and shedding of a large portion of the bottom and middle crop. The good picking weather in October and November, fortunate as it was, fell very far short in compensating for the loss during the earlier part of the season; and but for the long, open fall, three millions of bales could not have been gathered, as it turned out the old hills have this year yielded the best, and the low, rich lands the poorest crops, especially in the extreme South, where the caterpillar did very extensive damage. The diversion of land from cotton to grain, in the northern portion of the Confederacy, was of itself, greatly instrumental in reducing the aggregate yield in 1861; during the present year, the same will be, to some extent, the case everywhere; but in Texas, and all the northern part of the cotton-growing states, the crop planted will be very much smaller than last year; and should the season not be very favorable, it is scarcely possible that three millions of bales will be raised.

Since the foregoing was written, later accounts are at hand, showing the stock actually in Liverpool the 1st of January to have been 623,000 bales, or about 80,000 more than was expected—the increase being chiefly in American descriptions; this, at 40,000 bales per week for consumption and export, would be consumed by the 20th of April. Only about 80,000 bales were known to be afloat to arrive by April, which will give two more weeks supply. *These facts are extracted from a private letter.* The receipts from other sources than the United States the first four months of 1860 were 350,000 bales, and much larger last year. This bears out the opinion before expressed, that the East India supply has been exhausted. Without having access to an annual Liverpool statement, we have published accounts said to have come from that source, to the effect that the consumption of Great Britain in 1861 was 2,391,000 bales, and of the continent of Europe 2,030,000. If this be correct, the increase in the amount manufactured on the continent is much greater than we were justified in predicting. "King Cotton" holds the balance of power, and will make his influence felt.

If the published accounts of the large consumption of continental Europe prove to be correct, the raw material there must be almost entirely exhausted. The English consumption was nearly equal to that of 1860, notwithstanding the enhanced value of the raw material; so that we may infer not only that the pressure upon foreign governments will compel them to get cotton by some means before summer, but that high prices must continue to rule for some time to come.

James H. Thornwell

OUR DANGER AND OUR DUTY

James H. Thornwell (1812–62) was a Presbyterian clergyman, college professor and president, and, after 1860, an ardent southern nationalist. Born in South Carolina, Thornwell experienced a difficult childhood after the early death of his father. Educated at South Carolina College in Columbia and later at Andover (Mass.) Theological Seminary and Harvard College, Thornwell became a Presbyterian minister in 1834. From 1837 until 1851, he held various professorships at South Carolina College, as well as two brief ministerial appointments. He was appointed president of the college in 1851, a post he held until 1855, when he resigned to become professor of theology at the Presbyterian Theological Seminary in Columbia. In addition to his educational duties, he was active in the Presbyterian denomination and established the Southern Presbyterian Review *in 1847. An advocate of the separation of church and state, he nevertheless became an ardent supporter of the Confederacy in 1860. He lent his talents as a propagandist to the southern cause before his early death from tuberculosis in 1862.*

"Our Danger and Our Duty" was originally prepared as a pamphlet that had wide circulation in the Confederate army. When Thornwell wrote, the early confidence of the South in the superiority of its cause and its armies had begun to fade under the northern onslaughts. In April, 1862, a Union force under Admiral David G. Farragut captured New Orleans. In Kentucky and Tennessee, the Union armies under U. S. Grant were on the move and in early April defeated the Confederates at Shiloh. During much of the spring, George B. McClellan was trying to get the Union army in position to take the Confederate capital at Richmond, Virginia. Thus, the dangers to which Thornwell alluded were very real.

Thornwell astutely noted the high stakes for which both sides were playing and tried to rouse the southern spirit to meet the challenge. He appealed to southerners' fears of the probable aftermath of a northern victory, their public spirit, and their faith in a just Providence. If only all southerners would do their duty, put aside selfishness and sin, and

Vol. XXXIII (May/August, 1862), pp. 43–51.

dedicate themselves to God, they might "become the fit instruments of
a holy Providence in a holy cause." Writing as he must often have
preached, Thornwell urged his countrymen to take up their duties
cheerfully so as to earn the "glorious future" that lay before them.

The ravages of Louis XIV in the beautiful valleys of the Rhine, about
the close of the seventeenth century, may be taken as a specimen of the
appalling desolation which is likely to overspread the Confederate
States, if the Northern army should succeed in its schemes of subjugation and of plunder. Europe was then outraged by atrocities inflicted
by Christians upon Christians, more fierce and cruel than even Ma-
hometans could have had the heart to perpetrate. Private dwellings
were razed to the ground, fields laid waste, cities burnt, churches demolished, and the fruits of industry, wantonly and ruthlessly destroyed. But three days of grace were allowed to the wretched inhabitants to flee their country, and in a short time, the historian tells us,
"the roads and fields, which then lay deep in snow, were blackened by
innumerable multitudes of men, women and children, flying from their
homes. Many died of cold and hunger; but enough survived to fill the
streets of all the cities of Europe with lean and squalid beggars, who
had once been thriving farmers and shopkeepers." And what have we
to expect if our enemies prevail? Our homes, too, are to be pillaged,
our cities sacked and demolished, our property confiscated, our true
men hanged, and those who escape the gibbet, to be driven as vagabonds and wanderers in foreign climes. This beautiful country is to
pass out of our hands. The boundaries which mark our States are, in
some instances, to be effaced, and the States that remain are to be converted into subject provinces, governed by Northern rulers and by
Northern laws. Our property is to be ruthlessly seized and turned over
to mercenary strangers, in order to pay the enormous debt which our
subjugation has cost. Our wives and daughters are to become the prey
of brutal lust. The slave, too, will slowly pass away, as the red man did
before him, under the protection of Northern philanthropy; and the
whole country, now like the garden of Eden in beauty and fertility, will
first be a blackened and smoking desert, and then the minister of
Northern cupidity and avarice. Our history will be worse than that of
Poland and Hungary. There is not a single redeeming feature in the
picture of ruin which stares us in the face, if we permit ourselves to be

conquered. It is a night of thick darkness, that will settle upon us. Even sympathy, the last solace of the afflicted, will be denied to us. The civilized world will look coldly upon us, or even jeer us with the taunt that we have deservedly lost our own freedom in seeking to perpetuate the slavery of others. We shall perish under a cloud of reproach and of unjust suspicions, sedulously propagated by our enemies, which will be harder to bear than the loss of home and of goods. Such a fate never overtook any people before.

The case is as desperate with our enemies as with ourselves. They must succeed or perish. They must conquer us or be destroyed themselves. If they fail, national bankruptcy stares them in the face; divisions in their own ranks are inevitable, and their Government will fall to pieces under the weight of its own corruption. They know they are a doomed people if they are defeated. Hence their madness. They must have our property to save them from insolvency. They must show that the Union cannot be dissolved, to save them from future secessions. The parties, therefore, in this conflict can make no compromises. It is a matter of life and death with both—a struggle in which their *all* is involved.

But the consequences of success on our part will be very different from the consequences of success on the part of the North. If *they* prevail, the whole character of the Government will be changed, and instead of a federal republic, the common agent of sovereign and independent States, we shall have a central despotism, with the notion of States forever abolished, deriving its powers from the will, and shaping its policy according to the wishes, of a numerical majority of the people; we shall have, in other words, a supreme, irresponsible democracy. The will of the North will stand for law. The Government does not now recognize itself as an ordinance of God, and when all the checks and balances of the Constitution are gone, we may easily figure to ourselves the career and the destiny of this godless monster of democratic absolutism. The progress of regulated liberty on this continent will be arrested, anarchy will soon succeed, and the end will be a military despotism, which preserves order by the sacrifice of the last vestige of liberty. We are fully persuaded that the triumph of the North in the present conflict will be as disastrous to the hopes of mankind as to our own fortunes. They are now fighting the battle of despotism. They have put their Constitution under their feet; they have annulled its most sacred provisions; and in defiance of its solemn guaranties, they are now engaged, in the halls of Congress, in discussing and maturing bills which make Northern notions of necessity the paramount laws of the land. The avowed end of the present war is, to make the Government a government of force. It is to settle the principle, that whatever may be its corruptions and abuses, however unjust and tyrannical its legislation, there is no redress, except in vain petition or empty remonstrance. It was as a protest against this principle, which sweeps away the last security for liberty, that Virginia, North Carolina, Tennessee, and Missouri seceded, and if the Government should be reëstablished, it must be reëstablished with this feature of remorseless despotism fully and indelibly fixed. The future fortunes of our children, and of this continent, would then be determined by a tyranny which has no parallel in history.

On the other hand, we are struggling for constitutional freedom. We are upholding the great principles which our fathers bequeathed us, and if we should succeed, and become, as we shall, the dominant nation of this continent, we shall perpetuate and diffuse the very liberty for which Washington bled, and which the heroes of the Revolution achieved. We are not revolutionists—we are resisting revolution. We are upholding the true doctrines of the Federal Constitution. We are conservative. Our success is the triumph of all that has been considered established in the past. We can never become aggressive; we may absorb, but we can never invade for conquest, any neighboring State. The peace of the world is secured if our arms prevail. We shall have a Government that acknowledges God, that reverences right, and that makes law supreme. We are, therefore, fighting not for ourselves alone, but, when the struggle is rightly understood, for the salvation of this whole continent. It is a noble cause in which we are engaged. There is everything in it to rouse the heart and to nerve the arm of the freeman and the patriot; and though it may now seem to be under a cloud, it is too big with the future of our race to be suffered to fail. It cannot fail; it must not fail. Our people must not brook the infamy of betraying their sublime trust. This beautiful land we must never suffer to pass into the hands of strangers. Our fields, our homes, our firesides and sepulchres, our cities and temples, our wives and daughters, we must protect at every hazard. The glorious inheritance which our fathers left us we must never betray. The hopes with which they died, and which buoyed their spirits in the last conflict, of making their country a blessing to the world, we must not permit to be unrealized. We must seize the torch from their hands, and transmit it with increasing brightness to distant generations. The word failure must not be pronounced among us. It is not a thing to be dreamed of. We must settle it that we *must* succeed. We must not sit down to count chances. There is too much at stake to think of discussing probabilities—we must make success a certainty, and that, by the blessing of God, we can do. If we are prepared to do our duty, and our whole duty, we have nothing to fear. But what is our duty? This is a question which we must gravely consider. We shall briefly attempt to answer it.

In the first place, we must shake off all apathy, and become fully alive to the magnitude of the crisis. We must look the danger in the face, and comprehend the real grandeur of the issue. We shall not exert ourselves until we are sensible of the need of effort. As long as we cherish a vague hope that help may come from abroad, or that there is something in our past history, or the genius of our institutions, to protect us from overthrow, we are hugging a fatal delusion to our bosoms. This apathy was the ruin of Greece at the time of the Macedonian invasion. This was the spell which Demosthenes labored so earnestly to break. The Athenian was as devoted as ever to his native city and the free institutions he inherited from his fathers; but somehow or other he could not believe that his country could be conquered. He read its safety in its ancient glory. He felt that it had a prescriptive right to live. The great orator saw and lamented the error; he poured forth his eloquence to dissolve the charm; but the fatal hour had come, and the spirit of Greece could not be roused. There was no more real patriotism at the time of the second Persian invasion than in the age of Philip; but then there was no apathy, every man appreciated the danger; he saw the crash that was coming, and prepared himself to resist the blow. He knew that there was no safety except in courage and in desperate effort. Every man, too, felt identified with the State; a part of its weight rested on his shoulders. It was this sense of personal interest and personal responsibility—the profound conviction that every one had something to do, and that Greece expected him to do it—this was the public spirit which turned back the countless hordes of Xerxes, and saved Greece to liberty and man. This is the spirit which we must have, if we, too, would succeed. We must be brought to see that all, under God, depends on ourselves; and, looking away from all foreign alliances, we must make up our minds to fight desperately and fight long, if we would save the country from ruin, and ourselves from bondage. Every man should feel that he has an interest in the State, and that the State in a measure leans upon him; and he should rouse himself to efforts as bold and heroic as if all depended on his single right arm. Our courage should rise higher than the danger, and whatever may be the odds against us, we must solemnly resolve by God's blessing, that we will not be conquered. When, with a full knowledge of the danger, we are brought to this point, we are in the way of deliverance, but until this point is reached, it is idle to count on success.

It is implied in the spirit which the times demand, that all private interests are sacrificed to the public good. The State becomes everything, and the individual nothing. It is no time to be casting about for expedients to enrich ourselves. The man who is now intent upon money, who turns public necessity and danger into means of speculation, would, if very shame did not rebuke him, and he were allowed to follow the natural bent of his heart, go upon the field of battle after an engagement and strip the lifeless bodies of his brave countrymen of the few spoils they carried into the fight. Such men, unfit for anything generous or noble themselves, like the hyena, can only suck the blood of the lion. It ought to be a reproach to any man, that he is growing rich while his country is bleeding at every pore. If we had a Themistocles among us, he would not scruple to charge the miser and extortioner with stealing the Gorgon's head; he would search their stuff, and if he could not find that, he would find what would answer his country's needs much more effectually. This spirit must be rebuked; every man must forget himself, and think only of the public good.

The spirit of faction is even more to be dreaded than the spirit of avarice and plunder. It is equally selfish, and is, besides, distracting and divisive. The man who now labors to weaken the hands of the Government, that he may seize the reins of authority, or cavils at public measures and policy, that he may rise to distinction and office, has all the selfishness of a miser, and all the baseness of a traitor. Our rulers are not infallible; but their errors are to be reviewed with candor, and their authority sustained with unanimity. Whatever has a tendency to destroy public confidence in their prudence, their wisdom, their energy, and their patriotism, undermines the security of our cause. We must not be divided and distracted among ourselves. Our rulers have great responsibilities; they need the support of the whole country; and nothing short of a patriotism which buries all private differences, which is ready for compromises and concessions, which can make charitable allowances for differences of opinion, and even for errors of judgment, can save us from the consequences of party and faction. We must be united. If our views are not carried out, let us sacrifice private opinion to public safety. In the great conflict with Persia, Athens yielded to

Sparta, and acquiesced in plans she could not approve, for the sake of the public good. Nothing could be more dangerous now than scrambles for office and power, and collisions among the different departments of the Government. We must present a united front.

It is further important that every man should be ready to work. It is no time to play the gentleman; no time for dignified leisure. All cannot serve in the field; but all can do something to help forward the common cause. The young and the active, the stout and vigorous, should be prepared at a moment's warning for the ranks. The disposition should be one of eagerness to be employed; there should be no holding back, no counting the cost. The man who stands back from the ranks in these perilous times, because he is unwilling to serve his country as a private soldier, who loves his ease more than liberty, his luxuries more than his honor, that man is a dead fly in our precious ointment. In seasons of great calamity the ancient pagans were accustomed to appease the anger of their gods by human sacrifices; and if they had gone upon the principle of selecting those whose moral insignificance rendered them alike offensive to heaven and useless to earth, they would always have selected these drones, and loafers, and exquisites. A Christian nation cannot offer them in sacrifice, but public contempt should whip them from their lurking holes, and compel them to share the common danger. The community that will cherish such men without rebuke, brings down wrath upon it. They must be forced to be useful, to avert the judgments of God from the patrons of cowardice and meanness.

Public spirit will not have reached the height which the exigency demands, until we shall have relinquished all fastidious notions of military etiquette, and have come to the point of expelling the enemy by any and every means that God has put in our power. We are not fighting for military glory; we are fighting for a home, and for a national existence. We are not aiming to display our skill in tactics and generalship; we are aiming to show ourselves a free people, worthy to possess and able to defend the institutions of our fathers. What signifies it to us how the foe is vanquished, provided it is done? Because we have not weapons of the most approved workmanship, are we to sit still and see our soil overrun, and our wives and children driven from their homes, while we have in our hands other weapons that can equally do the work of death? Are we to perish if we cannot conquer by the technical rules of scientific warfare? Are we to sacrifice our country to military punctilio? The thought is monstrous. We must be prepared to extemporize expedients. We must cease to be chary, either about our weapons or the means of using them. The end is to drive back our foes. If we cannot procure the best rifles, let us put up with the common guns of the country; if they cannot be had, with pikes, and axes, and tomahawks; anything that will do the work of death is an effective instrument in a brave man's hand. We should be ready for the regular battle or the partisan skirmish. If we are too weak to stand an engagement in the open field, we can waylay the foe, and harass and annoy him. We must prepare ourselves for a guerilla war. The enemy must be conquered; and any method by which we can honorably do it must be resorted to. This is the kind of spirit which we want to see aroused among our people. With this spirit, they will never be subdued. If driven from the plains, they will retreat to the mountains; if beaten in the field, they will hide in swamps and marshes, and when their enemies are least expecting it, they will pounce down upon them in the dashing exploits of a Sumter, a Marion, and a Davie. It is only when we have reached this point that public spirit is commensurate with the danger.

In the second place, we must guard sacredly against cherishing a temper of presumptuous confidence. The cause is not ours but God's; and if we measure its importance only by its accidental relation to ourselves, we may be suffered to perish for our pride. No nation ever yet achieved anything great that it did not regard itself as the instrument of Providence. The only lasting inspiration of lofty patriotism and exalted courage is the inspiration of religion. The Greeks and Romans never ventured upon any important enterprise without consulting their gods. They felt that they were safe only as they were persuaded that they were in alliance with heaven. Man, though limited in space, limited in time, and limited in knowledge, is truly great, when he is linked to the Infinite, as the means of accomplishing lasting ends. To be God's servant, that is his highest destiny, his sublimest calling. Nations are under the pupilage of Providence; they are in training themselves, that they may be the instruments of furthering the progress of the human race.

Polybius, the historian, traces the secret of Roman greatness to the profound sense of religion which constituted a striking feature of the national character. He calls it, expressly, the firmest pillar of the Roman State; and he does not hesitate to denounce, as enemies to public order and prosperity, those of his own contemporaries who sought to undermine the sacredness of these convictions. Even Napoleon sustained his vaulting ambition by a mysterious connection with the invisible world. He was a man of destiny. It is the relation to God, and His providential training of the race, that imparts true dignity to our struggle; and we must recognize ourselves as God's servants, working out His glorious ends, or we shall infallibly be left to stumble upon the dark mountains of error. Our trust in Him must be the real spring of our heroic resolution to conquer or to die. A sentiment of honor, a momentary enthusiasm, may prompt and sustain spasmodic exertions of an extraordinary character; but a steady valor, a self-denying patriotism, protracted patience, a readiness to do, and dare, and suffer, through a generation or an age, this comes only from a sublime faith in God. The worst symptom that any people can manifest, is that of pride. With nations, as with individuals, it goes before a fall. Let us guard against it. Let us rise to the true grandeur of our calling, and go forth as servants of the Most High, to execute His purposes. In this spirit we are safe. By this spirit our principles are ennobled, and our cause translated from earth to heaven. An overweening confidence in the righteousness of our cause, as if that alone were sufficient to insure our success, betrays gross inattention to the Divine dealings with communities and States. In the issue betwixt ourselves and our enemies, we may be free from blame; but there may be other respects in which we have provoked the judgments of Heaven, and there may be other grounds on which God has a controversy with us, and the swords of our enemies may be His chosen instruments to execute His wrath. He may first use them as a rod, and then punish them in other forms for their own iniquities. Hence, it behooves us not only to have a righteous cause, but to be a righteous people. We must abandon all our sins, and put ourselves heartily and in earnest on the side of Providence.

Hence, this dependence upon Providence carries with it the necessity of removing from the midst of us whatever is offensive to a holy God. If the Government is His ordinance, and the people His instruments, they must see to it that they serve Him with no unwashed or defiled hands. We must cultivate a high standard of public virtue. We must renounce all personal and selfish sins, and we must rebuke every custom or institution that tends to deprave the public morals. Virtue is power, and vice is weakness. The same Polybius, to whom we have already referred, traces the influence of the religious sentiment at Rome in producing faithful and incorruptible magistrates, who were strangers alike to bribery and favor in executing the laws and dispensing the trusts of the State, and that high tone of public faith which made an oath of absolute security for faithfulness. This stern simplicity of manners we must cherish, if we hope to succeed. Bribery, corruption, favoritism, electioneering, flattery, and every species of double-dealing; drunkenness, profaneness, debauchery, selfishness, avarice, and extortion; all base material ends must be banished by a stern integrity, if we would become the fit instruments of a holy Providence in a holy cause. Sin is a reproach to any people. It is weakness; it is sure, though it may be slow, decay. Faith in God—that is, the watchword of martyrs, whether in the cause of truth or of bribery. That alone ennobles and sanctifies.

"All other nations," except the French, as Burke has significantly remarked, in relation to the memorable revolution which was doomed to failure in consequence of this capital omission, "have begun the fabric of a new Government, or the reformation of an old, by establishing originally, or by enforcing with greater exactness, some rites or other of religion. All other people have laid the foundations of civil freedom in severer manners, and a system of a more austere and masculine morality." To absolve the State, which is the society of rights, from a strict responsibility to the Author and Source of justice and of law, is to destroy the firmest security of public order, to convert liberty into license, and to impregnate the very being of the commonwealth with the seeds of dissolution and decay. France failed, because France forgot God; and if we tread in the footsteps of that infatuated people, and treat with equal contempt the holiest instincts of our nature, we too may be abandoned to our folly, and become the hissing and the scorn of all the nations of the earth. "Be wise now, therefore, O ye kings! be instructed, ye Judges of the earth. Kiss the Son, lest He be angry, and ye perish from the way, when His wrath is kindled but a little. Blessed are all they that put their trust in Him."

In the third place, let us endeavor rightly to interpret the reverses which have recently attended our arms. It is idle to make light of them. They are serious—they are disastrous. The whole end of Providence in any dispensation it were presumptuous for any one, independently of a special revelation, to venture to decipher. But there are tendencies which lie upon the surface, and these obvious tendencies are designed for our guidance and instruction. In the present case, we may humbly believe that one purpose aimed at has been to rebuke our confidence and our pride. We had begun to despise our enemy, and to prophesy safety without much hazard. We had laughed at his cowardice, and boasted of our superior prowess and skill. Is it strange that, while indulging such a temper, we ourselves should be made to turn our backs, and to become a jest to those whom we had jeered? We had grown licentious, intemperate and profane; is it strange that, in the midst of our security, God should teach us that sin is a reproach to any people? Is it strange that He should remind us of the moral conditions upon which alone we are authorized to hope for success? The first lesson, therefore, is one of rebuke and repentance. It is a call to break off our sins by righteousness, and to turn our eyes to the real secret of national security and strength.

The second end may be one of trial. God has placed us in circumstances in which, if we show that we are equal to the emergency, all will acknowledge our right to the freedom which we have so signally vindicated. We have now the opportunity for great exploits. We can demonstrate to the world what manner of spirit we are of. If our courage and faith rise superior to the danger, we shall not only succeed, but we shall succeed with a moral influence and character that shall render our success doubly valuable. Providence seems to be against us—disaster upon disaster has attended our arms—the enemy is in possession of three States, and beleaguers us in all our coasts. His resources and armaments are immense, and his energy and resolution desperate. His numbers are so much superior, that we are like a flock of kids before him. We have nothing to stand on but the eternal principles of truth and right, and the protection and alliance of a just God. Can we look the danger unflinchingly in the face, and calmly resolve to meet it and subdue it? Can we say, in reliance upon Providence, that, were his numbers and resources a thousand fold greater, the interests at stake are so momentous, that we will not be conquered? Do we feel the moral power of courage, of resolution, of heroic will, rising and swelling within us, until it towers above all the smoke and dust of the invasion? Then we are in a condition to do great deeds. We are in the condition of Greece when Xerxes hung upon the borders of Attica with an army of five millions that had never been conquered, and to which State after State of Northern Greece had yielded in its progress. Little Athens was the object of his vengeance. Leonidas had fallen—four days more would bring the destroyer to the walls of the devoted city. There the people were, a mere handful. Their first step had been to consult the gods, and the astounding reply which they received from Delphi would have driven any other people to despair. "Wretched men!" said the oracle, which they believed to be infallible, "why sit ye there! Quit your land and city, and flee afar! Head, body, feet, and hands are alike rotten; fire and sword, in the train of the Syrian chariot shall overwhelm you; nor only *your* city, but other cities also, as well as many even of the temples of the gods, which are now sweating and trembling with fear, and foreshadow, by drops of blood on their roofs, the hard calamities impending. Get ye away from the sanctuary, with your souls steeped in sorrow." *We* have had reverses, but no such oracle as this. It was afterwards modified so as to give a ray of hope, in an ambiguous allusion to wooden walls. But the soul of the Greek rose with the danger, and we have a succession of events, from the desertion of Athens to the final expulsion of the invader, which make that little spot of earth immortal. Let us imitate, in Christian faith, this sublime example. Let our spirit be loftier than that of the pagan Greek, and we can succeed in making every pass a Thermopylæ, every strait a Salamis, and every plain a Marathon. We can conquer and we *must*. We must not suffer any other thought to enter our minds. If we are overrun, we can at least die; and if our enemies get possession of our land, we can leave it a howling desert. But, under God, we shall not fail. If we are true to him, and true to ourselves, a glorious future is before us. We occupy a sublime position. The eyes of the world are upon us; we are a spectacle to God, to angels, and to men. Can our hearts grow faint, or our hands feeble, in a cause like this? The spirits of our fathers call to us from their graves. The heroes of other ages and other countries are beckoning us on to glory. Let us seize the opportunity, and make to ourselves an immortal name, while we redeem a land from bondage, and a continent from ruin.

J. D. B. De Bow

A TALK WITH RADICAL LEADERS

In this, one of the last major articles he wrote before his death on February 27, 1867, De Bow attempted to defend the actions of the South over the preceding six years and to convince northern leaders to adopt a reconstruction policy of reconciliation rather than vengeance. An avid secessionist in the late fifties and early sixties, De Bow made no apology for his earlier views or for the actions of the South. He still believed in the theoretical right of secession, though the northern victory had eliminated it as a practical course of action. He accepted, though not cheerfully, the northern triumph and dedicated his revived Review *to the "honor and prosperity of the Country" and to "the reestablishment of Southern Prosperity."*

De Bow, however, like many other former Confederates, had not entirely given up trying to win by peaceful means what the South had lost in war. Reconstruction in 1865–66 under the policies of President Andrew Johnson allowed southerners a considerable measure of self-control. Men like De Bow argued that the South would use the opportunity to rebuild a strong Union and to solve the "negro question" in its own way. For southerners, reconstruction meant retaining as much of their prewar world as possible, but especially continuing the subordination of blacks to whites. Several states were reluctant even to do the minimum required by Johnson: repudiate slavery, secession, and the Confederate debt. Even more disturbing to northern leaders were the black codes enacted by most southern states. Designed to replace the slave codes, the black codes, although accepting the abolition of slavery, hedged the freedman with restrictions that limited his freedom and ensured white domination. By mid-1866, these and similar actions prompted many northerners to wonder who had won the war.

When De Bow wrote his article, the Radical leaders in the Republican party had become convinced of the need for harsher reconstruction measures and had begun to take steps to remove reconstruction from the control of President Johnson. De Bow argued that such steps were unnecessary and could only produce more suffering and bitterness. Like many southerners, he believed that the war and defeat were suffi-

Vol. II, After War Series (October, 1866), pp. 337–46.

cient punishment for whatever sins the South might have committed. A harsh reconstruction policy, in his view, could only sow the seeds of future discord. He was particularly concerned that the South be allowed to resolve the "negro question" in its own fashion—in other words, to find new means to enforce Negro subordination. De Bow's pleas, however eloquent, fell on deaf ears, for the Radicals in Congress were determined not to allow the South to win the peace.

"While Vengeance pondered o'er new plans of pain,
And staunched the blood she saves to shed again."
Byron.—*Corsair.*

You are the head and front of that offending, which for so many long years has reaped its fruits in the alienation of the people of this great country, in the array of section against section, of neighborhood against neighborhood, until the whole land has been converted into a Pandemonium, and civil war has run its career of blood, rapine, devastation and death. Some of you are men of scholarly attainments, of much research, taught in history and philosophy, and outside the limits of your proclivities as agitators, we are informed, are men of many social and personal qualities. The errors of such men are more dangerous, their very sincerity and earnestness are the harbingers of greater woe to their country.

Granting which, I am reluctant to admit that personal grievances have had much to do with raising many of you to your present bad eminence, and that you have been cheered onward by thousands as misguided as yourselves, and giving you even the benefit of the statement, that those against whom your ire is aroused are not free from offence (if you please, have themselves been active offenders), can there be found in all of this justification for the savage and merciless warfare which you wage? It is no longer the noble and manly warfare of the field, of armed host against armed host, of bayonet, ball and shell; but a war of the armed against the disarmed, of the strong against the weak, of the conqueror against his prisoners, for it is to this condition that the event of the recent great war has reduced the millions of the South!

And, sirs, who are these people of the South, that having overcome by overwhelming millions from your Northern hive, it is the end of your philosophy, by every ingenious contrivance of discriminating legislation, of restrictions, of agrarian and revolutionary manœuvring, to humiliate, degrade and crush hopelessly and forever? Who are they?

When your ancestors of the *Mayflower*, in the dim antiquity of our country, were struggling with the savages of the North, ours enduring equal hardship, and with like spirit and determination, were grappling with those by the waters of the James and the Roanoke, in the sandy dells and among the flowery slopes of the Cooper and the Ashley, the beautiful May and the Savannah. These hardy pioneers made the wilderness to smile and blossom, and transferred from the Old to the New World their high notions of liberty and independence, bequeathing them as an inheritance to their children. Among those pioneers who landed at Port Royal, in South Carolina, in the century which first disturbed the repose of Cape Cod, were the ancestors of the present writer.

Two centuries came of marvelous life and energy, the record of which is scarcely preserved to us more than in tradition or doubtful history; wigwams and cabins, tomahawks and rifles, Indian councils and woodman's axes, King Philips and Yemasees, and the people by the Connecticut, the James, or the Savannah, emerged from the wilderness and talked to kings and Parliaments, and ministers of rights, of independence and liberty, and backed their noble language by blows, fast and thick, from which despotism at last recoiled. These workers of the forest, descendants of Winslow or Standish, of Berkley or Craven, cemented by the memories of common toils and dangers, came together in council, banded together in the field, and presented to the world an example of heroic devotion, intrepidity, courage, and valor, which has ever since lived in song and story. Were the fights less sanguinary when led by Sumter or Marion, than when led by Putnam? Was not the path of the invader tracked with blood, whether he landed by the Hudson, the Chesapeake, or along the Southern bays? Were the Washingtons, the Lees, the Randolphs, Henrys, Rutledges, the Middletons and Pinckneys, in retirement, while the Hancocks and Adamses were carrying through the Glorious War, and when that struggle was over, and the nations of the world anxiously awaited results, were the councils of Jefferson and Madison and the Pinckneys rejected, whilst that of the Hamiltons and Jays was left free and untrammeled to build up the colossal fabric of American liberty? Is it needful to forget all of this?

Three-quarters of a century again. The infant nation has reached to vigorous manhood. Westward Ho! is the cry from the Penobscot to the St. Johns. Texas and Arkansas, Arizona and Missouri, alike with Oregon and Nebraska, bespeak the venturous enterprise and daring of the sections. They meet shoulder to shoulder and breast to breast in fighting against Britain the second battle of independence: in the same Union they brave death from the Seminole in the glades of Florida, and carry the banner of the Stars through all the desperate encounters of Mexico, from the Castle de Ulloa to the very capital of the Aztecs. Washington, Jackson, Scott, Taylor, chosen chieftains in these great encounters, sons of the South all, do their glories pale by the side of Northern heroes? And in the great field of State-craft and diplomacy, was not the national honor and repute preserved untarnished, and the national rights vindicated and upheld through all this period, though for two-thirds of it the sceptre was in Southern hands, and in nearly all of it Southern intellect was represented everywhere, at home and abroad? In enterprise and wealth, section went hand in hand with section, though perhaps in different degrees; and whilst Northern factories and workshops peopled densely its sterile shores, and foreign immigration sought the teeming prairies of the West, the exhaustless agricultural regions of the South freighted the great navies of the country with its splendid products, brought back the fabrics for which they were exchanged, and raised the nation to the rank of almost the first maritime power upon earth!

What secret causes were at work, during all this period, to undermine the noble structure, what teachings of statesmen or demagogues, what seeds of bitterness were sown or reaped, or who is responsible for the final catastrophe, it is needless here to inquire. John Randolph, who saw the Government inaugurated, claimed to have seen, even then, the "poison under its wing." In the times of the embargo, and the war which followed; when Louisiana was purchased or Missouri was admitted; when the tariff policy sought to become a vehicle of oppression; or when the Mexican war left its Pandora's box of territorial evils, the poison continued to manifest and diffuse itself, until the whole body politic was threatened with incurable disease. The end was sure, however delayed. The statesmen of Massachusetts, when pressed, alike with those of Virginia and Carolina, taught the doctrines of State rights and State remedies, and among these, that of breaking up the compact and resuming sovereignty. The question was argued in Congress, as it had been in all the State conventions which adopted the Constitution, and, to say the least, was left undecided; it was argued by the press, in the courts, and by great political parties. The South, in the main, accepted one view, and the North another. Acting upon its own theory, the blow was struck. Thirteen States seceded!

There was nowhere a more sincere and earnest believer in the right of secession, nor a more earnest advocate of its practice at this particular juncture than ourselves, believing, as we did, that it would be for the interest of both sections, on account of irreconcilable differences, to establish independent but friendly nationalities. The energies of each would thus be left free and untrammeled, and their mutual action upon each other would be favorable to the liberties of the whole. It is not clear yet, but that history will pronounce the same verdict when the generations now upon the stage shall have long since passed away. We regarded it a peaceable measure, and believe that had a more rational policy actuated the North, war could not have resulted. The idea of *permanent* separation was not yet entertained by Southern masses, and it was altogether practicable, with slight concessions, to have reconstructed the Union without one drop of blood. We thought this result highly probable, whether desirable or not, and believe that ninety-nine in the hundred of the people of the South entertained the same secret expectations. Mr. Lincoln's call for troops, to repossess, by force of arms, those forts and navy yards which it had been thought were possessed of right, and in virtue of the doctrine of State sovereignty, dissipated the illusion.

Throwing aside, however, the question of *responsibility*, when the decision against us was the sword, we will do the Southern people the justice to say, there was no longer any hesitation. The day of debate was ended. The talent, the worth, the intellect, all that was noble and distinguished in the States, from Virginia to Texas, the descendants of the men who fought with Washington at Yorktown, of the heroes who figured in all the great fights where the national eagle floated, or who vindicated the fame of the nation on the ocean, on the floors of Congress, in the chair of the Presidency, or the Cabinet, or in positions of honor abroad, buckled on their armor, marshaled their cohorts, and in hot haste rushed to the front. The exceptions were so few as not to affect the rule, and we are not now, nor ever have been, willing to impugn the motives, or to denounce the men, scattered here and there, in most of the States, who constitute the exceptions. Let them defend their record as we do our own.

Was this a rebellion? were these traitors, or did the struggle rise to a greater and nobler altitude? The question can remain for history. Name it, if you please, however harshly, and where do you find, in all the histories that you have read, from those of Thucidides and Livy, down to Bancroft and Hildreth, so unequal a struggle, maintained with so much fire and energy; such deeds of valor and prowess performed; such privations and sufferings endured; such heroism displayed. How many great armies were driven back; what captains' fortunes were ruined, what Saragossa defences, as at Charleston and Vicksburg! Six millions of men were in the death struggle against four times that number; six millions without a ship, with scarcely a gun-boat, cut off from all the world by rigorous blockade, without clothing, without arms, and often without food! Yet the fight went on for four long years, until some of your leading writers and thinkers began to express the opinion that Southern independence was virtually achieved. These deeds of daring and of heroism, this record of energy and endurance, startled the European world, and extorted its admiration if not its friendship. Are the men of the North less impressible by the morally sublime, when exhibited by those once their enemies? Can they not recognize heroism, and claim it as their common heritage in the future? Even heroism, if you please to say so, in a wrong cause.

This people have not been degraded or humbled. It is not in your power, and if you are true statesmen it cannot be your desire to do either. They are your countrymen, and for good or for ill, your descendants and theirs, in all the ages that are to come, are likely to mingle together. Their crest is erect! Let their losses be ever so severe, they do not embrace Honor. That survives, and fortunately for America it does, for what a picture would its republicanism present, were the people of one-third of the States, self-acknowledged, to be degraded and debased! Neither revenge nor policy could dictate this. Revenge could not be gratified by sowing the storm to reap the whirlwind. Policy, ancient and modern, teaches differently. The Greeks and Romans conquered the world by conciliation, laws, liberties, institutions, as well as by arms. English liberties and the English Constitution have been maintained by the descendants of York and Lancaster, of Cromwell and the Cavaliers. On the field of Bosworth, after the star of Richard had set in blood, the princely Richmond could exclaim:

> "Proclaim a pardon to the soldiers fled
> That in submission will return to us;

And then, as we have taken the Sacrament,
We will unite the White Rose and the Red;
Smile Heaven upon this fair conjunction
That long hath frowned upon their enmity."

A people with such antecedents as those of the South cannot submit permanently to be lorded over and acknowledge the authority of a master race. They may endure for a time, but the wound will rankle and bleed afresh, and they will strike back and bite the heel of the oppressor. Inextinguishable hatred will grow up, and their children and children's children, like the infant Hannibal, will be sworn upon the altars of vengeance. Nor ought the power of such a race to be despised. Weak it may be to-day, disorganized and overwhelmed by defeat, and colossal, disciplined, and organized may be the power which is brought in threatening attitude against it. There are small accidents in history which change the relations of peoples. The weak have but to wait upon opportunity. Ireland, Poland, Italy, Hungary, will rise and rise again. History is full of these examples. A vast military establishment, great standing armies, garrisons will be needed here, and whilst their force is expended in crushing rebellion in one quarter, in such wide domain, it will be aroused and rampant in a hundred others. The Tyrant, the Oppressor, and the Despot will in vain seek to prevent opportunities which the great political relations of the world involve, and he will, even in the grandeur of his pretensions, tremble before them.

"Who would be free
Themselves *will* strike the blow."

But why drive a brave and earnest people to despair? What great public purpose can be answered? In what respect will the North be happier, wealthier, more powerful by such a course? What Christian or patriotic instinct can be gratified by it? You have said that freemen work better than slaves, and is not the doctrine as applicable to white men as to negroes? Do you not hasten to get rid of the expense and charge of territories by converting them into States? Has not Britain realized a thousand times over profit by the change which made her colonies independent States?

Do you wish to make secession odious and prevent the possibility of its recurrence? If sharp, fierce, and sanguinary war has not accomplished this, do you think that the meaner remedies of the thumbscrew and the galleys will avail? What a compliment are you paying to a people whose standards have all gone down and the debris only of whose power survives? Methinks

"There be *six* Richmonds in the field—
Five have I slain to-day!"

The South went down under your cohorts and your legions, else would she be in arms now; but having gone down with her broad and teeming lands wasted, with her cities destroyed, her warriors scattered, and bleeding, and dead, her resources exhausted, and her people clothed in sackcloth and in ashes, yours is a magnificent tribute, when behind every lash you see her bayonets gleaming still. Compose yourselves. The work is done—done efficiently and finally. The issue which was made fairly, was as fairly decided. In appealing to the sword, its arbitrament was accepted. People knew no higher Courts, and Congresses may decide as they please—*the bayonet gives the law*! From the Chesapeake to El Paso, the South tells you this. Her legislatures, her statesmen, her disarmed warriors, her people of high and low degree all solemnly and emphatically declare it, and having discovered their truth and earnestness, when they told you that they meant *war*, can you not trust them now when they tell you that they mean *peace*, permanent and lasting peace? Moreover, the issues which resulted in war are extinct. If new ones arise, they are as likely to be such as will disturb the peace of the North as ours. No man in our domain, unless within the walls of a lunatic asylum, dreams of resistance to a power which in the heyday of our prosperity and might, bore so overwhelmingly and resistlessly upon us. The Government of the United States is our *only* government, and in its honor and glory must we find ours!

But perhaps you expect to help the negro. Well now:

"In the name of all the gods at once
On what meat was this our *darkey* fed
That he is grown so great?"

Is all the machinery of this vast government, its Congress, courts, purse, sword, but so many ingenious contrivances to take care of Cuffee and his rights? Now, gentlemen radicals, let us reason a little. Have you not done enough for Ethiopia? You enslaved the negro. Well! you vowed his emancipation and removed his shackles. At the cost of five thousand millions of treasure and perhaps a million of lives you have made him free. There he stands. On the basis of these figures each puling infant of the Freedmen's Bureau has been purchased by the nation with twelve hundred and fifty dollars in gold, and wherever you see four of them together, recollect that the forfeit has been the death of one white citizen! We are not complaining of this, however, but stating the fact. *All that the negro has earned in bondage for the white man has been returned to him with interest.* Have you not done enough, then? Will you find a better stopping-point? *He is free!* If he be a man, if he has thoughts, will, instincts, appetites, capacities, can he not take care of himself as you and we have done; and if he has not these attributes, can you give them? Nobody wishes now his enslavement. The Gordian knot has been cut. The responsibility, from which, as Christian men, we shrunk, is yours. The problem baffled us and our fathers. It baffles no longer! With us the negro is to live and not with you. The wealth of the nation could not colonize him. We want his labor—there are thousands of avenues of employment in which it can be absorbed. Will it not be our interest to make him a contented laborer and an efficient one, and will not the laws of competition settle questions of remuneration for one race as well as for another? *The ties of sympathy between the negro and the white man, his former master, are not dissolved because slavery has ceased.* The negro has been associated with our youth, our manhood, and our homes, and by no act of his is he dissociated now. He has the double protection of our sympathies and interests. There will be parties, too, growing up at the South who will gradually avail themselves of the negro element. The North may be sure that in the contestation the negro will in time get every right and privilege. That day cannot be hurried. All attempt to do so will bring an "Iliad of Woes" to the luckless negro. Trust at least to time and the new social elements that will be brought into play. Millions of your own people and people from all the nationalities of Europe will seek the golden treasures of the South, and we are inviting them by immigration, societies and associations, in all the States and cities. Let them come. We are not afraid of, but invite the inundation. We shall live happily and prosperously with us, each minding our own affairs, and each building up one vast empire. Let it be kept upon record, too, that African freedom is no new thing at the South. When the war opened there were a half million of emancipated blacks within our domain, and it was never alleged, even by Fred Douglass, that they were possessed of fewer social rights, immunities, and privileges than those of his own section. We believe that he even asserted the contrary, but if he did not, we will read a little from the Compendium of the Census of 1850, page 81. By the table it appears, that of the free colored population in New York sixty were clerks, doctors, druggists, merchants, ministers, printers, students, and teachers, or one in fifty-five of the whole, and in New Orleans there were one hundred and sixty-five in similar occupations, or one in eleven! The proportion of negroes occupying positions requiring education was in Connecticut one in one hundred of the whole, and in Louisiana one in *twelve*! The following is quoted also from page 196 of the same Census:

"In Connecticut $215,535 in real estate was owned by free blacks, and $88,000 by mulattoes; total $303,535. In Louisiana $311,465 by free blacks, and $3,958,830 by mulattoes; total $4,270,295. New York city owned by free blacks, $65,310, by mulattoes $44,000. New Orleans owned by free blacks $222,970, mulattoes $1,991,000. In Barnwell, Beaufort and Charleston, S.C., fifty-eight free colored owned under $1,000 each of real estate, ten owned between $1,000 and $5,000 *each*, two between $5,000 and $10,000, etc."

Do you expect to advance the prosperity of the Union? The whole land is covered by one vast mortgage created by the war—a mortgage which bears sharply upon its industry and threatens its future safety. This mortgage must be raised. The Southern fields, which have been the great creators of wealth in the past, can create again, and from this source, if left free and untrammeled, and not otherwise, you may expect princely contributions to the National exchequer. Under even the partially "let alone" policy before the war, she furnished five hundred millions of dollars annually as a trading capital to the North. Grant that she is crippled; you cannot mend one wing by breaking the other. There is power yet in her soil, and power in her energies, which have been wonderfully developed and brought forth by war, not dreamed of in your philosophy. Her mineral as well as agricultural wealth is limitless. Witness her marvelous achievements in the past few months. In the moment which sheathed the sword she grasped the plow-handle, and amid all the embarrassments of the negro question, reclaimed from the wilderness whole principalities which had once blossomed as the rose. This, too, without money and without credit. She has repaired and put in working order her vast railroad system, which was left without bridges, without iron, without locomotives, and without cars, and not satisfied, she has revived every projected route, and is seeking, by organized companies, to connect every part of her interior.

She is erecting factories and workshops at a rate which was never seen before. She is rebuilding her country mansions, and her towns, Selma, Atlanta, Columbia, Charleston arise, Phoenix like, from the flames. Witness, too, the improvement on her newspapers. Her periodical press issues two numbers where but one was issued before. Each charity is fostered and sustained. Churches go up, asylums for the disabled, hospitals for the sick, relief establishments for the widow and the child; schools on every hill, colleges and academies more numerous, better organized, and more largely attended than ever. Despondency nowhere. What a people!

A word in conclusion to what are called *Southern radicals*. There are such scattered through all the States with greater or less power. Is it your *interest* to keep up these agitations? Your leaders deceive, if they do not tell you that you are in a small minority. You were not strong enough to prevent secession. The wave went over you. You yielded. Grant that you were wronged, grant that you suffered; do you not mistake your remedy? Those who opposed the old Revolutionary War returned after peace, and their children and children's children reaped the glories of that event. Even the property that had been sequestered was restored. Your condition would have been much better than these. There are stronger reasons now to ignore the past. There is room enough in the country for all. We can all prosper, grow rich, and according to merit share political power. Better the friendship of your neighbor across the road or in the next county, than your neighbor in Boston or New Hampshire. You cannot successfully oppose an overwhelming public opinion. Insist upon it, and sooner or later you go down. Acknowledge the fact; graciously, manfully, generously and intelligently, and you will be received back into the family fold, and in a few years all that existed of strife and bitterness will be things of the past, trifles light as air in the comparison of our harmonious Union and accord. We are not without hope. The Convention which was recently held in Philadelphia, where all of the States from the St. Lawrence to the Pacific affiliated harmoniously after six years of separation, was a magnificent and stirring event, and will cast its influences over all the land. Good and true men will look up. Hope will revive, and even the worst radical, we care not who, will see the necessity of bending to the storm. If you have sinned, sin no more—

> "While yet the lamp holds out to burn,
> The vilest sinner may return."

George Fitzhugh

CAMP LEE AND THE FREEDMAN'S BUREAU

Before the Civil War, George Fitzhugh was one of the most militant defenders of slavery in the South. In his books, Sociology for the South *(1854) and* Cannibals All! *(1859), and in* De Bow's Review *he repeatedly defended a patriarchal social system and argued that slavery, either chattel or wage, was the natural condition of most men. Fitzhugh believed that chattel slavery was better for the slave than the "wage slavery" of the North and Europe because it offered the slave greater protection. Fitzhugh was resigned to the outcome of the war and the abolition of slavery. He retained, however, his interest in the condition of the former slaves, especially because he suspected they could not long survive without the protection of their masters.*

In spite of his proslavery views, Fitzhugh took a position with the Freedman's Bureau after the war. Many white southerners hated the Freedman's Bureau for its efforts to ease the transition from slavery to freedom. The bureau faced the almost insurmountable problems of relief, education, health and sanitation, land and labor contract disputes, and southern hostility. In each district, the bureau established a special court to decide minor disputes. To each of these courts, two agents were attached, one white and one black. Fitzhugh was chosen as an agent for the Richmond, Virginia, district where he served as an associate judge in the Freedman's Bureau court from October, 1865, until late 1866. Fitzhugh's court was at Camp Lee outside of Richmond, and in this piece he recounted his experiences.

Fitzhugh's observations on the blacks and the Freedman's Bureau were both genial and patronizing. He conceded that the bureau was necessary only because he retained his longstanding conviction that blacks could not survive without masters of some sort. Even while a bureau judge, he looked forward to the day when the South would regain the management of the Negroes and again make them work profitably. He would not have long to wait: Congress terminated most functions of the Freedman's Bureau in 1869, its educational work in 1870, and all remaining responsibilities in 1872, leaving the former slaves in the care of their former masters.

Vol. II, After War Series (October, 1866), pp. 346–55.

Camp Lee, about a mile from Richmond, is but a branch or appendage of the Freedman's Bureau in that city. For this reason, and because we ourselves live at Camp Lee, and until recently held our court in Richmond, we have thought it would be appropriate to treat of the two in connection. Admitted behind the curtains, were we curious, prying, or observant, we might have collected materials for an article at once rich, racy and instructive; but we are, unfortunately, abstracted, and see or hear very little that is going on around us. What we have seen and heard, so far as we deem it interesting, we will relate, without breach of confidence, because nothing has been told us in confidence, and we have seen or heard nothing at all discreditable to any officer of the Bureau.

The institution has a very pretty name, but unlike the rose, "would not smell as sweet by any other name." In truth, it is simply and merely a negro nursery; a fact which would have been obvious even to the blind, if led into our little court-room, where the stove was in full blast, and about a hundred cushites were in attendance, as suitors, witnesses or idle lookers-on. You may be sure, Mr. Editor, we smoked desperately and continuously. As this habit of ours, of smoking whilst sitting on the Bench, has been made the subject of remark in some of the Northern papers, we deem this explanation due to our contemporaries and to posterity; for as part, parcel, or appurtenance of the Negro Nursery, we shall certainly descend to posterity. Indeed, a good many of our Federal friends will be obliged to us for this explanation, for our soldiers smoked terribly in Richmond, quite as terribly as Uncle Toby's soldiers swore in Flanders.

This Negro Nursery is an admirable idea of the Federals, which, however, they stole from us. For we always told them the darkeys were but grown-up children that needed guardians, like all other children. They saw this very soon, and therefore established the Freedmen's Bureau; at first for a year, thinking that a year's tuition under Yankee school ma'ams and Federal Provost Marshals would amply fit them for self-support, liberty and equality, and the exercise of the right of suffrage. They have now added two years more to the duration of the Bureau, because they now see that the necessity for nursing the negroes is twice as urgent as they thought it at first. At the end of that time, they will discover that their pupils are irreclaimable "*mauvais sujets*," aand will be ready to throw up "in divine disgust" the whole negro-nursing and negro-teaching business, and to turn the affair over to the State authorities.

The American people, by that time, must become satisfied that they have expended enough, aye, and far too much, of blood and treasure in the hopeless attempt to make citizens of negroes. They must first be made men, and the Bureau is a practical admission and assertion that they are not men, and will not be for two years hence. By that time they think the Ethiopian will change his skin. We are sure he will not. Negro he is, negro he always has been, and negro he always will be. Never has he been, and never will he be a man, physically, morally, or intellectually, in the European or American sense of the term. None are so thoroughly aware that the term "negro" is, in its ordinary acceptation, the negation of manhood, as the abolitionists and the negroes themselves. They are no longer negroes, but "colored people." Those who call them other than negroes, are acting falsely and hypocritically, for they thereby as good as assert that these blacks have changed their natures, moral and intellectual, and risen to an equality with the whites.

They are our fellow-beings, children, not men, and therefore to be compassionated and taken care of.

The Bureau has occasioned much irritation, and in some instances, no doubt, been guilty of wrong and injustice to our people; but it has saved the South a world of money and of trouble, and expended a great deal of money among us, at a time when we could spare neither men nor money to keep order among the negroes, or to support the helpless ones. We can bear it for two years longer, but after that time we must have negro-nurseries of our own; that is, like the Federals, we must institute a distinct and separate government for the negroes. A majority of those living in the country will subside, if they have not already subsided, into the "*statu quo ante bellum.*" The crowds of paupers, beggars, rogues, and vagabonds, infesting our cities and their suburbs, must be summarily dealt with by State bureaux located in each considerable town. No bureaux or bureau officers will be needed in the country, or in villages—nor are they even now needed.

We have resided at Camp Lee for more than a year. During that whole time there have been from three to five hundred negroes here, furnished with houses by the Federal authorities, part of which were built by the Confederates during the war for military purposes, and part by the State Agricultural Society. The grounds are still owned by that Society. The brick house, however, in which we reside was originally erected by Colonel John Mayo, deceased, father-in-law of General Winfield Scott. The dwelling-house, called the Hermitage, was burned down many years ago. The Society added a story to these brick buildings, and erected two-storied porticos in front and at the sides of them. They now make quite an imposing appearance, with a portico of a hundred and fifty feet in front, and wings of about eighty on the lower floor, and one of equal extent on the upper floor. We are, just now, the sole occupant of the lower floor, and a French lady the sole occasional occupant of the upper floor.

Most of this building, until a few weeks since, was occupied by Mrs. Gibbons, her daughter and Miss Ellison. Whilst they were here, Camp Lee was tolerable, and often very agreeable, even to us, separated as we are from our family. We hope, and have reason to expect, that they will return during this fall. In front of this building, we have a market-garden of two acres, which so far, owing to the drought, has been a great failure, but which Daniel Coleman (Freedman), our gardener, assures us will do wonderfully well as a fall garden. But we are quite incredulous. We are great at theory, and hence generally fail in practice.

Just beside our vegetable-garden stands Mrs. Gibbons' zoological-garden. Here she would sometimes have as many as a hundred and twenty negro orphans, of both sexes, and various ages. The buildings for them were ample and commodious. Mrs. G.'s attention and kindness to her wards was assiduous, untiring, and very successful. When she first took these infants in charge, some time last fall, the mortality among them was fearful; but after about two months, by frequent ablutions, close shaving of their heads, abundance of warm and clean clothing, and plenty of good and various food, they were rendered remarkably healthy, and so continued until their removal to Philadelphia. Mrs. G. removed, in all, about two hundred to that city. We presume they have not been so healthful there, for we learn, indirectly, that the Board of Health of that city has advised, or required, their removal. Poor things! Camp Lee was a Paradise to them. Immorality and crime in every form, want and disease, will fill up the balance of their existence. They will be feeble, hated, persecuted and despised. They lost nothing in losing their parents; but lost all in losing their masters. They will meet with no more kind Mrs. Gibbons in this cold, harsh, cruel world.

Mrs. Gibbons is a member of the Society of Friends, deputed by an association of ladies, of Philadelphia, belonging to that society, to superintend the negro orphan asylum at this place. The Bureau furnishes the ordinary rations to these infants, and the association abundance of whatever else that is needed for their comfortable subsistence. When Mrs. Gibbons left, she had on hand some fifty-five new comers, not yet prepared to be sent North. These were sent over to Howard Grove, another branch of the Negro Nursery at Richmond. We believe most of the sick, aged and infirm negroes are sent there. It was a Confederate hospital during the war, and is now a negro nursery and hospital. We have never visited it since the war. Near it is Chimborazo Hospital, now Nursery, and this also was a Confederate hospital. There were a great many negroes there last winter, but we believe the Bureau has succeeded in getting rid of all but the infants and infirm. We learn there are nine ladies there, teaching literary or industrial schools.

Miss Ellison was the teacher at this place. This teaching, however, is, we fear, but a cruel farce, that but incites to insubordination, and will induce the negroes to run a muck against the whites, in which Cuffee will come off second best. These negro orphans have lost their parents, but we feel quite positive that in three instances out of four their parents are not both dead. Negroes possess much amiableness of feeling but not the least steady, permanent affection. "Out of sight, out of mind," is true of them all. They never grieve twenty-four hours for the death of parents, wives, husbands, or children. Some of the negroes at this place informed us, many months ago, that many of Mrs. Gibbons' orphans had parents in Richmond. About four weeks since, a very interesting little negro child, about two years old, was deserted by its mother, picked up in the streets of Richmond, and brought to Mrs. Gibbons. Not ten days since, just at the approach of a terrific storm, a negro mother left her little daughter, of about five years old, exposed in the field, within a few hundred yards of this place. It was picked up by some kind-hearted negro, and is now in the keeping of the French lady. It is clever, and extremely emaciate. It has been starved. But we do not blame the poor mother. She, too, deprived of a master, was no doubt starving, and the best she could possibly do was thus to expose her child, with the hope that some humane person able to provide for it might find it and take it in charge. . . .

The negroes in the country are contented, and valuable laborers. Having no rent to pay, abundance of food and fuel, and money enough at all times to buy plain necessary clothing, they are never punished by absolute want, never become restless or insubordinate. Besides, they dwell too far apart to combine for any mischievous purposes. But the excessive numbers of negroes about our towns, for want of employment, are continually in a state bordering on actual starvation, and all starving men are desperate and dangerous. We know from daily and careful observation that the Bureau in Richmond has and still is exerting itself to the utmost of its very limited powers to abate this nuisance, by refusing rations, and advising and persuading the negroes to remove into the country, where they can all find employment. Force, not "moral suasion," governs all men, whether white or black. If the Bureau had the power to take these idle negroes up, and hire them out to the highest bidder, or put them out to the lowest, and were about to exercise the power, the negroes would at once squander, and find masters in the country. But the Radicals are afraid that if negroes are treated no better than poor white people, it will be said that they are re-enslaved, and subjected to a worse form of slavery than that from which they have just escaped. The result of all this must be, that a very large standing army must be kept up in the South by the Federal Government; portions of it stationed at every town south of the Ohio and Mason and Dixon's line; or the Constitution must be amended so as to authorize the several States to maintain standing armies. But even after all this is done, there will be frequent bloody collisions between the races in all of our Southern towns. Negroes, so useful in the country, are an abominable nuisance in town. Mobs at the South, after a time, will drive them out, as mobs have often done at the North. The Radicals hold the wolf by the ears. They have not tamed him, and instead of letting him go, are trying to mend their hold. This wolf is the opposing races in our towns and cities. In conquering the South and freeing the negroes, they but bought the elephant—and now they know not what to do with him. But he is *their* elephant, not ours, and we are of opinion should be left with them to be nursed and cared for. In two more years they will grow heartily tired of nursing this elephant and holding the wolf by the ears. Standing armies and Freedmen's Bureaus are rather more expensive cages than the country can now afford. These negro nurseries will be broken up, and their inmates, probably, be turned over to us at the South, to try our hands at nursing. If the North, after turning them over to us, will not intermeddle in their management, we will at once tame them, and make them useful, and instead of costing the nation some thirty millions a year, they will yield a neat annual profit to it of some two hundred millions. Then you will hear no more of idle, discontented, starving negroes. All will be well provided for, and all happy and contented.

We have the highest respect for all the offices of the Bureau in Richmond, from the commanding general down. They have even treated us with great courtesy and kindness; and we are witness to the fact that they discharge their duties with zeal, industry and integrity. Therefore, in calling the Bureau a negro nursery or a congeries of negro nurseries, we intend no disrespect—but only wish to convey to the public a full, accurate and comprehensive idea of the true character of the institution. Besides, we have been one of the nurses ourselves, and would not bring discredit on our own calling. . . .

George Fitzhugh

CUI BONO?—THE NEGRO VOTE

When "Camp Lee" was published in October, 1866, George Fitzhugh had been confident that the work of the Freedman's Bureau was both necessary and temporary. He was certain that the care and control of southern blacks would be quickly returned to the capable direction of white southerners. In the year that intervened between that article and "Cui Bono?" reconstruction had passed from Andrew Johnson's mild direction to the harsher measures enacted under Radical leadership in Congress. Part of the Radical plan was to create a Republican party in the South by winning the support of white Unionists and the newly enfranchised blacks. Radical measures ensured black participation in the writing of new constitutions for the southern states and in the ensuing state governments. Blacks participated extensively in the various constitutional conventions, but only in South Carolina did they constitute a majority (61 percent) of the delegates. In the reconstruction governments that were established in 1867 and 1868, blacks played important roles, but they never really dominated any state government and at no time and in no state did they rule.

Fitzhugh's analysis of the growing political power of blacks greatly exaggerated their actual power and suggests more about the fears of white southerners. Fitzhugh accused the blacks of planning a social and cultural revolution, but most historians agree that no such revolution was ever plotted or attempted. Blacks wanted and demanded their legal, civil, and political rights, but they made no effort to degrade the whites and establish black supremacy. Of course, for southerners like Fitzhugh, the very idea of equality of the races, let alone the reality, was revolutionary, and Fitzhugh voiced the concerns of many of his countrymen in this piece on Negro voting.

Port Royal, Va., September 17th, 1867

Messrs. Editors—The Radicals have overreached themselves. The negroes throughout the South are determined not to become their allies

Vol. IV, After War Series (October, 1867), pp. 289–92.

and supple tools, but to set up a party of their own, and to vote for none but negro candidates for office. They naturally reject with scorn and contempt the Radical proposition that henceforth there shall be no distinctions of color or race, but that all men shall stand on their own merits. They see, that under a thin disguise, this is a proposition that the negroes shall do the voting, and the Radicals fill all the offices. Four millions of negroes in the South, they insist, by virtue of their numbers and their loyalty, are entitled to fill most of the Federal and State offices at the South, and not to become mere hewers of wood and drawers of water for a handful of false, hypocritical, newly-converted white Unionists. Thrown upon their individual merit regardless of color or race, and they know that no negroes would be elected or appointed to office, for more capable white men are everywhere to be found. Obliterate all distinctions of race, and the negroes at the South, like those at the North, would become outcasts, pariahs, paupers and criminals. They would be confined to the most loathsome and least lucrative employments, and spend half their time in prisons, work-houses and poor-houses. They know that mere political equality would at once condemn them to social slavery—and they see at the North, that this social slavery, or slavery to skill and capital, of an inferior to a superior race, is the worst possible condition in which human beings can be placed. You, and your readers, must see that the negroes will not be satisfied with a nominal, but deceptive equality, but are everywhere determined to become masters of those who lately owned them as slaves. We admire their pluck. They are all armed and ready; all burning for a fight. They are impatient at the tedious process of reconstruction, and lavish much more abuse upon the Federal soldiers, the Freedman's Bureau and the Radicals, than upon the Secessionists. So soon as invested with the voting franchise, they will be full masters of the situation, for they constitute a majority on every acre of good land (except a little about the mountains) from Maryland to Florida, from the Atlantic to the Mississippi, and from the Rio Grande to Memphis. By mere voting, and selecting none but negroes as county, state and federal officers, in the favored regions where they constitute the majority, in two or three years they might expel the whites from all the fertile sections of the South, and turn those sections into hunting, ranging, fowling and fishing grounds, just as they were held, or infested by the Indians. Nature seems to have intended all the fertile portions of the South for mere roaming grounds for savages, for no where else on the globe would bountiful Nature enable savages to live with so little labor. It would be far easier for negro savages to live without labor on the sea, gulf and river coasts in the South, than in any parts of Africa. Wild fruits are ten-times as abundant in these favored sections of the South as in any parts of Africa; and so are fish, oysters, water fowl, and forest game. Give the negroes the right of suffrage, and at once they become masters of the situation throughout every acre of good land in the South, except about the mountains. They would only have to elect negro judges, sheriffs, justices of the peace, constables, jurors, etc., in order to expel the whole white population, except here and there a few old, infirm, silly, infatuated landholders. Our mechanics have nothing to do, and are rapidly emigrating. White common laborers or hirelings have all disappeared. We have not seen a single one since the war. There is nothing for our educated, enterprising young men to do here, and they are all removing. We have no industrial pursuits, except farming, and that is carelessly, lazily and languidly pursued by a few white land-owners, and by troops of freedmen, who work occasionally, in a desultory way—say, on the average, three days in the week. The negro tenants, next year, will claim half of our lands, and negro judges, jurors, justices, etc., will sustain their claims—that is, provided, negro suffrage turns over the South to negro rule. It is a monstrous absurdity, cruelty and attempted deception, to invite white men from the North to settle in the South, subject themselves to negro rule, and probably, ere long, to be massacred by negroes. No! Let the whites at the North first expel the Radicals from power, deny to the negro the rights of citizenship, make him a subordinate, or mere coarse, common laborer, as God and Nature designed he should be, and these white men from the North will find the South a delightful residence. Now, no sane man would live here longer than he could make arrangements to quit but for the hope and expectation that Radical rule is nearly ended, and that the Northern Democrats, soon to come into power, will do justice to the whites of the South, and the whites of the North, by putting the negro to work, and leaving voting, legislating, and governing, to the whites.

We have said that the negroes, so soon as they become invested with the right of suffrage, will become masters of the situation, and may seize on and hold all of the property of the whites, without redress on their parts; for negro jurors, justices and judges, taught by Northern Abolition emissaries that they (the negroes) are the rightful owners of all Southern lands and other property, would be sure to profit by the lessons they have thus learned. But they are impatient. This is too slow a process for them. We assure you, and your readers, and the entire North, that the freedmen (with very few exceptions) are anxious, impatient, burning with desire to begin the fight—the war of races—at once. They hold incendiary meetings, caucuses and conventions every day. They are all around; they are continually drilling in defiance of law. They have every where secret military organizations; they daily defy and insult the Federal troops and the Freedman's Bureau. They are ready and anxious to fight all the whites both North and South. They believe themselves far better soldiers than the whites, and are ready to attempt the expulsion or extermination of the whites. Unless the elections at the North, this fall, show a decided Democratic gain, the war of the races will begin ere the commencement of another year. And what will be the consequences? Why, a few hundreds or thousands, whites, men, women and children, will be massacred by the negroes; and then, in retaliation, hundreds of thousands negroes will be exterminated by the infuriated whites. This war of races will brutalize whites as well as blacks. Yet, knowingly, willfully, premeditatedly and advisedly, the Radical leaders are bringing about this inhuman and bloody result. And for why? Not to make allies of the negroes, for the negroes hate and despise them, and are everywhere busy in building up a negro party and in nominating negro candidates for office. They are equally the enemies of radical measures and radical men. In all their meetings in the cotton states, they denounce the direct tax on cotton, and will be sure to oppose the protective tariff; or indirect tax on cotton and other necessaries of life; for such taxes fall most heavily on the laboring classes. They will, for like reasons, be sure to advocate the repudiation of the National debt; whilst white representatives from the South would vote for its payment to the uttermost cent; for such payment would obviously be part of the terms of Reconstruction, which no honest Southron would attempt to violate. Besides, this war of races would involve the North also in war, increase the National debt, greatly increase Federal taxation, destroy altogether the Northern market for her merchandise and manufactures at the South; put a stop to the production of cotton, rice, sugar and tobacco; render reconstruction equally hopeless and undesirable; divide, probably, the Union into a half dozen separate nations, and involve the whole country, without distinction of race or section, in one common, irremediable ruin. But we hope and believe that Northern men begin to see that the continuance of radical rule is rapidly bringing about these disastrous results, and that they will soon hurl these cruel, dishonest and disorganizing rulers from the seats of power, do justice to the South, restore the Union on constitutional terms, and renew amicable and profitable relations between the lately hostile sections.

With us in tidewater Virginia, and I presume the same is true every where south of us, all is indecision, confusion, chaos. Men live from day to day, from year to year, from hand to mouth, without any settled or fixed plans of future life. Houses innumerable have been burnt or destroyed, and not one is rebuilt. Dilapidated houses are not repaired. Fences and enclosures of all kinds have gone down, and no one thinks of renewing them. Lands are cultivated merely for present profit, without a thought or purpose or improving them, for no one knows how soon his lands may be confiscated by the Radicals, or seized upon by the negroes. Our native white population is deserting, and no immigrants coming in. Before, and up to the time of the war, our rivers were alive with Northern vessels, every family in tolerable circumstances had its Northern teacher, male or female, and our roads and court-yards swarmed with agents and drummers, peddlers, etc., from the North. Now, all this is changed, and not a single individual, male or female, visits us by land or water from the North. A "Live Yankee" has not been seen in these parts for the last six months. And why come to be subjected to negro competition,—and soon—still worse,—to negro rule? No! Let the Northern men stay at home, and first put down the negroes and the Radicals. Then, the South, and not till then, will be a place fit to live in. Then, we will find room and extend the most cordial welcome to five millions of Northerners, if they will come among us,— without regard to their opinions, political, social, or religious. We know, when they see things here with their own eyes, and become identified with us in interest, that they will all make most valuable citizens. But at present, none but a negro amalgamationist should remove to the South.

Selected Bibliography

This bibliography is not intended to be comprehensive. The work. cited should guide further study on De Bow, his *Review*, and the topics discussed. For the most part, we have confined our citations to the recent secondary literature.

De Bow and his *Review* have been the subjects of only two full-length studies: Otis C. Skipper, *J. D. B. De Bow, Magazinist of the Old South* (Athens, Ga.: University of Georgia Press, 1958); and Diffee W. Standard, *"De Bow's Review,* 1846–1880: A Magazine of Southern Opinion" (Ph.D. dissertation, University of North Carolina, 1970). Skipper hangs a history of the *Review* on a biography of De Bow, while Standard is primarily concerned with the journal's contents and operation. Both works, however, should be used with caution because of numerous errors. The place of *De Bow's Review* in the periodical literature of the mid-nineteenth century is discussed in Frank Luther Mott, *A History of American Magazines* (5 vols.; Cambridge: Harvard University Press, 1938–68), Vols. I and II. The difficulties encountered by editors and publishers of southern magazines, in general, are briefly discussed in Jay B. Hubbell, *The South in American Literature* (Durham, N.C.: Duke University Press, 1954).

During the last twenty-five years, slavery and race have been the subjects of a rapidly growing body of literature. Kenneth M. Stampp, *The Peculiar Institution: Slavery in the Antebellum South* (New York: Alfred A. Knopf, 1956), began the modern reassessment of slavery with his general study. Stanley Elkins, *Slavery: A Problem in American Institutional and Intellectual Life* (Chicago: University of Chicago Press, 1959), raised considerable controversy by comparing plantations to concentration camps. Robert Fogel and Stanley Engerman used cliometrics and quantitative data to study the economy of slavery in *Time On the Cross: The Economics of American Negro Slavery* (2 vols.; Boston: Little, Brown, 1974). Their methods and conclusions have been sharply criticized by Herbert Gutman, *Slavery and the Numbers Game* (Urbana: University of Illinois Press, 1975), and Paul

A. David, *et al.*, *Reckoning With Slavery* (New York: Oxford University Press, 1976). Eugene Genovese has published several significant studies of the plantation system and slavery, including *The Political Economy of Slavery* (New York: Pantheon Books, 1965), and *Roll Jordan, Roll: The World the Slaves Made* (New York: Pantheon Books, 1974). Herbert Gutman, *The Black Family in Slavery and Freedom* (New York: Pantheon Books, 1976), and John Blassingame, *The Slave Community: Plantation Life in the Antebellum South* (Rev. ed.; New York: Oxford University Press, 1979), examine the black family and Afro-American culture. Leon Litwack, *Been in the Storm Too Long: The Aftermath of Slavery* (New York: Alfred A. Knopf, 1979), carries the story of black Americans into the immediate postwar years. William Stanton, *The Leopard's Spots: Scientific Attitudes Toward Race in America, 1815–59* (Chicago: University of Chicago Press, 1960); William Sumner Jenkins, *Pro-Slavery Thought in the Old South* (Chapel Hill: University of North Carolina Press, 1935); and George M. Frederickson, *The Black Image in the White Mind: The Debate on Afro-American Character and Destiny, 1817–1914* (New York: Harper and Row, 1971), analyze the racial attitudes of proslavery southerners.

The subject of southern agriculture is intimately bound up with the matters of slavery and race. In addition to the works on slavery cited above, the reader should also consult the classic study by Paul W. Gates, *The Farmer's Age: Agriculture, 1815–1860* (New York: Holt, Rinehart and Winston, 1960); Sam Bowers Hilliard, *Hogmeat and Hoecake: Food Supply in the Old South, 1840–1860* (Carbondale: Southern Illinois University Press, 1972); and Gavin Wright, *The Political Economy of the Cotton South: Households, Markets, and Wealth in the Nineteenth Century* (New York: W. W. Norton, 1978), which provides a rigorous analysis of the southern economy before and after the Civil War. Other useful discussions of southern economic life after the war are: Stephen J. DeCanio, *Agriculture in the Postbellum South* (Cambridge: M.I.T. Press, 1974), and Roger Ransom and Richard L. Sutch, *One Kind of Freedom: The Economic Consequences of Emancipation* (New York: Cambridge University Press, 1977).

Like slavery and race relations, nineteenth-century southern economic growth and development have received considerable attention from economic historians and economists. While the studies of Hilliard and Wright address a number of important specific questions, more general studies of antebellum economic development, North and South, are: George Rogers Taylor, *The Transportation Revolution, 1815–1860* (New York: Holt, Rinehart and Winston, 1951); Douglass C. North,

The Economic Growth of the United States, 1790–1860 (Englewood Cliffs, N.J.: Prentice-Hall, 1961); Stuart Bruchey, *The Roots of American Economic Growth, 1607–1861: An Essay in Social Causation* (New York: Harper and Row, 1965); and Albert Fishlow, *Railroads and the Transformation of the Ante-Bellum Economy* (Cambridge: Harvard University Press, 1965).

Among the works particularly useful to an understanding of southern culture and society in this period are: Clement Eaton, *Freedom of Thought in the Old South* (Durham, N.C.: Duke University Press, 1940); and *The Growth of Southern Civilization, 1790–1860* (New York: Harper and Row, 1961); William R. Taylor, *Cavalier and Yankee: The Old South and American National Character* (New York: George Braziller, 1961); and W. J. Cash, *The Mind of the South* (New York: Alfred A. Knopf, 1941). Russel B. Nye, *Society and Culture in America, 1830–1860* (New York: Harper and Row, 1974), is a more general survey of antebellum culture.

The work of David M. Potter figures prominently in the historiography of the disintegration of the Union. His *The Impending Crisis, 1848–1861*, completed and edited by Don E. Fehrenbacher (New York: Harper and Row, 1976), provides an indispensable overview of the conflict between North and South on the territorial question. The literature dealing with particular aspects of the issue includes William J. Cooper, *The South and the Politics of Slavery, 1828–1856* (Baton Rouge: Louisiana State University Press, 1978); Don E. Fehrenbacher, *The Dred Scott Case: Its Significance in American Law and Politics* (New York: Oxford University Press, 1978), and *The South and Three Sectional Crises* (Baton Rouge: Louisiana State University Press, 1980); and James A. Rawley, *Race & Politics: "Bleeding Kansas" and the Coming of the Civil War* (Philadelphia: Lippincott, 1969).

The larger question of relations between the North and the South before the Civil War has produced a massive body of literature. The previously cited works of David M. Potter, William J. Cooper, Jr., and Don E. Fehrenbacher, as well as David Brion Davis, *The Slave Power Conspiracy and the Paranoid Style* (Baton Rouge: Louisiana State University Press, 1969), and John McCardell, *The Idea of a Southern Nation: Southern Nationalists and Southern Nationalism* (New York: W. W. Norton, 1979), provide valuable discussions of the increasing alienation between the sections. Antislavery agitation was one of the most divisive issues of the period and, like the broader question, has engendered a plethora of historical studies. Among the most significant are Louis Filler, *The Crusade Against Slavery, 1830–1860* (New

York: Harper and Row, 1960); Eric Foner, *Free Soil, Free Labor, Free Men: The Ideology of the Republican Party Before the Civil War* (New York: Oxford University Press, 1970); Aileen S. Kraditor, *Means and Ends in American Abolitionism: Garrison and His Critics on Strategy and Tactics, 1834–1850* (New York: Pantheon Books, 1969); James Brewer Stewart, *Holy Warriors: The Abolitionists and American Society* (New York: Hill and Wang, 1976); and Ronald G. Walters, *The Antislavery Appeal: American Abolitionism After 1830* (Baltimore: Johns Hopkins University Press, 1976).

    The Civil War has generated continuing debate on its causes, course, and consequences. Classic studies include Avery O. Craven, *The Coming of the Civil War* (New York: Charles Scribner's Sons, 1942); Roy F. Nichols, *The Disruption of American Democracy* (New York: Macmillan, 1948); and Allan Nevins, *The War for the Union* (4 vols.; New York: Charles Scribner's Sons, 1959–71). A recent short study of the whole period is David Herbert Donald, *Liberty and Union* (Lexington, Mass.: D. C. Heath, 1978), while Emory Thomas recounts the history of the Confederacy in *The Confederate Nation, 1861–1865* (New York: Harper and Row, 1979). Diplomatic maneuvering during the war, particularly southern efforts to enlist European aid, is examined by Frank L. Owsley, *King Cotton Diplomacy* (Chicago: University of Chicago Press, 1959); David P. Crook, *The North, The South, and the Powers* (New York: Wiley, 1974); and Brian Jenkins, *Britain & the War for the Union* (Montreal: McGill and Queen's University Press, 1974). Southern efforts to deal with the ending of slavery are treated in James L. Roark, *Masters Without Slaves: Southern Planters in the Civil War and Reconstruction* (New York: W. W. Norton, 1977), and Roger Ransom and Richard L. Sutch, *One Kind of Freedom: The Economic Consequences of Emancipation* (New York: Cambridge University Press, 1977). Reliable surveys of Reconstruction include John Hope Franklin, *Reconstruction After the Civil War* (Chicago: University of Chicago Press, 1961), and Kenneth M. Stampp, *The Era of Reconstruction* (New York: Alfred A. Knopf, 1965). C. Vann Woodward, *The Strange Career of Jim Crow* (3rd ed.; New York: Oxford University Press, 1974), and Michael Perman, *Reunion Without Compromise: The South and Reconstruction, 1865–1868* (New York: Cambridge University Press, 1973), deal with the efforts of southern whites to maintain their domination.